COMPUTERS IN EDUCATION

COMPUTERS IN EDUCATION

Arul Jothi
M.Sc., M.Ed.
Principal, Arcot Sri Mahalakshmi Women's Teacher Training Institute,
Villapakkam, Vellore Dist.-632521 T.N.

Dr. D.L. Balaji
B.Com., M.A., M.Phil., D.Lit.,
Correspondent, Arcot Sri Mahalakshmi Educational Institutions,
Villapakkam, Vellore Dist.-632521 T.N.

Dr. Rajesh Verma
Lecturer, School of Education,
Nalanda Open University,
Patna

CENTRUM PRESS
NEW DELHI-110002 (INDIA)

CENTRUM PRESS
H.O.: 4360/4, Ansari Road, Daryaganj,
New Delhi-110 002 (India)
Ph.: 23278000, 23261597

B.O.: No. 1015, Ist Main Road, BSK IIIrd Stage
IIIrd Phase, IIIrd Block,
Bangalore - 560 085 (India)
Tel.: 080-41723429
Visit us at: www.centrumpress.com

Computers in Education

First Edition, 2009

PRINTED IN INDIA

Printed at Balaji Offset, Delhi

Contents

Preface

The history of computers in education has been variously characterized as an "accidental revolution" or "unthinking man and his thinking machines." Others have said that the computer revolution has changed the adage that "necessity is the mother of invention" to "in a computer world, invention is the mother of necessity." However characterized, it is clear that innovators in this field have created some of the most provocative and stimulating ideas in the history of education.

Broadly speaking, the two major functions of education are to transmit the culture, values and lessons of the past to the current generation; and to prepare our children for the world in which they will live. Preparing children for the world in which they will live is becoming more difficult than ever. In retrospect, there has been a confluence of changes that have significantly impacted the direction of modern education.

Modern, high-speed computers and telecommunications have facilitated the rapid movement of financial resources, goods and services, and have created an interdependence among the world economies. To benefit from these markets, nations must be competitive, and to be competitive they must have a well-educated work force.

In India, the use of computers in schools for educational purposes began very late. Nowadays, we find every good school is equipped with computers for educating children. Teachers and students can use computers in many ways, for teaching the use of computers, assessing various data banks, viewing films, listening to music and browsing the Internet. But it is the compact disc revolution which has influenced the use of computers in schools in a big way.

This book has given emphasize on Information Technology and Education. The book is a thoughtful work which provides rich knowledge both about computers and about the process of computer aided learning. It shows how computers can enhance student motivation and engagement.

— *Dr. Rajesh Verma*

Unit–I

Basics of Computer

Computer

A computer is a machine that manipulates data according to a list of instructions. Although mechanical examples of computers have existed throughout history, the first resembling a modern computer were developed in the mid-20th century (1940–1945). The first electronic computers were the size of a large room, consuming as much power as several hundred modern personal computers (PC). Modern computers based on tiny integrated circuits are millions to billions of times more capable than the early machines, and occupy a fraction of the space. Simple computers are small enough to fit into a wristwatch, and can be powered by a watch battery. Personal computers in their various forms are icons of the Information Age, what most people think of as a "computer", but the embedded computers found in devices ranging from fighter aircraft to industrial robots, digital cameras, and toys are the most numerous.

The ability to store and execute lists of instructions called programmes makes computers extremely versatile, distinguishing them from calculators. The Church–Turing thesis is a mathematical statement of this versatility: any computer with a certain minimum capability is, in principle, capable of performing the same tasks that any other computer can perform. Therefore computers ranging from a personal digital assistant to a supercomputer are all able to perform the same computational tasks, given enough time and storage capacity.

Definition

A computer is a device that accepts information (in the form of digitalized data) and manipulates it for some result based on a programme or sequence of instructions on how the data is to be processed. Complex computers also include the means for storing data (including the programme, which is also a form of data) for some necessary duration. A programme may be invariable and built into the computer (and called *logic circuitry* as it is on microprocessors) or different programmes may be provided to the computer (loaded into its storage and then started by an administrator or user). Today's computers have both kinds of programming.

Most histories of the modern computer begin with the Analytical Engine envisioned by Charles Babbage following the mathematical ideas of George Boole, the mathematician who first stated the principles of logic inherent in today's digital computer. Babbage's assistant and collaborator, Ada Lovelace, is said to have introduced the ideas of programme loops and subroutines and is sometimes considered the first programmer.

Apart from mechanical calculators, the first really useable computers began with the vacuum tube, accelerated with the invention of the transistor, which then became embedded in large numbers in integrated circuits, ultimately making possible the relatively low-cost personal computer.

Modern computers inherently follow the ideas of the stored programme laid out by John von Neumann in 1945. Essentially, the programme is read by the computer one instruction at a time, an operation is performed, and the computer then reads in the next instruction, and so on.

Recently, computers and programmes have been devised that allow multiple programmes (and computers) to work on the same problem at the same time in parallel. With the advent of the Internet and higher bandwidth data transmission, programmes and data that are part of the same overall project can be distributed over a network and embody the Sun Microsystems slogan: "The network is the computer."

Main Units

Central Processing Unit

A central processing unit (CPU) or processor is an electronic circuit that can execute computer programmes. This broad definition can easily be applied to many early computers that existed long before the term "CPU" ever came into widespread usage. The term itself and its initialism have been in use in the computer industry at least since the early 1960s (Weik 1961). The form, design and implementation of CPUs have changed dramatically since the earliest examples, but their fundamental operation has remained much the same. Early CPUs were custom-designed as a part of a larger, sometimes one-of-a-kind, computer.

However, this costly method of designing custom CPUs for a particular application has largely given way to the development of mass-produced processors that are made for one or many purposes. This standardization trend generally began in the era of discrete transistor mainframes and minicomputers and has rapidly accelerated with the popularization of the integrated circuit (IC). The IC has allowed increasingly complex CPUs to be designed and manufactured to tolerances on the order of nanometers. Both the miniaturization and standardization of CPUs have increased the presence of these digital devices in modern life far beyond the limited application of dedicated computing machines. Modern microprocessors appear in everything from automobiles to cell phones to children's toys.

History of CPU

Prior to the advent of machines that resemble today's CPUs, computers such as the ENIAC had to be physically rewired in order to perform different tasks. These machines are often referred to as "fixed-programme computers," since they had to be physically reconfigured in order to run a different programme. Since the term "CPU" is generally defined as a software (computer programme) execution device, the earliest devices that could rightly be called CPUs came with the advent of the stored-programme computer.

The idea of a stored-programme computer was already present during ENIAC's design, but was initially omitted so the machine could be finished sooner. On June 30, 1945, before ENIAC was even completed, mathematician John von Neumann distributed the paper entitled "First Draft of a Report on the EDVAC." It outlined the design of a stored-programme computer that would eventually be completed in August 1949 (von Neumann 1945). EDVAC was designed to perform a certain number of instructions (or operations) of various types. These instructions could be combined to create useful programmes for the EDVAC to run. Significantly, the programmes written for EDVAC were stored in high-speed computer memory rather than specified by the physical wiring of the computer. This overcame a severe limitation of ENIAC, which was the large amount of time and effort it took to reconfigure the computer to perform a new task. With von Neumann's design, the programme, or software, that EDVAC ran could be changed simply by changing the contents of the computer's memory.

While von Neumann is most often credited with the design of the stored-programme computer because of his design of EDVAC, others before him such as Konrad Zuse had suggested similar ideas. Additionally, the so-called Harvard architecture of the Harvard Mark I, which was completed before EDVAC, also utilized a stored-programme design using punched paper tape rather than electronic memory. The key difference between the von Neumann and Harvard architectures is that the latter separates the storage and treatment of CPU instructions and data, while the former uses the same memory space for both. Most modern CPUs are primarily von Neumann in design, but elements of the Harvard architecture are commonly seen as well.

Being digital devices, all CPUs deal with discrete states and therefore require some kind of switching elements to differentiate between and change these states. Prior to commercial acceptance of the transistor, electrical relays and vacuum tubes (thermionic valves) were commonly used as switching elements. Although these had distinct speed advantages over earlier, purely mechanical designs, they were unreliable for various reasons. For example, building direct current sequential logic circuits out of relays requires additional hardware to cope with the problem of contact bounce. While vacuum tubes do not suffer from contact bounce, they must heat up before becoming fully operational and eventually stop functioning altogether. Usually, when a tube failed, the CPU would have to be diagnosed to locate the failing component so it could be replaced. Therefore, early electronic (vacuum tube based) computers were generally faster but less reliable than electromechanical (relay based) computers.

Tube computers like EDVAC tended to average eight hours between failures, whereas relay computers like the (slower, but earlier) Harvard Mark I failed very rarely (Weik 1961:238). In the end, tube based CPUs became dominant because the significant speed advantages afforded generally outweighed the reliability problems. Most of these early synchronous CPUs ran at low clock rates compared to modern microelectronic designs (see below for a discussion of clock rate). Clock signal frequencies ranging from 100 kHz to 4 MHz were very common at this time, limited largely by the speed of the switching devices they were built with.

Discrete Transistor and IC CPUs

The design complexity of CPUs increased as various technologies facilitated building smaller and more reliable electronic devices. The first such improvement came with the advent of the transistor. Transistorized CPUs during the 1950s and 1960s no longer had to be built out of bulky, unreliable, and fragile switching elements like vacuum tubes and electrical relays. With this improvement more complex and reliable CPUs were built onto one or several printed circuit boards containing discrete (individual) components.

During this period, a method of manufacturing many transistors in a compact space gained popularity. The integrated circuit (IC) allowed a large number of transistors to be manufactured on a single semiconductor-based die, or "chip." At first only very basic non-specialized digital circuits such as NOR gates were miniaturized into ICs. CPUs based upon these "building block" ICs are generally referred to as "small-scale integration" (SSI) devices. SSI ICs, such as the ones used in the Apollo guidance computer, usually contained transistor counts numbering in multiples of ten. To build an entire CPU out of SSI ICs required thousands of individual chips, but still consumed much less space and power than earlier discrete transistor designs. As microelectronic technology advanced, an increasing number of transistors were placed on ICs, thus decreasing the quantity of individual ICs needed for a complete CPU. MSI and LSI (medium- and large-scale integration) ICs increased transistor counts to hundreds, and then thousands.

In 1964 IBM introduced its System/360 computer architecture which was used in a series of computers that could run the same programmes with different speed and performance. This was significant at a time when most electronic computers were incompatible with one another, even those made by the same manufacturer. To facilitate this improvement, IBM utilized the concept of a microprogram (often called "microcode"), which still sees widespread usage in modern CPUs (Amdahl *et al.* 1964). The System/360 architecture was so popular that it dominated the mainframe computer market for the decades and left a legacy that is still continued by similar modern computers like the IBM zSeries. In the same year (1964), Digital Equipment Corporation (DEC) introduced another influential computer aimed at the scientific and research markets, the PDP-8. DEC would later introduce the extremely popular PDP-11 line that originally was built with SSI ICs but was eventually implemented with LSI components once these became practical. In stark contrast with its SSI and MSI predecessors, the first LSI implementation of the PDP-11 contained a CPU composed of only four LSI integrated circuits (Digital Equipment Corporation 1975).

Transistor-based computers had several distinct advantages over their predecessors. Aside from facilitating increased reliability and lower power consumption, transistors also allowed CPUs to operate at much higher speeds because of the short switching time of a transistor in comparison to a tube or relay. Thanks to both the increased reliability as well as the dramatically increased speed of the switching elements (which were almost exclusively transistors by this time), CPU clock rates in the tens of megahertz were obtained during this period. Additionally while discrete transistor and IC CPUs were in heavy usage, new high-performance designs like SIMD (Single Instruction Multiple Data) vector processors began to appear. These early experimental designs later gave rise to the era of specialized supercomputers like those made by Cray Inc.

Microprocessors

The introduction of the microprocessor in the 1970s significantly affected the design and implementation of CPUs. Since the introduction of the first microprocessor (the Intel 4004) in 1970 and the first widely used microprocessor (the Intel 8080) in 1974, this class of CPUs has almost completely overtaken all other central processing unit implementation methods. Mainframe and minicomputer manufacturers of the time launched proprietary IC development programmes to upgrade their older computer architectures, and eventually produced instruction set compatible microprocessors that were backward-compatible with their older hardware and software. Combined with the advent and eventual vast success of the now ubiquitous personal computer, the term "CPU" is now applied almost exclusively to microprocessors.

Previous generations of CPUs were implemented as discrete components and numerous small integrated circuits (ICs) on one or more circuit boards. Microprocessors, on the other hand, are CPUs manufactured on a very small number of ICs; usually just one. The overall smaller CPU size as a result of being implemented on a single die means faster switching time because of physical factors like decreased gate parasitic capacitance. This has allowed synchronous microprocessors to have clock rates ranging from tens of megahertz to several gigahertz. Additionally, as the ability to construct exceedingly small transistors on an IC has increased, the complexity and number of transistors in a single CPU has increased dramatically. This widely observed trend is described by Moore's law, which has proven to be a fairly accurate predictor of the growth of CPU (and other IC) complexity to date.

While the complexity, size, construction, and general form of CPUs have changed drastically over the past sixty years, it is notable that the basic design and function has not changed much at all. Almost all common CPUs today can be very accurately described as von Neumann stored-programme machines. As the aforementioned Moore's law continues to hold true, concerns have arisen about the limits of integrated circuit transistor technology. Extreme miniaturization of electronic gates is causing the effects of phenomena like electromigration and subthreshold leakage to become much more significant. These newer concerns are among the many factors causing researchers to investigate new methods of computing such as the quantum computer, as well as to expand the usage of parallelism and other methods that extend the usefulness of the classical von Neumann model.

CPU Operation

The fundamental operation of most CPUs, regardless of the physical form they take, is to execute a sequence of stored instructions called a programme. The programme is represented by a series of numbers that are kept in some kind of computer memory. There are four steps that nearly all CPUs use in their operation: fetch, decode, execute, and writeback.

The first step, fetch, involves retrieving an instruction (which is represented by a number or sequence of numbers) from programme memory. The location in programme memory is determined by a programme counter (PC), which stores a number that identifies the current position in the programme. In other words, the programme counter keeps track of the CPU's place in the current programme. After an instruction is fetched, the PC is incremented by the length of the instruction word in terms of memory units. Often the instruction to be fetched must be retrieved from relatively slow memory, causing the CPU to stall while waiting for the instruction to be returned. This issue is largely addressed in modern processors by caches and pipeline architectures.

The instruction that the CPU fetches from memory is used to determine what the CPU is to do. In the decode step, the instruction is broken up into parts that have significance to other portions of the CPU. The way in which the numerical instruction value is interpreted is defined by the CPU's instruction set architecture (ISA). Often, one group of numbers in the instruction, called the opcode, indicates which operation to perform. The remaining parts of the number usually provide information required for that instruction, such as operands for an addition operation. Such operands may be given as a constant value (called an immediate value), or as a place to locate a value: a register or a memory address, as determined by some addressing mode. In older designs the portions of the CPU responsible for instruction decoding were unchangeable hardware devices. However, in more abstract and complicated CPUs and ISAs, a microprogram is often used to assist in translating instructions into various configuration signals for the CPU. This microprogram is sometimes rewritable so that it can be modified to change the way the CPU decodes instructions even after it has been manufactured.

After the fetch and decode steps, the execute step is performed. During this step, various portions of the CPU are connected so they can perform the desired operation. If, for instance, an addition operation was requested, an arithmetic logic unit (ALU) will be connected to a set of inputs and a set of outputs. The inputs provide the numbers to be added, and the outputs will contain the final sum. The ALU contains the circuitry to perform simple arithmetic and logical operations on the inputs (like addition and bitwise operations). If the addition operation produces a result too large for the CPU to handle, an arithmetic overflow flag in a flags register may also be set.

The final step, writeback, simply "writes back" the results of the execute step to some form of memory. Very often the results are written to some internal CPU register for quick access by subsequent instructions. In other cases results may be written to slower, but cheaper and larger, main memory. Some types of instructions manipulate the programme counter rather than directly produce result data. These are generally called "jumps" and facilitate behavior like loops, conditional programme execution (through the use of a conditional jump), and functions in programmes. Many instructions will also change the state of digits in a "flags" register. These flags can be used to influence how a programme behaves, since they often indicate the outcome of various operations. For example, one type of "compare" instruction considers two values and sets a number in the flags register according to which one is greater. This flag could then be used by a later jump instruction to determine programme flow.

After the execution of the instruction and writeback of the resulting data, the entire process repeats, with the next instruction cycle normally fetching the next-in-sequence instruction because of the incremented value in the programme counter. If the completed instruction was a jump, the programme counter will be modified to contain the address of the instruction that was jumped to, and programme execution continues normally. In more complex CPUs than the one described here, multiple instructions can be fetched, decoded, and executed simultaneously. This section describes what is generally referred to as the "Classic RISC pipeline," which in fact is quite common among the simple CPUs used in many electronic devices (often called microcontroller). It largely ignores the important role of CPU cache, and therefore the access stage of the pipeline.

Characteristics

Super Computer

The biggest in size, the most expensive in price than any other is classified and known as super computer. It can process trillions of instructions in seconds. This computer is not used as a PC in a home neither by a student in a college.

Governments specially use this type of computer for their different calculations and heavy jobs. Different industries also use this huge computer for designing their products.

In most of the Hollywood's movies it is used for animation purposes. This kind of computer is also helpful for forecasting weather reports worldwide.

Mainframes

Another giant in computers after the super computer is Mainframe, which can also process millions of instruction per second and capable of accessing billions of data.

This computer is commonly used in big hospitals, air line reservations companies, and many other huge companies prefer mainframe because of its capability of retrieving data on a huge basis.

This is normally to expensive and out of reach from a salary-based person who wants a computer for his home.

This kind of computer can cost up to thousands of dollars.

Minicomputer

This computer is next in he line but less offers less than mainframe in work and performance. These are the computers, which are mostly preferred by the small type of business personals, colleges, etc.

Personal Computers

Almost all the computer users are familiar with the personal computers. They normally know what the personal computer is and what are its functions.

This is the computer mostly preferred by the home users. These computers are lesser in cost than the computers given above and also, small in size; they are also called PCs in short for Personal computers.

This computer is small in size and you can easily arrange it to fit in your single bedroom with its all accommodation. Today this is thought to be the most popular computer in all.

Notebook Computers

Having a small size and low weight the notebook is easy to carry to anywhere. A student can take it with him/her to his/her school in his/her bag with his/her book.

This is easy to carry around and preferred by students and business people to meet their assignments and other necessary tasks. The approach of this computer is also the same as the Personal computer. It can store the same amount of data and having a memory of the same size as that of a personal computer. One can say that it is the replacement of personal desktop computer.

Generation of Computers

The history of computer development is often referred to in reference to the different generations of computing devices. Each generation of computer is characterized by a major technological development that fundamentally changed the way computers operate, resulting in increasingly smaller, cheaper, more powerful and more efficient and reliable devices.

Read about each generation and the developments that led to the current devices that we use today.

First Generation-1940-1956: Vacuum Tubes

The first computers used vacuum tubes for circuitry and magnetic drums for memory, and were often enormous, taking up entire rooms. They were very expensive to operate and in addition to using a great deal of electricity, generated a lot of heat, which was often the cause of malfunctions.

First generation computers relied on machine language, the lowest-level programming language understood by computers, to perform operations, and they could only solve one problem at a time. Input was based on punched cards and paper tape, and output was displayed on printouts.

The UNIVAC and ENIAC computers are examples of first-generation computing devices. The UNIVAC was the first commercial computer delivered to a business client, the U.S. Census Bureau in 1951.

Key Terms To Understanding The Five Generations of Computers:

- computer
- magnetic drums
- binary

- integrated circuit
- semiconductor
- nanotechnology

Second Generation-1956-1963: Transistors

Transistors replaced vacuum tubes and ushered in the second generation of computers. The transistor was invented in 1947 but did not see widespread use in computers until the late 50s. The transistor was far superior to the vacuum tube, allowing computers to become smaller, faster, cheaper, more energy-efficient and more reliable than their first-generation predecessors. Though the transistor still generated a great deal of heat that subjected the computer to damage, it was a vast improvement over the vacuum tube. Second-generation computers still relied on punched cards for input and printouts for output.

Second-generation computers moved from cryptic binary machine language to symbolic, or assembly, languages, which allowed programmers to specify instructions in words. High-level programming languages were also being developed at this time, such as early versions of COBOL and FORTRAN. These were also the first computers that stored their instructions in their memory, which moved from a magnetic drum to magnetic core technology.

The first computers of this generation were developed for the atomic energy industry.

Third Generation-1964-1971: Integrated Circuits

The development of the integrated circuit was the hallmark of the third generation of computers. Transistors were miniaturized and placed on silicon chips, called semiconductors, which drastically increased the speed and efficiency of computers.

Instead of punched cards and printouts, users interacted with third generation computers through keyboards and monitors and interfaced with an operating system, which allowed the device to run many different applications at one time with a central programme that monitored the memory. Computers for the first time became accessible to a mass audience because they were smaller and cheaper than their predecessors.

Fourth Generation-1971-Present: Microprocessors

The microprocessor brought the fourth generation of computers, as thousands of integrated circuits were built onto a single silicon chip. What in the first generation filled an entire room could now fit in the palm of the hand. The Intel 4004 chip, developed in 1971, located all the components of the computer - from the central processing unit and memory to input/output controls - on a single chip.

In 1981 IBM introduced its first computer for the home user, and in 1984 Apple introduced the Macintosh. Microprocessors also moved out of the realm of desktop computers and into many areas of life as more and more everyday products began to use microprocessors.

As these small computers became more powerful, they could be linked together to form networks, which eventually led to the development of the Internet. Fourth generation computers also saw the development of GUIs, the mouse and handheld devices.

Fifth Generation-Present and Beyond: Artificial Intelligence

Fifth generation computing devices, based on artificial intelligence, are still in development, though there are some applications, such as voice recognition, that are being used today. The use of parallel processing and superconductors is helping to make artificial intelligence a reality. Quantum computation and molecular and nanotechnology will radically change the face of computers in years to come. The goal of fifth-generation computing is to develop devices that respond to natural language input and are capable of learning and self-organization.

Computers are available in different shapes, sizes and weights, due to these different shapes and sizes they perform different sorts of jobs from one another. They can also be classified in different ways. All the computers are designed by the qualified computer architectures that design these machines as their requirements.

A computer that is used in a home differs in size and shape from the computer being used in a hospital. Computers act as a server in large buildings, while the computer also differs in size and shape performing its job as a weather forecaster.

A student carrying a laptop with him to his college is different in shape and size from all the computers mentioned above.

Here we are going to introduce different classifications of computers one by one. We will discuss what are in classifications and what job they perform.

Classification of Computers

Computers can be classified many different ways — by size, by function, and/or by processing capacity. We will study the classification of computers by size. The size of a computer often determines its function and processing capacity. The size of computers varies widely from tiny to huge and is usually dictated by computing requirements. For example, it is clear that the IRS will have different requirements than those of a college student.

The largest computers are *supercomputers*. They are the most powerful, the most expensive, and the fastest. They are capable of processing trillions of instructions per second. Examples of users of these computers are governmental agencies, such as the IRS, the National Weather Service, and the National Defense Agency. Also, they are used in the making of movies, space exploration, and the design of many other machines. The Cray supercomputer is nicknamed "Bubbles", because of its bubbling coolant liquids. Cray supercomputers, the first of which was invented by Seymour Cray, now maintain 75 percent of the supercomputer market. Supercomputers are used for tasks that require mammoth data manipulation.

Large computers are called mainframes. Mainframe computers process data at very high rates of speed, measured in the millions of instructions per second. They are very expensive, costing millions of dollars in some cases. Mainframes are designed for multiple users and process vast amounts of data quickly. Banks, insurance companies, manufacturers, mail-order companies, and airlines are typical users. Mainframes are often 'servers'— computers that control the networks of computers for large companies like catalog merchandiser L. L. Bean.

Microcomputers can be divided into two groups — personal computers and workstations. Workstations are specialized computers that approach the speed of mainframes. Often microcomputers are connected to networks of other computers. The price of a microcomputer varies greatly from less than $1000 to several thousand dollars, depending on the capacity and features of the computer. Microcomputers make up the vast majority of computers.

Another classification of computer is the *notebook* computer. A notebook computer can fit into a briefcase and weigh fewer than two pounds, yet it can compete with the microcomputer. A larger, heavier version is called a *laptop* computer. Notebooks generally cost more than microcomputers but can run most of the microcomputer software and are more versatile. Like other computers, notebook computers are getting faster, lighter, and more functional.

The smallest computer is the handheld computer called a *personal digital assistant* or a *PDA*. PDAs are used to track appointments and shipments as well as names and addresses. PDAs are called pen-based computers because they utilize a pen-like stylus that accepts hand-written input directly on a touch-sensitive screen. You have probably noticed delivery employees using these.

Speed, Reliability, Storage Capacity and Productivity

Computers of all sizes have common characteristics — speed, reliability, storage capacity, and productivity. Computers are the foundation of business, travel, and leisure life today. Computers provide the processing speed required by all facets of society. The quick service we expect at the bank, at the grocery store, on the stock exchange, and on the Internet are dependent on the speed of computers. Can you imagine our world without computers?

Computers are extremely reliable as well. Most errors are caused by humans, not computers. Computers are capable of storing enormous amounts of data that must be located and retrieved very quickly. The capability to store and retrieve volumes of data is at the core of the Information Age.

Hardware and Software

The Computer Hardware and Software industry of Bangalore is regarded as the focal point of advanced technology that acts as the prime catalyst in the economic growth of the city. Housing the biggest international names of Information Technology, Bangalore is referred as the Silicon Valley of India.

With the widening of the global business horizon, Bangalore has emerged as the key player in the field of Information Technology and Information Technology enabled services. From proposed plans of Hardware Park to a thriving Business Process Outsourcing sector, Bangalore is progressing beyond leaps and bounds. The city deals with the latest models of Hardware tools, Computer parts, Software programmes and accessories. The newest developments in the Software programming domain enable Bangalore to compete with the best IT brands of the world. Facilitated by a remarkably skilled and efficient lot of Hardware and Software professionals, the city truly fulfills all the criterion of being the IT capital of the country.

The major IT and ITes organizations of global repute that add credibility to the Computer Hardware and Software contours of Bangalore are:

- Microsoft Corporation
- IBM Global Services Ltd.
- Infosys Technologies Ltd.

- Intel Asia Electronics Inc.
- ITC Ltd.–Information Systems Div.
- Oracle Software (I) Ltd.
- SAP India Pvt. Ltd.
- Satyam Computer Services Ltd.
- Tata Consultancy Services
- Wipro Infotech Group
- Dell Asia Pacific SDN
- Citicorp
- CMC Ltd.
- Aptech Ltd.
- Compaq India
- Tata Infotech Ltd.
- Verifone
- TVS Electronics South Asia (P) Ltd.
- Tata Honeywell Ltd.
- Tektronix India Ltd.

To take India to greater heights of virtual development, the Computer Hardware and Software segment of Bangalore is consistently making new and globally acclaimed technological strides.

Computer Software

Computer software, or just software is a general term used to describe a collection of computer programmes, procedures and documentation that perform some task on a computer system.

The term includes:

- Application software such as word processors which perform productive tasks for users.
- Firmware which is software programmed resident to electrically programmable memory devices on board

mainboards or other types of integrated hardware carriers.

- Middleware which controls and co-ordinates distributed systems.
- System software such as operating systems, which interface with hardware to provide the necessary services for application software.
- Software testing is a domain independent of development and programming. It consists of various methods to test and declare a software product fit before it can be launched for use by either an individual or a group. Many tests on functionality, performance and appearance are conducted by modern testers with various tools such as QTP, Load runner, Black box testing etc to edit a checklist of requirements against the developed code. ISTQB is a certification that is in demand for engineers who want to pursue a career in testing.
- Testware which is an umbrella term or container term for all utilities and application software that serve in combination for testing a software package but not necessarily may optionally contribute to operational purposes. As such, testware is not a standing configuration but merely a working environment for application software or subsets thereof.

Software includes websites, programmes, video games, etc. that are coded by programming languages like C, C++, etc.

"Software" is sometimes used in a broader context to mean anything which is not hardware but which is *used* with hardware, such as film, tapes and records.

Overview

Computer software is often regarded as anything but hardware, meaning that the "hard" are the parts that are tangible while the "soft" part is the intangible objects inside the computer. Software encompasses an extremely wide array of products and technologies developed using different techniques like programming languages, scripting languages or even microcode or a FPGA state. The types of software include web pages developed by technologies like HTML, PHP, Perl, JSP, ASP.NET, XML, and desktop applications like Microsoft Word, OpenOffice developed by technologies like C, C++, Java, C#, etc. Software usually runs on an underlying software operating systems such as the Microsoft Windows or Linux. Software also includes video games and the logic systems of modern consumer devices such as automobiles, televisions, toasters, etc.

Relationship to Computer Hardware

Computer software is so called to distinguish it from computer hardware, which encompasses the physical interconnections and devices required to store and execute (or run) the software. At the lowest level, software consists of a machine language specific to an individual processor. A machine language consists of groups of binary values signifying processor instructions which change the state of the computer from its preceding state. Software is an ordered sequence of instructions for changing the state of the computer hardware in a particular sequence. It is usually written in high-level programming languages that are easier and more efficient for humans to use (closer to natural language) than machine language. High-level languages are compiled or interpreted into machine language object code. Software may also be written in an assembly language, essentially, a mnemonic representation of a machine language using a natural language alphabet. Assembly language must be assembled into object code via an assembler.

The term "software" was first used in this sense by John W. Tukey in 1958. In computer science and software engineering, computer software is all computer programmes. The theory that is the basis for most modern software was first proposed by Alan Turing in his 1935 essay *Computable numbers with an application to the Entscheidungsproblem.*

Types of Software

Practical computer systems divide software systems into three major classes: system software, programming software and application software, although the distinction is arbitrary, and often blurred.

System Software

System software helps run the computer hardware and computer system. It includes:

- device drivers,
- operating systems,
- servers,
- utilities,
- windowing systems,

(these things need not be distinct)

The purpose of systems software is to unburden the applications programmer from the details of the particular computer complex being used, including such accessory devices as communications, printers, readers, displays, keyboards, etc. And also to partition the computer's resources such as memory and processor time in a safe and stable manner.

Programming Software

Programming software usually provides tools to assist a programmer in writing computer programmes, and software using different programming languages in a more convenient way. The tools include:

- compilers,
- debuggers,
- interpreters,
- linkers,
- text editors,

An Integrated development environment (IDE) is a single application that attempts to manage all these functions.

Computer Hardware

Personal Computers (PCs) can be obtained in desktop, laptop, notebook and other portable formats.

They are used in all areas of society.

This module describes the parts of typical desktop personal computers.

please add your contributions

Note: Should this stuff be moved to other pages?

Computer hardware:

- The Motherboard and things directly attached to it.
- Computer chassis and screen, preferly with standard sizes (i.e. ISO A4 for notebook chassis).
- Storage media
- Other peripherals

Class 1 Components

Class 1 components are integral to the function of the computer.

CPU

The CPU (Central Processing Unit) is the 'brain' of the computer. It's typically a square ceramic package plugged into the motherboard, with a large heat sink on top (and often a fan on top of that heat sink).

All instructions the computer will process are processed by the CPU. There are many "CPU architectures", each of which has its own characteristics and trade-offs. The dominant CPU architectures used in personal computing are x86 and PowerPC. x86 is easily the most popular processor for this class of machine (the dominant manufacturers of x86 CPUs are Intel and AMD). The other architechtures are used, for istance, in workstations, servers or embedded systems CPUs contain a small amount of static RAM (SRAM) called a cache. Some processors have two or three levels of cache, containing as much as several megabytes of memory.

Dual Core

Some of the new processors made by Intel and AMD are Dual core. The Intel designation for dual core are "Pentium D",

"Core Duo" and "Core 2 Duo" while AMD has its "X2" series and "FX-6x".

The core is where the data is processed and turned into commands directed at the rest of the computer. Having two cores increases the data flow into the processor and the command flow out of the processor potentially doubling the processing power, but the increased performance is only visible with multithreaded applications and heavy multitasking.

Hyper Threading

Hyper Threading is a technology that uses one core but adds a virtual processor to an additional thread at the same time. Normally the processor carries out one task and then proceeds onto the next task. But with Hyper Threading the processor continually switches in-between each task as if to do them at the same time.

Case

Most modern computers have an "ATX form factor" case in which ATX-compatible power supplies, Mainboards and Drives can be mounted. The Mini-ITX is much different in important ways unlike its relatives the Micro-ATX and the Flex-ATX. The mainboard size can be up to 170mm x 170 mm which is smaller than the Flex and Micro-ATX can be. Usually at less than 100 watts, the Mini-ITX PSU is energy efficient. The Mini-ITX is also backward-compatible with the Flex/Micro-ATX models.

During the 1980's and 1990's almost all cases were beige, even Apple's Macintosh line. A few rare exceptions to this were black. Only recently have computer case designers realized that there was a worthwhile market for other colours and designs. This has led to all sorts of modifications to the basic design of a computer case. Now it is easy to find cases with transparent windows and glowing lights illuminating their insides.

Power Supply

All computers have some sort of power supply. This converts the supply voltage (AC 110 or 220V) to different voltages such as DC 5V, 12V and 3.3V. These are needed inside the computer system by nearly every component inside the computer.

There will be a bunch of connectors coming off of the supply, called Molex connectors. They come in varying sizes, meant for different applications, such as the motherboard (usually the largest of the connectors), the hard and optical drives (a bunch of medium-sized connectors), as well as the floppy drive (a relatively small connector, also saw usage among videocards in 2004). As newer standards come out, the types of connectors have changed. Many power supplies now come with power connectors for Serial ATA hard drives. These are smaller and are "hot-swappable", meaning they can be removed and plugged in again without fear of data loss or electrical problems.

The power supply also has an exhaust fan that is responsible for cooling the power supply, as well as providing a hot air exhaust for the entire case. Some power supplies have two fans to promote this effect.

It is important to buy a power supply that can accommodate all of the components involved. Some may argue that it is the most important part of a computer, and therefore it is worth spending the money to get a decent one.

Motherboard

The Motherboard (also called Mainboard) is a large, thin, flat, rectangular fiberglass board (typically green) attached to the case. The Motherboard carries the CPU, the RAM, the chipset and the expansion slots (PCI, AGP - for graphics -, ISA, etc.). The Motherboard also holds things like the BIOS (Basic Input Output System) and the CMOS Battery (a coin cell that keeps an embbeded RAM in the motherboard -often NVRAM-powered to keep various settings in effect).

Most modern motherboards have onboard sound and LAN controller, some of them even have on-board graphics. These are adequate for standard office work and system sounds. But dedicated sound and graphics cards plugged into the expansion slots offer much better quality and performance.

The expansion slots (PCI, PCI-e, PCI-X, AGP, ISA, etc.) allow additional functions.

RAM

Random Access Memory (RAM) is a memory that the microprocessor uses to store data during processing. This memory is volatile (loses its contents at power-down). When a software application is launched, the executable programme is loaded from hard drive to the RAM. The microprocessor supplies address into the RAM to read instructions and data from it. RAM is needed because hard drives are too slow to operate with the speed of a microprocessor.

Some of the types of RAM are SDRAM, DDR RAM, Rambus RAM, SIMM, DIMM.

UNIT-II

Computer Hardware

Hardware : Definition

Computer hardware has advanced drastically since the early days when computers took up entire rooms and required teams of people to run. Modern computer systems fit in a small case and can draw power from a standard wall jack. It is important to learn about the components of your computer so that you can diagnose problems or replace equipment as it becomes outdated.

Function

Hardware is the corporeal and tangible portion of a computer system that you interact with to take advantage of computer programmes. It is distinct from software in that it is built of physical material and generally does not perform logical operations or change its state frequently.

Main System

The central piece of hardware for any computer is the motherboard, which is a circuit board that contains all of the sockets, slots, and chip sets that all of the other hardware devices will be connected into. The central processing unit, which handles all of the mathematical calculations that the computer needs to perform, is attached to the main socket of the motherboard. The two main companies that produce processors, AMD and Intel, each make a variety of different processor types that work with different motherboards. The random access memory attaches to slots in the motherboard and it controls the speed that computations occur. The hard drive is the component that actually stores all of the data in the computer such as files, music or games. All of these units are run by a power supply that plugs into a wall socket. Computers with more advanced hardware will require a higher voltage power supply to run at peak efficiency. Some sort of cooling system must also be used, such as a fan or liquid cooling tubes, to prevent the other devices from overheating and shutting down. All of these components are held inside of a metal or plastic case.

Media

Media hardware devices allow external types of media to be used by the computer. The main media drive will be a CD or DVD that is allows you to install programmes from CDs or play music. A graphics card, which will either plug into a PCI, AGP or PCI-Express slot on the motherboard, controls the level of graphical options that can be utilized for video games or graphics editing programmes. Sound cards are used so that your computer can use different kinds of speaker systems. The final media hardware types are ports on the front or back of the computer that allow devices to be connected through USB, Fireware, Serial or Ethernet cables.

Input

In order to interact with your computer system, you will need some kind of input hardware. Most computer systems require one or more input devices to be connected or it will not boot up at all. The most popular input devices are a mouse for navigating the screen, a keyboard for typing text and a microphone for sending voice over the internet or activating voice command software.

Output

The fastest or most advanced computer in the world is useless without a means of displaying information to the user. Output hardware devices solve this problem by visually displaying graphics or text or playing sounds. A monitor is the most common type of output device. Older and bulkier cathode-ray tube monitors worked much like early televisions but most modern monitors are flat panel liquid crystal displays. Printers can also be considered output devices as they can print information from a software programme.

Input Devices: Keyboard

Keyboard : The keyboard is used to type information into the computer or input information. There are many different keyboard layouts and sizes with the most common for Latin based languages being the QWERTY layout (named for the first 6 keys). The standard keyboard has 101 keys. Notebooks have embedded keys accessible by special keys or by pressing key combinations (CTRL or Command and P for example). Ergonomically designed keyboards are designed to make typing easier.

Some of the keys have a special use. There are referred to as command keys. The 3 most common are the Control or CTRL, Alternate or Alt and the Shift keys though there can be more (the Windows key for example or the Command key). Each key on a standard keyboard has one or two characters. Press the key to get the lower character and hold Shift to get the upper.

Mouse

Most modern computers today are run using a mouse controlled pointer. Generally if the mouse has two buttons the left one is used to select objects and text and the right one is used to access menus. If the mouse has one button (Mac for instance) it controls all the activity and a mouse with a third button can be used by specific software programmes.

One type of mouse has a round ball under the bottom of the mouse that rolls and turns two wheels which control the direction of the pointer on the screen. Another type of mouse uses an optical system to track the movement of the mouse.

Note: It is important to clean the mouse periodically, particularly if it becomes sluggish. A ball type mouse has a small circular panel that can be opened, allowing you to remove the ball. Lint can be removed carefully with a tooth pick or tweezers and the ball can be washed with mild detergent. A build up will accumulate on the small wheels in the mouse. Use a small instrument or finger nail to scrape it off taking care not to scratch the wheels. Track balls can be cleaned much like a mouse and touch-pad can be wiped with a clean, damp cloth. An optical mouse can accumulate material from the surface that it is in contact with which can be removed with a finger nail or small instrument.

Joystick ABCs

The Joystick is a hardware input device used for games and/or flight simulators. This device is used to maneuver a particular item throughout locations.

Along with the capability of maneuvering items, the joystick will also have a series of buttons which can be programmed to fire weapons, add acceleration as well as several other possibilities, depending upon the programme.

Touch Screen

Add industrial computer, rugged computer and touch screen computer to the many products produced by Greco Systems. Flexible design allow these products to be customized to meet your specific needs. Touch Screen Computer is also listed with Greco CNC Software and Hardware because some of our customers prefer mouse and keyboard free operation of their DNC software as well as other shop floor applications. Contact us and speak with one of our specialists that can help you with your decision with a Touch Screen Computer, Rugged Computer or Industrial Computer.

Touchpad

A touchpad is a pointing device consisting of specialized surface that can translate the motion and position of a user's fingers to a relative position on screen. They are a common feature of laptop computers and also used as a substitute for a computer mouse where desk space is scarce. Touchpads vary in size but are rarely made larger than 40 square centimeters (about 6 square inches). They can also be found on personal digital assistants (PDAs) and some portable media players.

Operation and Function

Touchpads operate in one of several ways, including capacitance and conductance sensing. The most common technology used today entails sensing the capacitance of a finger, or the capacitance between sensors. Because of the property being sensed, capacitance-based touchpads will not sense the tip of a pencil or other similar implement. Gloved fingers will generally also be problematic (such as in a cleanroom environment). Likewise, moist, sweaty, or callused fingers will also affect capacitance sensing. However, some touchpads, such as have been manufactured by Elographics, sensed electrical conductance. In the case of the Elographics touchpads, there were little nipples that separated a flexible top surface from a lower surface. When the top surface was pushed into contact with the bottom surface, using either a finger or any other device, the point of contact could be sensed due to the signal being conducted. In this case, one could use a finger or a wooden stylus, and performance would not be affected by sweat or calluses, for example.

Like mice, touchpads are relative motion devices. This means that the relative motion of a finger on the touchpad surface causes the relative motion of the cursor on the screen. The buttons below or above the pad serve as standard mouse buttons. Depending on the model of touchpad and drivers behind it, you may also click by tapping your finger on the touchpad, and drag with a tap followed by a continuous pointing motion (a 'click-and-a-half'). Touchpad drivers can also allow the use of multiple fingers to facilitate the other mouse buttons (commonly two-finger tapping for the center button).

Some touchpads also have "hotspots": locations on the touchpad that indicate user intentions other than pointing. For example, on certain touchpads, moving the finger along an edge of the touch pad will act as a scroll wheel, controlling the scrollbar and scrolling the window that has the focus vertically or horizontally depending on which edge is stroked. However, these are driver dependent functions and can be disabled. Also, certain touchpad drivers allow for tap zones, regions whereby a tap will execute a function. For example, pausing the media player or launching an application.

Touchpads in Devices

Early Apollo desktop computers were equipped with a touchpad on the right side of the keyboard.

Touchpads are primarily used in portable laptop computers, because a standard mouse requires a flat surface near the keyboard not always available outside of a standard computing environment. Because the touchpad's position is fixed relative to the keyboard, and very short finger movements are required to move the cursor across the display screen, many users find touchpads preferable, and desktop keyboards with built-in touchpads are available from specialist manufacturers. However, these features can also cause frustration when a user's thumb accidentally swipes over the touchpad while typing.

Touchpads are also the primary control interface for menu navigation on all of the currently produced iPod portable music players (except the iPod shuffle and iPod Touch), where they are referred to as "click wheels". Creative Labs also uses a touchpad for their Zen line of MP3 players, beginning with the Zen Touch and most recently featured in the Zen Vision:M. The new Zune product line (the Zune 80 and Zune 4/8) uses touch for the Zune Pad.

Apple's PowerBook 500 series was the first laptop to carry such a device, which Apple refers to as a "trackpad". When introduced in May 1994, it replaced the trackball of previous PowerBook models. Apple's more recent laptops feature trackpads that can sense up to four fingers simultaneously, providing more options for input, such as the ability to bring up the context menu by tapping two fingers.

Psion PLC's Psion MC 200/400/600/WORD Series, introduced in 1989, came with a new mouse-replacing touchpad; however, the Psion's device more closely resembles a graphics tablet than a touchpad, as one would position the cursor by clicking on a specific point on the pad, instead of moving it in the direction of a stroke.

Theory of Operation

There are two principal means by which touchpads work. In the *matrix approach*, a series of conductors are arranged in an array of parallel lines in two layers, separated by an insulator and crossing each other at right angles to form a grid. A high frequency signal is applied sequentially between pairs in this two-dimensional grid array. The current that passes between the nodes is proportional to the capacitance. When a virtual ground, such as a finger, is placed over one of the intersections between the conductive layer some of the electrical field is shunted to this ground point, resulting in a change in the apparent capacitance at that location. This method received U.S. Patent 5,305,017 awarded to George Gerpheide in April 1994. The *capacitive shunt method*, described in an application note by Analog Devices, senses the change in capacitance between a transmitter and receiver that are on opposite sides of the sensor. The transmitter creates an electric field which oscillates at 200-300 kHz. If a ground point, such as the finger, is placed between the transmitter and receiver, some of the field lines are shunted away, decreasing the apparent capacitance.

Magnetic Ink Character Reader

Magnetic Ink Character Recognition, or MICR, is a character recognition technology adopted mainly by the banking industry to facilitate the processing of cheques. The process was demonstrated to the American Bankers Association in July 1956, and was almost universally employed in the U.S. by 1963.. On September 12, 1961, Stanford Research Institute (now SRI International) was awarded U.S. Patent Number 3,000,000 for invention of MICR; the patent was assigned to General Electric. MICR is standardized by ISO 1004.

The major MICR fonts used around the world are E-13B and CMC-7. The E-13B font was chosen by George Jacobi, who was working for General Electric at the time. Almost all Indian, US, Canadian and UK checks now include MICR characters at the bottom of the paper in the E-13B font. Some countries, including France, use the CMC-7 font developed by Bull.

The 14 characters of the E-13B font. The control characters bracketing each numeral block are (from left to right) *transit*, *on-us*, *amount*, and *dash*.

An example of the CMC-7 MICR font. Shown are the 15 characters of the CMC-7 font. The control characters after the numerals are (from left to right) *internal*, *terminator*, *amount*, *routing*, and an unused character.

In addition to their unique fonts, MICR characters are printed with a magnetic ink or toner, usually containing iron oxide. Magnetic printing is used so that the characters can be reliably read into a system, even when they have been overprinted with other marks such as cancellation stamps. The characters are first magnetized in the plane of the paper with a North pole on the right of each MICR character. Then they are usually read with a MICR read head which is a device similar in nature to the playback head in an audio tape recorder, and the letterforms' bulbous shapes ensure that each letter produces a unique waveform for the character recognition system to provide a reliable character result. Examples of MICR waveforms have been developed and can be displayed using spreadsheet applications like Microsoft Excel or compatible. The error rate for the magnetic scanning of the numbers at the bottom of a typical check is smaller than with optical character recognition systems. For well printed MICR, the can't read rate is usually less than 1% while the substitution rate (misread rate) is in the order of 1 per 100,000 characters.

In 1960s, the MICR fonts became a symbol of modernity or futurism, leading to the creation of lookalike "computer" typefaces that imitated the appearance of the MICR fonts, but, unlike real MICR fonts, had a full character repertoire.

In 1991, Advantage Laser Products became the first toner cartridge manufacturer to offer MICR toner in lieu of MICR Ink for desktop laser printers. This revolutionized the check printing business. Prior to 1991 checks were printed with magnetic ink on an offset press. With the advent of MICR toner, checks could be printed on almost any desktop laser printer.

Optical Mark Reader

The Optical Mark Reader is a device the "reads" pencil marks on NCS compatible scan forms such as surveys or test answer forms. If that all seems overly technical to you, just think of it as the machine that checks multiple choice computer forms. In this document The Optical Mark Reader will be referred to as the scanner or OMR. The computer test forms designed for the OMR are known as NCS compatible scan forms. Tests and surveys completed on these forms are read in by the scanner, checked, and the results are saved to a file. This data file can be converted into an output file of several different formats, depending on which type of output you desire.

The OMR is a powerful tool that has many features. If you are using casstat (grading tests), the OMR will print the number of correct answers and the percentage of correct answers at the bottom of each test. It will also record statistical data about each question. This data is recorded in the output file created when the forms are scanned. You'll find out more about the data file and output formats available later on in this document.

The NCS compatible scan forms are the green and blue scan forms seen below.

NCS Compatible Scan Forms

These forms can be purchased at the campus bookstore or the convenience store located in the union. The green form has ten choices for each answer and the blue form has five choices for each answer. When students fill out these forms it is important that the name field is filled out with the appropriate letters filled in below the name. See the Example of a Correct Student Scan Form for more information. If this is not done the scanner will report an error. Also make sure none of the forms are damaged. Damaged forms cannot be checked. There are two sets of preprinted marks that help the scanner read the form. They are the "Skunk Marks" and the "Timing Marks". See the picture below for the location of these marks.

It is important that you use NCS compatible forms as the OMR is specifically designed to check these forms. The five and ten response NCS forms are the standard forms used for surveys and tests. If you wish to use other NCS forms, contact Information Technology at 766-2082 to find out what support we can offer.

Once you have the filled in the scan forms and wish to process them, here is what you must do. First complete a cover scan form. For test grading this will be an answer key, for teacher evaluations this will be a form filled out with the instructor's information, and for surveys this may be general information about the survey.

Once this is completed you will need to go to the Ivinson Building to process the forms. The OMR is located in the computer lab in Ivinson Rm136. When you come into the lab go behind the lab assistant's desk. The OMR and the computer connected to it are located there on the table just left of the colour printer. Printed versions of Test Grading, Generic Teacher Evaluations, College of Education Teacher Evaluations, and A&S Teacher Evaluations pages explaining how to scan, process, and print are located in a folder near the computer. Also inside the folder is a printed version of Scanning Errors. It is a handy reference when problems occur. In the folder there should also be an End of Forms page as well as some blank NCS blue and green scan forms in the back. The blank forms are there in case someone removed the End of Forms page from the lab. There is also a document that explains the numbers the scanner will print on the bottom of graded tests.

At this point you should determine what kind of forms you are going to process, test forms, 45 question teacher evaluations, Cafeteria teacher evaluations, or surveys. Those links will take you to the How To Pages of processing each type. Before you start it is important to note that the system is case sensitive. You will need to type in all responses exactly how they appear in the How To Pages for the type of forms you will be scanning.

If you do not, problems will occur. Sit down at the computer and follow the directions for the type of forms you will be scanning. When you start, the computer prompt should be Ready>. If not ask the computer lab assistant for help; they will correct the problem. In the second step of the How To Pages the directions specify to accept the defaults. Advanced users and users with more than one answer key may want to change these. For directions on changing these defaults see the Changing Scan Defaults page. Most users will not need to do this. We recommend pressing return on the keyboard at each prompt to accept the defaults. After completing the first few steps in the How To Pages for your form type, the computer will prompt you to PUT THE STACK OF FORMS IN THE INPUT HOPPER. Meaning it is time to load the scanner with your scan forms. There are a few things you should know about the Optical Mark Reader that will help you understand how to scan the forms. In the How To documents there are OMR related terms that may seem confusing. Use the following picture to guide you when you come across terms referring to the parts of the scanner.

The Optical Mark Reader

The input hopper holds the forms to be scanned. The Sheet Guide is used to keep forms aligned in the hopper. This is important as forms not properly aligned will become jammed in the scanner. Actual scanning occurs on the Transport bed. Once a form is scanned it comes to rest in the Output Stacker. The Operator Panel displays the scanner status and any error messages. If the scanner stops scanning in the middle of a job check the Operator Panel for information. To load the scanner place your forms in the hopper so that they are readable to you and the timing marks are on the same side as the Operator Panel. The picture below shows how to load the scanner. Never place more than 200 forms in the input hopper at a time as this causes the scanner to jam.

Barcode Reader

A barcode reader (or barcode scanner) is an electronic device for reading printed barcodes. Like a flatbed scanner, it consists of a light source, a lens and a light sensor translating optical impulses into electrical ones. Additionally, nearly all barcode readers contain *decoder* circuitry analyzing the barcode's image data provided by the sensor and sending the barcode's content to the scanner's output port.

Scanner

In computing, a scanner is a device that optically scans images, printed text, handwriting, or an object, and converts it to a digital image. Common examples found in offices are variations of the *desktop (or flatbed) scanner* where the document is placed on a glass window for scanning. *Hand-held scanners*, where the device is moved by hand, have evolved from text scanning "wands" to 3D scanners used for industrial design, reverse engineering, test and measurement, orthotics, gaming and other applications. Mechanically driven scanners that move the document are typically used for large-format documents, where a flatbed design would be impractical.

Modern scanners typically use a charge-coupled device (CCD) or a Contact Image Sensor (CIS) as the image sensor, whereas older *drum scanners* use a photomultiplier tube as the image sensor. A *rotary scanner,* used for high-speed document scanning, is another type of drum scanner, using a CCD array instead of a photomultiplier. Other types of scanners are planetary scanners, which take photographs of books and documents, and 3D scanners, for producing three-dimensional models of objects.

Another category of scanner is digital camera scanners, which are based on the concept of reprographic cameras. Due to increasing resolution and new features such as anti-shake, digital cameras have become an attractive alternative to regular scanners. While still having disadvantages compared to traditional scanners (such as distortion, reflections, shadows, low contrast), digital cameras offer advantages such as speed, portability, gentle digitizing of thick documents without damaging the book spine. New scanning technologies are combining 3D scanners with digital cameras to create full-colour, photo-realistic 3D models of objects.

In the biomedical research area, detection devices for DNA microarrays are called scanners as well. These scanners are high-resolution systems (up to 1 µm/ pixel), similar to microscopes. The detection is done via CCD or a photomultiplier tube (PMT).

Webcamera

Webcams are video capturing devices connected to computers or computer networks, often using USB or, if they connect to networks, ethernet or Wi-Fi. They are well known for their low manufacturing costs and flexible applications.

History

Started in 1991, the first such camera, called the CoffeeCam, was pointed at the Trojan room coffee pot in the computer science department of Cambridge University. The camera was finally switched off on August 22, 2001. The final image captured by the camera can still be viewed at its homepage.

The coffee machine was repaired for free by Krups.

The oldest webcam, as the technology came to be known, still operating is FogCam at San Francisco State University, which has been running continuously since 1994.

One of the most widely reported-on webcam sites was JenniCam, started in 1996, which allowed internet users to constantly observe the life of its namesake, somewhat like reality TV series Big Brother, launched three years later. More recently, the website Justin.tv has shown a continuous video and audio stream from a mobile camera mounted on the head of the site's star.

Recently, Apple and other computer hardware manufactures began building webcams directly into laptop and desktop screens. This eliminates the need to use an external USB or Firewire webcam.

Video Conferencing

As webcam capabilities have been added to instant messaging text chat services such as AOL Instant Messenger, one-to-one live video communication over the internet has now reached millions of mainstream PC users worldwide. Increased video quality has helped webcams encroach on traditional video conferencing systems. New features such as lighting, real-time enhancements (retouching, wrinkle smoothing and vertical stretch) can make users more comfortable, further increasing popularity. Features and performance vary between programmes.

Videoconferencing support is included in programmes as Yahoo Messenger, AOL Instant Messenger (AIM), Windows Live Messenger, Skype, iChat, Paltalk (now PaltalkScene), Ekiga, Stickam,Tokbox, Camfrog and meetcam.

Some online video broadcasting sites have taken advantage of this technology to create internet television programmes centered around two (or more) people "diavlogging" with each other from two different places. Among others, BloggingHeads.tv uses this technology to set up conversations between prominent journalists, scientists, bloggers, and philosophers.

Video Security

Webcams are being used for security purposes. Software is available allowing PC-connected cameras to watch for movement and sound, recording both when they are detected; these recordings can be saved to the computer, e-mailed or uploaded to the internet. In one well-publicised case, a computer e-mailed out images as the burglar stole it, allowing the owner to give police a clear picture of the burglar's face even after the computer had been stolen.

As a Control Input Device

Special software can use the video stream from a webcam to assist or enhance a user's control of applications and games. Video features, including faces, shapes, models and colours can be observed and tracked to produce a corresponding form of control. For example, the position of a single light source can be tracked and used to emulate a mouse pointer, a head mounted light would allow hands-free computing and would greatly improve computer accessibility. This can also be applied to games, providing additional control, improved interactivity and immersiveness.

FreeTrack is a free webcam motion tracking application for Microsoft Windows that can track a special head mounted model in up to six degrees of freedom and output data to mouse, keyboard, joystick and FreeTrack supported games.

The EyeToy for the PlayStation 2 (The updated PlayStation 3 equivalent is the PlayStation Eye) and similarly the Xbox Live Vision Camera for the Xbox 360 and Xbox Live are colour digital cameras that have been used as control input devices by some games.

Small webcam-based PC games are available as either standalone executables or inside web browser windows using Adobe Flash.

Aggregators

Due to the increasing volume of webcams throughout the world, aggregator websites have arisen, allowing users to find live video streams based on location or other criteria. Aggregators provide collections of thousands of live video streams or up-to-date still pictures. In the sector of recreation and leisure, Webcams.travel is evolving as another such aggregator with a special focus on webcams interesting for traveling and holiday planning. These travel webcams are of such interest that they are also in the gallery of Google Earth as a default layer. Additionally, the webcams of Webcams.travel are now also part of the Google Maps standard layers.

Technology

Webcams typically include a lens, an image sensor, and some support electronics. Various lenses are available, the most common being a plastic lens that can be screwed in and out to set the camera's focus. Fixed focus lenses, which have no provision for adjustment, are also available. As a camera system's depth of field is greater for small imager formats and is greater for lenses with a large f/number (small aperture), the systems used in webcams have sufficiently large depth of field that the use of a fixed focus lens does not impact image sharpness much. Image sensors can be CMOS or CCD, the former being dominant for low-cost cameras, but CCD cameras do not necessarily outperform CMOS-based cameras in the low cost price range. Most consumer webcams are capable of providing VGA-resolution video at a frame rate of 30 frames per second. Many newer devices can produce video in multi-megapixel resolutions, and a few can run at high frame rates such as the PlayStation Eye, which can produce 320×240 video at 120 frames per second.

Support electronics are present to read the image from the sensor and transmit it to the host computer. The camera pictured to the right, for example, uses a Sonix SN9C101 to transmit its image over USB. Some cameras - such as mobile phone cameras - use a CMOS sensor with supporting electronics "on die", i.e. the sensor and the support electronics are built on a single silicon chip to save space and manufacturing costs. Most webcams feature built in microphones to make video conferencing more convenient.

The USB video device class (UVC) specification allows for interconnectivity of webcams to computers even without proprietary drivers installed. Microsoft Windows Vista, Linux and Mac OS X 10.4 & 10.5 have UVC drivers built in and do not require extra drivers, although they are often installed in order to add additional features.

Privacy

Some 'Trojan horse' programmes can allow malicious hackers to activate a computer's camera without the user's knowledge, providing the hacker with a live video feed from the unfortunate user's camera. Cameras such as Apple's older external iSight cameras include lens covers to thwart this. Most other webcams have a built-in LED that lights up whenever the camera is active (such as Apple's newer internal iSight), although the malicious nature of a trojan horse could have the LED programmed to be disabled even when the webcam is online.

In mid-January 2005 some search engine queries were published in an on-line forum which allow anyone to find thousands of Panasonic- and Axis-made high-end web cameras, provided that they have a web-based interface for remote viewing. Many such cameras are running on default configuration, which does not require any password login or IP address verification, making them visible to anyone.

Effects on Modern Society

Positive Uses: Video chat is a good example of positive use, since it allows for cheap real-time communication from anywhere in the world. Webcasting is generally also a positive side of webcams, although terrorist groups also use it to spread their opinions. Webcasting has spun up a global community, based primarily on amateur video production. However, news websites like the BBC also produce professional live news videos. YouTube is yet another example of amateur production of extremely famous video material.

Possible Negative Uses: Internet privacy is the biggest concern of webcams. Children and teens under the legal age of consent have easy access to video broadcasting hardware and software, worrying their parents. Adult webcam related material is also a large portion of the webcam related sites on the internet and can be easily accessed through search engines if no parental control is enforced. On 2007-03-23, a man named Kevin Whitrick committed cyber suicide live on the internet in front of viewers in a chat room website.

Output Devices: Monitor

A visual display unit, often called simply a monitor or display, is a piece of electrical equipment which displays images generated from the video output of devices such as computers, without producing a permanent record. Most newer monitors typically consist of a TFT LCD, with older monitors based around a cathode ray tube (CRT). Almost all of the mainstream new monitors being sold on market now are LCD. The monitor comprises the display device, simple circuitry to generate and format a picture from video sent by the signals source, and usually an enclosure. Within the signal source, either as an integral section or a modular component, there is a display adapter to generate video in a format compatible with the monitor.

Screen Size

The size of a display is typically given as the distance between two opposite screen corners. One problem with this method is that it does not distinguish between the aspect ratios of monitors with identical diagonal sizes, in spite of the fact that a shape of a given diagonal span's area decreases as it becomes less square. For example, a 4:3 21" monitor has an area of ~211 square inches, while a 16:9 21" widescreen has an area of only ~188 square inches.

This method of measurement is from the first types of CRT television, when round picture tubes were in common use. Being circular, they only needed to use their diameter to describe their tube size. When round tubes were used to display rectangular images, the diagonal measurement was equivalent to the round tube's diameter. This method continued even when CRT tubes were manufactured as rounded rectangles.

Another historically problematic practice is the direct measurement of a monitor's imaging element as its quoted size in publicity and advertising materials. Especially on CRT displays, a substantial portion of the imaging element is concealed behind the case's bezel or shroud in order to hide areas outside the monitor's safe area due to overscan. Seen as deceptive, widespread consumer objection and lawsuits eventually forced most manufacturers to instead measure viewable size.

Imaging Technologies

As with television, many different hardware technologies exist for displaying computer-generated output:

- Liquid crystal display (LCD). TFT LCDs are currently the most popular display device for computers.
  - Passive LCDs are noted for poor contrast and slow response. They were used in laptops until the mid 1990s.

- Thin film transistor LCDs generate much better images. Nearly all modern LCD monitors are TFTs.
- Cathode ray tube (CRT)
    - Raster scan computer monitors produce images using pixels. These were the most popular display device for older computers.
    - Vector displays, as used on the Vectrex, scientific and radar applications, and several early arcade machines such as Asteroids use CRT displays because of requirement for a deflection system, although a raster-based display may be used, too.
    - Television sets were used by most early personal and home computers, connecting composite video to the television set using a modulator. Resolution and image quality were strongly limited by the display capabilities of television.
- Plasma display
- Video projectors use CRT, LCD, DLP, LCoS, and other technology to emit light to a projection screen. Front projectors use screens as reflectors to send light back, while rear projectors use screens as diffusers to refract light forward. Rear projectors are often integrated into the same case as their screen.
- Surface-conduction electron-emitter display (SED)
- Organic light-emitting diode (OLED) display
- Penetron military aircraft displays

Cathode Ray Tube

The CRT or cathode ray tube, is the *picture tube* of a monitor. The back of the tube has a negatively charged cathode. The electron gun shoots electrons down the tube and onto a charged screen. The screen is coated with a pattern of phosphor dots that glow when struck by the electron stream. Each cluster of three dots, one of each colour, is one pixel.

The image on the monitor's screen is usually made up from at least tens of thousands of such tiny dots glowing on command from the computer. The closer together the pixels are, the sharper the image on screen can be. The distance between pixels on a computer monitor screen is called its dot pitch and is measured in millimeters. Most monitors have a dot pitch of 0.28 mm or less.

There are two electromagnets around the collar of the tube which deflect the electron beam. The beam scans across the top of the monitor from left to right, is then blanked and moved back to the left-hand side slightly below the previous trace (on the next scan line), scans across the second line and so on until the bottom right of the screen is reached. The beam is again blanked, and moved back to the top left to start again. This process draws a complete picture, typically 50 to 100 times a second. The number of times in one second that the electron gun redraws the entire image is called the refresh rate and is measured in hertz (cycles per second). It is common in television or very early computer equipment, to use a technique called interlacing, in which all the odd-numbered lines of an image are traced, and then all the even-numbered lines; the circuitry of such an interlaced display need be capable of only half the speed of a non-interlaced display. An interlaced display, particularly at a relatively low refresh rate, can appear to some observers to flicker, and may cause eyestrain.

Performance Measurements

The performance of a monitor is measured in the following parameters:

- Luminance is measured in candelas per square meter.
- Viewable image size is measured diagonally. For CRTs, the viewable size is typically one inch (25 mm) smaller than the tube itself.
- Display resolution is the number of distinct pixels in each dimension that can be displayed. Maximum resolution is limited by dot pitch.
- Dot pitch is the distance between pixels of the same colour in millimeters. In general, the smaller the dot pitch, the sharper the picture will appear.

- Refresh rate is the number of times in a second that a display is illuminated. Maximum refresh rate is limited by response time.
- Response time is the amount of time a pixel in a monitor takes to go from active (black) to inactive (white) and back to active (black) again. It is measured in milliseconds. Lower numbers mean faster transitions and therefore fewer visible image artifacts.
- Contrast ratio is the ratio of the luminosity of the brightest colour (white) to that of the darkest colour (black) that the monitor is capable of producing.
- Power consumption is measured in watts.
- Aspect ratios is the ratio of the horizontal length to the vertical length. 4:3 is the standard aspect ratio, for example, so that a screen with a width of 1024 pixels will have a height of 768 pixels. If a widescreen display has an aspect ratio of 16:9, a display that is 1024 pixels wide will have a height of 576 pixels.
- Viewing angle is the maximum angle at which images on the monitor can be viewed, without excessive degradation to the images. It is measured in degrees horizontally and vertically.

Printers: Line Printer

The line printer is a form of high speed impact printer in which one line of type is printed at a time. They are mostly associated with the early days of computing, but the technology is still in use. Print speeds of 600 to 1200 lines-per-minute (approximately 10 to 20 pages per minute) were common.

Designs

Four principal designs existed:

- Drum printers
- Chain (train) printers
- Bar printers
- Comb printers

Drum Printer

In a typical drum printer design, a fixed font character set is engraved onto the periphery of a number of print wheels, the number matching the number of columns (letters in a line) the printer could print. The wheels, joined to form a large drum (cylinder), spin at high speed and paper and an inked ribbon are stepped (moved) past the print position. As the desired character for each column passes the print position, a hammer strikes the paper from the rear and presses the paper against the ribbon and the drum, causing the desired character to be recorded on the continuous paper. Because the drum carrying the letterforms (characters) remains in constant motion, the strike-and-retreat action of the hammers had to be very fast. Typically, they were driven by voice coils mounted on the moving part of the hammer.

Often the character sequences are staggered around the drum, shifting with each column. This obviates the situation whereby all of the hammers fire simultaneously when printing a line that consists of the same character in all columns, such as a complete line of dashes ("——").

Lower-cost printers did not use a hammer for each column. Instead, a hammer was provided for every other column and the entire hammer bank was arranged to shift left and right, driven by another voice coil. For this style of printer, two complete revolutions of the character drum were required with one revolution being used to print all the "odd" columns and another revolution being used to print all of the "even" columns. But in this way, only half the number of hammers, magnets, and the associated channels of drive electronics were required.

Data Products was a typical vendor of drum printers, often selling similar models with both a full set of hammers (and delivering, for example 600 lines-per-minute of output) and a half set of hammers (delivering 300 LPM).

Chain (train) Printer

Chain printers (also known as train printers) placed the type on moving bars (a horizontally-moving chain). As with the drum printer, as the correct character passed by each column, a hammer was fired from behind the paper. Compared to drum printers, chain printers had the advantage that the type chain could usually be changed by the operator. By selecting chains that had a smaller character set (for example, just numbers and a few punctuation marks), the printer could print much faster than if the chain contained the entire upper- and lower-case alphabet, numbers, and all special symbols. This was because, with many more instances of the numbers appearing in the chain, the time spent waiting for the correct character to "pass by" was greatly reduced. IBM was probably the best-known chain printer manufacturer and the IBM 1403 is probably the most famous example of a chain printer.

Bar Printer

Bar printers were similar to chain printers but were slower and less expensive. Rather than a chain moving continuously in one direction, the characters were on fingers mounted on a bar that moved left-to-right and then right-to-left in front of the paper. An example was the IBM 1443.

In all three designs, timing of the hammers (the so called "flight time") was critical, and was adjustable as part of the servicing of the printer. For drum printers, incorrect timing of the hammer resulted in printed lines that wandered vertically, albeit with characters correctly aligned horizontally in their columns. For train and bar printers, incorrect timing of the hammers resulted in characters shifting horizontally, albeit on vertically-level printed lines.

Most drum, chain, and bar printers were capable of printing up to 132 columns, but a few designs could only print 80 columns and some other designs as many as 160 columns.

Comb Printer

Comb printers, also called line matrix printers, represent the fourth major design. These printers were a hybrid of dot matrix printing and line printing. In these printers, a comb of hammers printed a portion of a row of pixels at one time (for example, every eighth pixel). By shifting the comb back and forth slightly, the entire pixel row could be printed (continuing the example, in just eight cycles). The paper then advanced and the next pixel row was printed. Because far less motion was involved than in a conventional dot matrix printer, these printers were very fast compared to dot matrix printers and were competitive in speed with formed-character line printers while also being able to print dot-matrix graphics as well as variable-sized characters.

Printronix and TallyGenicom are well-known vendors of comb printers. Because all of these printing methods produced a lot of noise, lineprinters of all designs were always enclosed in sound-absorbing cases of varying sophistication.

Serial Printers

The secret to success with printers on serial ports is understanding that the computer and the printer must agree on baud rate and flow control, and that you must have serial ports and wiring capable of supporting the parameters you have chosen.

It is often not important that your serial baud rate be particularly high. Although it is somewhat simplified, 9600 baud can be thought of as 9,600 bits per second. Given some overhead, we can roughly say that dividing that number by 10 gives characters per second. As very few low end printers can even come close to 960 characters per second, you can see that there is usually no need to go any faster. In fact, very few dot matrix printers can keep up with even 2400 baud. That's what flow control is needed for- the printer needs to be able to say "Hey, hold up a second- let me digest what you've already sent me".

There are two choices for flow control: software or hardware. Software flow control is often referred to as XON or XON/XOFF, and you may see hardware flow control referred to as "ctsflow" or sometimes "dtrflow". Under high speed conditions, hardware flow control is preferred, but you do need to know HOW the printer should be wired to set this up, so software flow control is simpler.

The purpose of flow control is so that the printer can tell the computer that it is momentarily overwhelmed, cannot handle any more input right now, and the computer should suspend sending data until the printer notifies it that it is once again ready to receive data. If the computer and the printer do not agree on flow control, you will lose data. Whether or not the printer notifies you that this has happened is entirely up to the designer of the printer, so HP laser printers, for example. will display an error message on their front panel, but many other printers simply throw away data. Most printers don't rely entirely on flow control. They usually also have a buffer that fills up with incoming data and gets emptied as it prints. If the buffer is larger than the print job, no flow control is necessarily needed. That's why small jobs print OK, but larger jobs may not- when the buffer fills, the printer needs to yell "Stop".

As the computer sending the data might not respond instantly to that request, the printer has a "high water mark" for the buffer. It might, for example, send the "Stop" signal when the buffer is 90% full. Some printers let you control that high-water mark. If yours does, setting it lower could help.

But by default, the Operating System provides NO flow control on a serial port. If nothing else has been done, a serial port will default to 9600 baud, 8 bit, no parity, and NO flow control. That means it will pay absolutely no attention to the printer telling it not to send any more. That's when garbled junk starts spitting out of the printer. You need to set flow control. How you set this depends on what you have for serial ports. The very first thing you want to do is DISABLE the serial port (example: "disable tty1a"). This may be confusing because you ENABLE a printer attached to a port, but you never, never want a printer port itself enabled for login. To be safe, check the upper case version of the port also ("disable tty1A").

Many intelligent serial ports (Digiboard, Equinox, Computone, Maxpeed) have ways to set and keep serial parameters on their ports. For example, if you have a Digiboard, you can type:

"ditty /dev/ttyb02 9600 ixon printer"

to force the port to stay at 9600 with software flow control.

If you are going to put these in a startup script, it may be necessary to delay their execution a few seconds to give the multiport drivers time to get their boards all set up. What I usually do if have a "setprint" script that gets called (/usr/local/bin/setprint &) from /etc/rc2.d/S99printers. That script starts of with a 15 second sleep and then does the "ditty's" and whatever else is needed. In many environments, I also explicitly disable the affected ports so that no accidental getty's are running, and may issue appropriate chmod commands if the ports are used for direct access.

However, for the standard com ports (tty1a, tty2a), it's not as easy, and you need what's called a "hold-open" script.

The problem is that while intelligent serial boards have special commands to set flow control and keep it set, the standard Unix stty command doesn't work that way. To set any option, you have to "open" the port, which is simply done by combining the stty command with a redirection symbol:

stty ixon < /dev/tty1a

Technically, this command actually works, but the problem is that the port will be reset to defaults -ixon the instant that the port is "closed", and that happens just microseconds after you press return! So, effectively, it does nothing.

SCO technical articles suggest the following command:

(stty 9600 ixon -ixany ; while : ; do sleep 3600; done) < /dev/tty1a &

The 9600 is the baud rate, and could be different, and of course your printer might be on a different port.

This command forces the port to be held open; therefor the stty command actually stays in effect.

You can't just type this at the command line. Well, you can, but unless you preface it with 'nohup' it will stop working the moment you log out, and if you reboot your machine you'll have to type it again. So the better idea is to create a file containing this command and place it somewhere where it will be executed at startup. The directory /etc/rc.d/8 is a good place on most SCO systems. Call it anything you like; I often use "setprinter". Don't forget to chmod 755 it.

Actually, nowadays there is no reason at all not to leave out the while and do:

(stty 9600 ixon ixoff -ixany; sleep 2000000000) < /dev/tty1a &

That's over 60 years of "sleep". There is an advantage to the "while" version: if the sleep gets killed, the other version will restart it.

It's also possible to control multiple printers with one shell; see Bela Lubkin's newsgroup post stty hold open scripts

For third-party devices such as Digiboard, etc. you have to be sure that the device is ready to accept commands when you issue them. Although Digi (for example) claims this is completely unnecessary, my experience is that it sometimes is, so my rc script calls "/usr/bin/setprint &", and that script looks something like:

#!/bin/sh

sleep 15

ditty ixon printer ttya15

Bill Vermillion made a really neat suggestion for these scripts:

If you set multiple printers in /etc/rc.d/8, if you use differing sleep times, it will be easy to kill the processes of any particular job by noting the sleep value in ps.

I also typically run a sleep of 300 - 5 minutes - instead of an hour - in case somethings goes awry it comes to life in 5 minutes.

My sleep times will be 300,301,302,303, ad nauseum.

— Bill Vermillion bv @ wjv.com

You can check how your port is set by typing "stty -a < /dev/tty1a" You will see something like:

speed 9600 baud; ispeed 9600 baud; ospeed 9600 baud;

line=0;intr=DEL;quit=^\;erase=^H;kill=^U;eof=^D;eol=^@;

swtch = ^@;susp = ^Z;start = ^Q;stop = ^S;

-parenb -parodd cs8 -cstopb hupcl cread -clocal -loblk -ortsfl -ctsflow -rtsflow

-ignbrk brkint ignpar -parmrk -inpck -istrip -inlcr -igncr icrnl -iuclc

ixon -ixany -ixoff

isig icanon -xcase echo echoe echok -echonl -noflsh -iexten -tostop -xclude

opost -olcuc onlcr -ocrnl -onocr -onlret -ofill -ofdel -isscancode

If the line referring to ixon instead says:

-ixon -ixany -ixoff

then you do not have software flow control set at all.

Generally speaking, you are better off with hardware flow control. Unfortunately, "better" is sometimes harder to attain, simply because there is no absolute standard way of implementing hardware flow control. Fortunately, it's not completely out of hand: serial printers usually either use the rts/cts pins or dtr. **Most** use cts/rts, or if they use dtr, it's probably wired to cts, so you can use:

stty rtsflow ctsflow -ortsfl -ixon -ixoff -ixany -clocal

Older versions (Xenix, particularly) didn't do this well. Sometimes it helped to leave out "rtsflow". One some Unix 3.2v4.0 to 4.2, it sometimes was necessary to use "ortsfl" instead. At one point, SCO used "crtsfl" to replace "rtsflow ctsflow". This is no longer true. You can read the gruesome details of this at Jeff Liebermann's site.

Even software flow control can have wiring problems: if the transmit line from the computer to the printer is correct, the printer will receive characters and will print. If the transmit back from the printer to the computer is wrong, or broken, the printer can't signal the computer to stop sending. You can check this sort of thing with a simple led device for serial ports

(Radio Shack sells part no. 276-1401) or even with just a continuity test.

Another test is to drag over a dumb terminal and hook it up as though it were the printer. If you are using software (ixon) flow control, hit CTRL-S as you send a print job (the data will be on the terminal's screen). If the data stops, then flow control is working- which means if your printer is still producing junk, there's something wrong with it.

For hardware flow control, leave the printer off-line and then send a print job. If it goes to the printer (disappears from the queue), then hardware flow control is not working. *For more on wiring, see Serial Wiring*

Note on printers: Okidata serial printers require DSR Invalid when using 3 wire xon/xoff flow control. Set this on the printer, using the front panel menus. The printer will not print with 3 wire (2-3-7) setups without this. If you've wired for hardware flow control, you don't need this, but if you are using xon-xoff you might as well do this anyway.

Baud Rate

Let's start with some basics: the SCO box is going to assume 8 data bits, no parity, and one stop bit. We"ll get to the baud rate in a minute, but first:

If you are otherwise set correctly but the SCO is set for EVEN parity, you'll be able to send lower case "a"'s and "b"'s, but not upper case, and upper case "C"'s, but not lower case.

If it's set ODD, it will be the other way around.

Why? Because the characters themselves are 7 bits, and the eighth (paity) bit will be set or unset depending on whether the number of bits set (in 7 bits) is even or odd. So an "a" is decimal 65, which is 2 bits set (64 and 1), while a "b" is decimal 66, which is still 2 bits (64 and 2), while "c" is 3 bits (64, 2 and 1). So if "even" parity is set, the "c" needs a parity bit added.

If the printer is set 7/even/1, you can send just about anything, but nothing happens.

If the baud rate is wrong, you'll get "garbage": wrong characters, no characters, characters with umlauts, etc.

Dot Matrix Printer

Typical output from a dot matrix printer operating in *draft* mode. This entire image represents an area of printer output approximately 4.5 cm × 1.5cm (1.75 × 0.6 inches) in size.

History of Printing

Woodblock printing	200
Movable type	1040
Intaglio	1430s
Printing press	1454
Lithography	1796
Chromolithography	1837
Rotary press	1843
Flexography	1873
Mimeograph	1876
Hot metal typesetting	1886
Offset press	1903
Screen-printing	1907
Dye-sublimation	1957
Phototypesetting	1960s
Photocopier	1960s
Pad printing	1960s
Laser printer	1969
Dot matrix printer	1970
Thermal printer	
Inkjet printer	1976
3D printing	1986
Stereolithography	1986
Digital press	1993

A dot matrix printer or impact matrix printer is a type of computer printer with a print head that runs back and forth, or in an up and down motion, on the page and prints by impact, striking an ink-soaked cloth ribbon against the paper, much like a typewriter.

Unlike a typewriter or daisy wheel printer, letters are drawn out of a dot matrix, and thus, varied fonts and arbitrary graphics can be produced. Because the printing involves mechanical pressure, these printers can create carbon copies and carbonless copies.

Each dot is produced by a tiny metal rod, also called a "wire" or "pin", which is driven forward by the power of a tiny electromagnet or solenoid, either directly or through small levers (pawls). Facing the ribbon and the paper is a small guide plate (often made of an artificial jewel such as sapphire or ruby) pierced with holes to serve as guides for the pins. The moving portion of the printer is called the print head, and when running the printer as a generic text device generally prints one line of text at a time.

Most dot matrix printers have a single vertical line of dot-making equipment on their print heads; others have a few interleaved rows in order to improve dot density.

These machines can be highly durable. When they do wear out, it is generally due to ink invading the guide plate of the print head, causing grit to adhere to it; this grit slowly causes the channels in the guide plate to wear from circles into ovals or slots, providing less and less accurate guidance to the printing wires. Eventually, even with tungsten blocks and titanium pawls, the printing becomes too unclear to read.

Although nearly all inkjet, thermal, and laser printers produce dot matrices, in common parlance these are seldom called "dot matrix" printers, to avoid confusion with dot matrix *impact* printers.

Early Dot Matrix Printers

The LA30 was a 30 character/second dot matrix printer introduced in 1970 by Digital Equipment Corporation of Maynard, Massachusetts. It printed 80 columns of uppercase-only 5x7 dot matrix characters across a unique-sized paper. The printhead was driven by a stepper motor and the paper was advanced by a somewhat-unreliable and definitely noisy solenoid ratchet drive. The LA30 was available with both a parallel interface and a serial interface; however, the serial LA30 required the use of fill characters during the carriage-return operation.

The LA30 was followed in 1974 by the LA36, which achieved far greater commercial success, becoming for a time the standard dot matrix computer terminal. The LA36 used the same print head as the LA30 but could print on forms of any width up to 132 columns of mixed-case output on standard green bar fanfold paper. The carriage was moved by a much-more-capable servo drive using a dc motor and an optical encoder/tachometer. The paper was moved by a stepper motor. The LA36 was only available with a serial interface but unlike the earlier LA30, no fill characters were required. This was possible because, while the printer never communicated at faster than 30 characters per second, the mechanism was actually capable of printing at 60 characters per second. During the carriage return period, characters were *buffered* for subsequent printing at full speed during a *catch-up* period. The two-tone buzz produced by 60 character-per-second catch-up printing followed by 30 character-per-second ordinary printing was a distinctive feature of the LA36.

Digital then broadened the basic LA36 line onto a wide variety of dot matrix printers including:

- LA180 — 180 c/s line printer
- LS120 — 120 c/s terminal
- LA120 — 180 c/s advanced terminal
- LA34 — Cost-reduced terminal
- LA38 — An LA34 with more features
- LA12 — A portable terminal

In 1970, Centronics (then of Hudson, New Hampshire) introduced a dot matrix printer, the Centronics 101. The search for a reliable printer mechanism led it to develop a relationship with Brother Industries, Ltd. of Japan, and the sale of Centronics-badged Brother printer mechanisms equipped with a Centronics print head and Centronics electronics. Unlike Digital, Centronics concentrated on the low-end line printer marketplace with their distinctive units. In the process, they designed the parallel electrical interface that was to become standard on most dot matrix printers (indeed, most printers in general) until it started to be replaced by the Universal Serial Bus (USB) in the late 1990s.

Dot Matrix Features

As with any technology product, feature-sets for dot-matrix printers vary by price, intended market, and year of introduction.

Inkjet Printer

History of Printing

Inkjet printers operate by propelling variably-sized droplets of liquid or molten material (ink) onto almost any sized page. They are the most common type of computer printer for the general consumer due to their low cost, high quality of output, capability of printing in different colours, and ease of use.

Like most modern technologies, the present-day inkjet has built on the progress made by many earlier versions. Among many contributors, Epson, Hewlett-Packard and Canon can claim a substantial share of the credit for the development of the modern inkjet. In the worldwide consumer market, four manufacturers account for the majority of inkjet printer sales: Canon, Hewlett-Packard, Epson, and Lexmark.

The emerging ink jet material deposition market also uses ink jet technologies, typically piezoelectric jets, to deposit materials directly on substrates.

Technologies

There are three main technologies in use in contemporary inkjet printers: thermal, piezoelectric, and continuous.

Thermal Inkjets

Most consumer inkjet printers (Lexmark, Hewlett-Packard, and Canon) use print cartridges with a series of tiny electrically heated chambers constructed by photolithography. To produce an image, the printer runs a pulse of current through the heating elements causing a steam explosion in the chamber to form a bubble, which propels a droplet of ink onto the paper (hence Canon's tradename of *Bubblejet* for its inkjets). The ink's surface tension as well as the condensation and thus contraction of the vapor bubble, pulls a further charge of ink into the chamber through a narrow channel attached to an ink reservoir.

The ink used is known as *aqueous* (i.e. water-based inks using pigments or dyes) and the print head is generally cheaper to produce than other inkjet technologies. The principle was discovered by Canon engineer Ichiro Endo in August 1977.

Note that thermal inkjets have no relation to thermal printers, which produce images by heating thermal paper, as seen on older fax machines, cash register, ATM receipt, and lottery ticket printers.

Certain Epson printers use special Durabrite Ultra ink which is a type of thermal ink.

Thermal Printer

History of Printing

A thermal printer (or direct thermal printer) produces a printed image by selectively heating coated thermochromic paper, or thermal paper as it is commonly known, when the paper passes over the thermal print head. The coating turns black in the areas where it is heated, producing an image. Two-colour direct thermal printers are capable of printing both black and an additional colour (often red), by applying heat at two different temperatures.

Thermal transfer printing is a related method that uses a heat-sensitive ribbon instead of heat-sensitive paper.

Essential Mechanisms

A thermal printer comprises these key components:

- Thermal head — generates heat; prints on paper

- Platen — a rubber roller that feeds paper
- Spring — applies pressure to the thermal head, causing it to contact the thermo-sensitive paper
- Controller boards — for controlling the mechanism

In order to print, one inserts thermo-sensitive paper between the thermal head and the platen. The printer sends an electrical current to the heating resistor of the thermal head, which in turn generates heat in a prescribed pattern. The heat activates the thermo-sensitive coloring layer of the thermo-sensitive paper, which manifests a pattern of colour change in response. Such a printing mechanism is known as a thermal system or direct system. The paper is impregnated with a solid-state mixture of a dye and a suitable matrix; a combination of a fluoran leuco dye and an octadecylphosphonic acid is an example. When the matrix is heated above its melting point, the dye reacts with the acid, shifts to its colored form, and the changed form is then conserved in metastable state when the matrix solidifies back quickly enough. See thermochromism.

Controller boards are embedded with firmware to manage the thermal printer mechanisms. The Firmware can manage multiple bar code types, graphics and logos. They enable the user to choose between different resident fonts (also including Asian fonts) and character sizes.

Controller boards can drive various sensors like paper low, paper out, door open, top of form etc., and they are available with the most commonly used interfaces (RS232, Parallel, USB, wireless). For POS application some boards can also control the cash drawer.

Applications

Thermal printers print faster and quieter than dot matrix printers. They are also more economical since their only consumable is the paper itself. Even though the paper is more expensive, printers can be rapidly refilled, leading to almost zero downtime. Commercial applications of thermal printers include filling station pumps, information kiosks, point of sale systems, and voucher printers in slot machines.

Through the 1990s, many fax machines used thermal printing technology. Toward the beginning of the 21st century, however, thermal wax transfer, laser, and inkjet printing technology largely supplanted thermal printing technology in fax machines in order to allow plain-paper printouts.

The Game Boy Printer, made in 1998, was a small thermal printer used to print out certain elements from some Game Boy games.

Early formulations of the thermo-sensitive coating used in thermal paper were sensitive to incidental heat, abrasion, friction (which can cause heat, thus darkening the paper), light (which can fade printed images), and water. However, more modern thermal coating formulations have resulted in exceptional image stability; *theoretically*, thermally-printed text should remain legible at least 50 years.

Hospitals commonly record fetal ultrasound scan images on thermal paper. This can cause problems if the parents wish to preserve the image by laminating it using a traditional laminator, as the heat will cause the entire page to darken. It is advisable to test the laminator using thermal fax paper, or an unwanted thermal POS receipt to see if this happens. As before, an option is to make a permanent ink duplicate of the image, and laminate that, testing first to ensure that the copying process won't darken the image either.

Primary Storage Devices : RAM

'*Random access memory* (usually known by its acronym, RAM) is a form of computer data storage. Today, it takes the form of integrated circuits that allows the stored data to be accessed in any order (i.e., at *random*). The word *random* thus refers to the fact that any piece of data can be returned in a constant time, regardless of its physical location and whether or not it is related to the previous piece of data.

By contrast, storage devices such as tapes, magnetic discs and optical discs rely on the physical movement of the recording medium or a reading head. In these devices, the movement takes longer than data transfer, and the retrieval time varies based on the physical location of the next item. The word RAM is often associated with volatile types of memory (such as DRAM memory modules), where the information is lost after the power is switched off. Many other types of memory are RAM, too, including most types of ROM and flash memory called *NOR-Flash*.

History

An early type of widespread *writable* random access memory was the magnetic core memory, developed from 1949 to 1952, and subsequently used in most computers up until the development of the static and dynamic integrated RAM circuits in the late 1960s and early 1970s. Before this, computers used relays, delay line memory or various kinds of vacuum tube arrangements to implement "main" memory functions (i.e., hundreds or thousands of bits), some of which were *random access*, some not. Latches built out of vacuum tube triodes, and later, out of discrete transistors, were used for smaller and faster memories such as registers and (random access) register banks. Prior to the development of integrated ROM circuits, *permanent* (or *read-only*) random access memory was often constructed using semiconductor diode matrices driven by address decoders.

Types of RAM

Modern types of *writable* RAM generally store a bit of data in either the state of a flip-flop, as in SRAM (static RAM), or as a charge in a capacitor (or transistor gate), as in DRAM (dynamic RAM), EPROM, EEPROM and Flash. Some types have circuitry to detect and/or correct random faults called *memory errors* in the stored data, using parity bits or error correction codes. RAM of the *read-only* type, ROM, instead uses a metal mask to permanently enable/disable selected transistors, instead of storing a charge in them.

As both SRAM and DRAM are *volatile*, other forms of computer storage, such as disks and magnetic tapes, have been used as persistent storage in traditional computers. Many newer products instead rely on flash memory to maintain data when not in use, such as PDAs or small music players. Certain personal computers, such as many rugged computers and netbooks, have also replaced magnetic disks with flash drives. With flash memory, only the NOR type is capable of true random access, allowing direct code execution, and is therefore often used instead of ROM; the lower cost NAND type is commonly used for bulk storage in memory cards and solid-state drives.

Memory Hierarchy

Many computer systems have a memory hierarchy consisting of CPU registers, on-die SRAM caches, external caches, DRAM, paging systems, and virtual memory or swap space on a hard drive. This entire pool of memory may be referred to as "RAM" by many developers, even though the various subsystems can have very different access times, violating the original concept behind the *random access* term in RAM. Even within a hierarchy level such as DRAM, the specific row, column, bank, rank, channel, or interleave organization of the components make the access time variable, although not to the extent that rotating storage media or a tape is variable. The overall goal of using a memory hierarchy is to obtain the higher possible average access performance while minimizing the total cost of entire memory system. (Generally, the memory hierarchy follows the access time with the fast CPU registers at the top and the slow hard drive at the bottom.)

In many modern personal computers, the RAM comes in an easily upgraded form of modules called memory modules or DRAM modules about the size of a few sticks of chewing gum. These can quickly be replaced should they become damaged or too small for current purposes. As suggested above, *smaller* amounts of RAM (mostly SRAM) are also integrated in the CPU and other ICs on the motherboard, as well as in hard-drives, CD-ROMs, and several other parts of the computer system.

ROM

Read-only memory (usually known by its acronym, ROM) is a class of storage media used in computers and other electronic devices. Because data stored in ROM cannot be modified (at least not very quickly or easily), it is mainly used to distribute firmware (software that is very closely tied to specific hardware, and unlikely to require frequent updates).

In its strictest sense, ROM refers only to mask ROM (the oldest type of solid state ROM), which is fabricated with the desired data permanently stored in it, and thus can never be modified. However, more modern types such as EPROM and flash EEPROM can be erased and re-programmed multiple times; they are still described as "read-only memory"(ROM) because the reprogramming process is generally infrequent, comparatively slow, and often does not permit random access writes to individual memory locations. Despite the simplicity of mask ROM, economies of scale and field-programmability often make reprogrammable technologies more flexible and inexpensive, so mask ROM is rarely used in new products as of 2007.

History

The simplest type of solid state ROM is as old as semiconductor technology itself. Combinational logic gates can be joined manually to map n-bit address input onto arbitrary values of m-bit data output (a look-up table). With the invention of the integrated circuit came mask ROM. Mask ROM consists of a grid of word lines (the address input) and bit lines (the data output), selectively joined together with transistor switches, and can represent an arbitrary look-up table with a regular physical layout and predictable propagation delay.

In mask ROM, the data is physically encoded in the circuit, so it can only be programmed during fabrication. This leads to a number of serious disadvantages:

1. It is only economical to buy mask ROM in large quantities, since users must contract with a foundry to produce a custom design.
2. The turnaround time between completing the design for a mask ROM and receiving the finished product is long, for the same reason.

3. Mask ROM is impractical for R&D work since designers frequently need to modify the contents of memory as they refine a design.
4. If a product is shipped with faulty mask ROM, the only way to fix it is to recall the product and physically replace the ROM.

Subsequent developments have addressed these shortcomings. PROM, invented in 1956, allowed users to programme its contents exactly once by physically altering its structure with the application of high-voltage pulses. This addressed problems 1 and 2 above, since a company can simply order a large batch of fresh PROM chips and programme them with the desired contents at its designers' convenience. The 1971 invention of EPROM essentially solved problem 3, since EPROM (unlike PROM) can be repeatedly reset to its unprogrammed state by exposure to strong ultraviolet light. EEPROM, invented in 1983, went a long way to solving problem 4, since an EEPROM can be programmed in-place if the containing device provides a means to receive the programme contents from an external source (e.g. a personal computer via a serial cable). Flash memory, invented at Toshiba in the mid-1980s, and commercialized in the early 1990s, is a form of EEPROM that makes very efficient use of chip area and can be erased and reprogrammed thousands of times without damage.

All of these technologies improved the flexibility of ROM, but at a significant cost-per-chip, so that in large quantities mask ROM would remain an economical choice for many years. (Decreasing cost of reprogrammable devices had almost eliminated the market for mask ROM by the year 2000.) Furthermore, despite the fact that newer technologies were increasingly less "read-only," most were envisioned only as replacements for the traditional use of mask ROM.

The most recent development is NAND flash, also invented by Toshiba. Its designers explicitly broke from past practice, stating plainly that "the aim of NAND Flash is to replace hard disks," rather than the traditional use of ROM as a form of non-volatile primary storage. As of 2007, NAND has partially achieved this goal by offering throughput comparable to hard disks, higher tolerance of physical shock, extreme miniaturization (in the form of USB flash drives and tiny microSD memory cards, for example), and much lower power consumption.

Use of ROM for Programme Storage

Every stored-programme computer requires some form of [[non-volatile]or erasable] storage to store the initial programme that runs when the computer is powered on or otherwise begins execution (a process known as bootstrapping, often abbreviated to "booting" or "booting up"). Likewise, every non-trivial computer requires some form of mutable memory to record changes in its state as it executes.

Forms of read-only memory were employed as non-volatile storage for programmes in most early stored-programme computers, such as ENIAC after 1948 (until then it was not a stored-programme computer as every programme had to be manually wired into the machine, which could take days to weeks). Read-only memory was simpler to implement since it required only a mechanism to read stored values, and not to change them in-place, and thus could be implemented with very crude electromechanical devices (see historical examples below). With the advent of integrated circuits in the 1960s, both ROM and its mutable counterpart static RAM were implemented as arrays of transistors in silicon chips; however, a ROM memory cell could be implemented using fewer transistors than an SRAM memory cell, since the latter requires a latch (comprising 5-20 transistors) to retain its contents, while a ROM cell might consist of the absence (logical 0) or presence (logical 1) of a single transistor connecting a bit line to a word line. Consequently, ROM could be implemented at a lower cost-per-bit than RAM for many years.

Most home computers of the 1980s stored a BASIC interpreter or operating system in ROM as other forms of non-volatile storage such as magnetic disk drives were too expensive. For example, the Commodore 64 included 64 KiB of RAM and

20 KiB of ROM contained a BASIC interpreter and the "KERNAL" (sic) of its operating system. Later home or office computers such as the IBM PC XT often included magnetic disk drives, and larger amounts of RAM, allowing them to load their operating systems from disk into RAM, with only a minimal hardware initialization core and bootloader remaining in ROM (known as the BIOS in IBM-compatible computers). This arrangement allowed for a more complex and easily upgradeable operating system.

In modern PCs, "ROM" (or Flash) is used to store the basic bootstrapping firmware for the main processor, as well as the various firmware needed to internally control self contained devices such as graphic cards, hard disks, DVD drives, TFT screens, etc, in the system. Today, many of these "read-only" memories – especially the BIOS – are often replaced with Flash memory (see below), to permit in-place reprogramming should the need for a firmware upgrade arise. However, simple and mature sub-systems (such as the keyboard or some communication controllers in the ICs on the main board, for example) may employ mask ROM or OTP (one time programmable).

ROM and successor technologies such as Flash are prevalent in embedded systems. This governs everything from industrial robots to appliances and consumer electronics (MP3 players, set-top boxes, etc) all of which are designed for specific functions, but nonetheless based on general-purpose microprocessors in most cases. With software usually tightly coupled to hardware, programme changes are rarely needed in such devices (which typically lack devices such as hard disks for reasons of cost, size, and/or power consumption). As of 2008, most products use Flash rather than mask ROM, and many provide some means for connection to a PC for firmware updates; a digital audio player's might be updated to support a new file format for instance. Some hobbyists have taken advantage of this flexibility to reprogram consumer products for new purposes; for example, the iPodLinux and OpenWRT projects have enabled users to run full-featured Linux distributions on their MP3 players and wireless routers, respectively.

ROM is also useful for binary storage of cryptographic data, as it makes them difficult to replace, which may be desirable in order to enhance information security.

ROM for Data Storage

Since ROM (at least in hard-wired mask form) cannot be modified, it is really only suitable for storing data which is not expected to need modification for the life of the device. To that end, ROM has been used in many computers to store look-up tables for the evaluation of mathematical and logical functions (for example, a floating-point unit might tabulate the sine function in order to facilitate faster computation). This was especially effective when CPUs were slow and ROM was cheap compared to RAM.

Notably, the display adapters of early personal computers stored tables of bitmapped font characters in ROM. This usually meant that the text display font could not be changed interactively. This was the case for both the CGA and MDA adapters available with the IBM PC XT. The use of ROM to store such small amounts of data has disappeared almost completely in modern general-purpose computers. However, Flash ROM has taken over a new role as a medium for mass storage or secondary storage of files.

Types of ROMs

Semiconductor Based

Classic mask-programmed ROM chips are integrated circuits that physically encode the data to be stored, and thus it is impossible to change their contents after fabrication. Other types of non-volatile solid-state memory permit some degree of modification:

- Programmable read-only memory (PROM), or one-time programmable ROM (OTP), can be written to or programmed via a special device called a PROM programmer. Typically, this device uses high voltages to permanently destroy or create internal links (fuses or antifuses) within the chip. Consequently, a PROM can only be programmed once.

- Erasable programmable read-only memory (EPROM) can be erased by exposure to strong ultraviolet light (typically for 10 minutes or longer), then rewritten with a process that again requires application of higher than usual voltage. Repeated exposure to UV light will eventually wear out an EPROM, but the endurance of most EPROM chips exceeds 1000 cycles of erasing and reprogramming. EPROM chip packages can often be identified by the prominent quartz "window" which allows UV light to enter. After programming, the window is typically covered with a label to prevent accidental erasure. Some EPROM chips are factory-erased before they are packaged, and include no window; these are effectively PROM.
- Electrically erasable programmable read-only memory (EEPROM) is based on a similar semiconductor structure to EPROM, but allows its entire contents (or selected banks) to be electrically erased, then rewritten electrically, so that they need not be removed from the computer (or camera, MP3 player, etc.). Writing or flashing an EEPROM is much slower (milliseconds per bit) than reading from a ROM or writing to a RAM (nanoseconds in both cases).
    - o Electrically alterable read-only memory (EAROM) is a type of EEPROM that can be modified one bit at a time. Writing is a very slow process and again requires higher voltage (usually around 12 V) than is used for read access. EAROMs are intended for applications that require infrequent and only partial rewriting. EAROM may be used as non-volatile storage for critical system setup information; in many applications, EAROM has been supplanted by CMOS RAM supplied by mains power and backed-up with a lithium battery.
    - o Flash memory (or simply flash) is a modern type of EEPROM invented in 1984. Flash memory can be erased and rewritten faster than ordinary EEPROM, and newer designs feature very high

endurance (exceeding 1,000,000 cycles). Modern NAND flash makes efficient use of silicon chip area, resulting in individual ICs with a capacity as high as 16 GB as of 2007; this feature, along with its endurance and physical durability, has allowed NAND flash to replace magnetic in some applications (such as USB flash drives). Flash memory is sometimes called flash ROM or flash EEPROM when used as a replacement for older ROM types, but not in applications that take advantage of its ability to be modified quickly and frequently.

By applying write protection, some types of reprogrammable ROMs may temporarily become read-only memory.

Other Technologies

There are other types of non-volatile memory which are not based on solid-state IC technology, including:

- Optical storage media, such CD-ROM which is read-only (analogous to masked ROM). CD-R is Write Once Read Many (analogous to PROM), while CD-RW supports erase-rewrite cycles (analogous to EEPROM); both are designed for backwards-compatibility with CD-ROM.

Historical Examples

- Diode matrix ROM, used in small amounts in many computers in the 1960s as well as electronic desk calculators and keyboard encoders for terminals. This ROM was programmed by installing discrete semiconductor diodes at selected locations between a matrix of *word line traces* and *bit line traces* on a printed circuit board.
- Resistor, capacitor, or transformer matrix ROM, used in many computers until the 1970s. Like diode matrix ROM, it was programmed by placing components at selected locations between a matrix of word lines and bit lines. ENIAC's Function Tables were resistor matrix

ROM, programmed by manually setting rotary switches. Various models of the IBM System/360 and complex peripherial devices stored their microcode in either capacitor (called BCROS for *Balanced Capacitor Read Only Storage* on the 360/50 & 360/65 or CCROS for *Card Capacitor Read Only Storage* on the 360/30) or transformer (called TROS for *Transformer Read Only Storage* on the 360/20, 360/40 and others) matrix ROM.

- Core rope, a form of transformer matrix ROM technology used where size and/or weight were critical. This was used in NASA/MIT's Apollo Spacecraft Computers, DEC's PDP-8 computers, and other places. This type of ROM was programmed by hand by weaving "word line wires" inside or outside of ferrite transformer cores.
- The perforated metal character mask ("stencil") in Charactron cathode ray tubes, which was used as ROM to shape a wide electron beam to form a selected character shape on the screen either for display or a scanned electron beam to form a selected character shape as an overlay on a video signal.
- Various mechanical devices used in early computing equipment. A machined metal plate served as ROM in the dot matrix printers on the IBM 026 and IBM 029 key punches.

Secondary Storage Devices : FDD

Feature Driven Development (FDD) is an iterative and incremental software development process. It is one of a number of Agile methods for developing software and forms part of the Agile Alliance. FDD blends a number of industry-recognized best practices into a cohesive whole. These practices are all driven from a client-valued functionality (feature) perspective. Its main purpose is to deliver tangible, working software repeatedly in a timely manner.

History

FDD was initially devised by Jeff De Luca to meet the specific needs of a 15 month, 50 person software development project at a large Singapore bank in 1997. Jeff De Luca delivered a set of five processes that covered the development of an overall model and the listing, planning, design and building of features. The first process is heavily influenced by Peter Coad´s approach to object modeling. The second process incorporates Peter Coad's ideas of using a feature list to manage functional requirements and development tasks. The other processes and the blending of the processes into a cohesive whole is a result of Jeff De Luca's experience. Since its successful use on the Singapore project there have been several implementations of FDD.

The description of FDD was first introduced to the world in Chapter 6 of the book *Java Modeling in Colour with UML* by Peter Coad, Eric Lefebvre and Jeff De Luca in 1999. In Stephen Palmer and Mac Felsing´s book *A Practical Guide to Feature-Driven Development* (published in 2002) a more general description of FDD, decoupled from java modeling in colour, is given.

The original and latest FDD processes can be found on Jeff De Luca´s website under the ´Article´ area. There is also a Community website available at which people can learn more about FDD, questions can be asked, and experiences and the processes themselves are discussed.

Overview

FDD is a model-driven short-iteration process that consists of five basic activities. For accurate state reporting and keeping track of the software development project, milestones that mark the progress made on each feature are defined. This section gives a high level overview of the activities.

Activities

FDD describes five basic activities that are within the software development process. In the figure on the right the meta-process model for these activities is displayed. During the first three sequential activities an overall model shape is established. The final two activities are iterated for each feature. For more detailed information about the individual sub-activities have a look at Table 2 (derived from the process description in the ´Article´ section of Jeff De Luca´s website). The concepts involved in these activities are explained in Table 3.

Develop Overall Model

The project starts with a high-level walkthrough of the scope of the system and its context. Next, detailed domain walkthroughs are held for each modeling area. In support of each domain, walkthrough models are then composed by small groups which are presented for peer review and discussion. One of the proposed models or a merge of them is selected which becomes the model for that particular domain area. Domain area models are merged into an overall model, the overall model shape being adjusted along the way.

HDD

A hard disk drive (often shortened as "hard disk" or "hard drive"), is a non-volatile storage device which stores digitally encoded data on rapidly rotating platters with magnetic surfaces. Strictly speaking, "drive" refers to a device distinct from its medium, such as a tape drive and its tape, or a floppy disk drive and its floppy disk. Early HDDs had removable media; however, an HDD today is typically a sealed unit (except for a filtered vent hole to equalize air pressure) with fixed media.

History

HDDs (introduced in 1956 as data storage for an IBM accounting computer) were originally developed for use with general purpose computers. During the 1990s, the need for large-scale, reliable storage, independent of a particular device, led to the introduction of embedded systems such as RAID arrays, network attached storage (NAS) systems and storage area network (SAN) systems that provide efficient and reliable access to large volumes of data. In the 21st century, HDD usage expanded into consumer applications such as camcorders, cellphones (e.g. the Nokia N91), digital audio players, digital video players (e.g. the iPod Classic), digital video recorders, personal digital assistants and video game consoles.

Technology

HDDs record data by magnetizing ferromagnetic material directionally, to represent either a 0 or a 1 binary digit. They read the data back by detecting the magnetization of the material. A typical HDD design consists of a spindle which holds one or more flat circular disks called platters, onto which the data are recorded. The platters are made from a non-magnetic material, usually aluminum alloy or glass, and are coated with a thin layer of magnetic material. Older disks used iron(III) oxide as the magnetic material, but current disks use a cobalt-based alloy.

The platters are spun at very high speeds. Information is written to a platter as it rotates past devices called read-and-write heads that operate very close (tens of nanometers in new drives) over the magnetic surface. The read-and-write head is used to detect and modify the magnetization of the material immediately under it. There is one head for each magnetic platter surface on the spindle, mounted on a common arm. An actuator arm (or access arm) moves the heads on an arc (roughly radially) across the platters as they spin, allowing each head to access almost the entire surface of the platter as it spins. The arm is moved using a voice coil actuator or in some older designs a stepper motor.

The magnetic recording media are CoCrPt-based magnetic thin films of about 10-20nm in thickness. The thin films are normally deposit on glass/ceramic/metal substrate and covered by thin carbon layer for protection. The Co-based alloy thin films are polycrystalline and the size of grains has an order of 10 nm. Because the sizes of each grain are tiny, they are typical single domain magnets. The media are magnetically hard (coercivity is about 0.3T) so that a stable remnant magnetization can be achieved. The grain boundaries turn out to be very important. The reason is that, the grains are very small and close to each other, so the coupling between each grains are very strong. When one grain is magnetized, the adjacent grains tend to be aligned parallel to it or demagnetized. Then both the stability of the data and signal-to-noise ratio will be sabotaged A clear grain boundary can weaken the coupling of the grains and subsequently increase the signal-to-noise ratio. During writing process, ideally one grain can store one bit (1/0). However, current technology can not reach that far yet. In practice, a group of grains (about 100) are magnetized as one bit. So, in order to increase the data density, smaller grains are required. From microstructure point of view, longitudinal and perpendicular recording are the same. Also, similar Co-based thin films are used in both longitudinal and perpendicular recording. However, the fabrication processes are different to gain different crystal structure and magnetic properties. In longitudinal recording, the single-domain grains have uniaxial anisotropy with easy axes lying in the film plane. The consequence of this arrangement is that adjacent magnets repel each other. Therefore the magnetostatic energy is so large that it is difficult to increase areal density. Perpendicular recording media, on the other hand, has the easy axis of the grains oriented perpendicular to the disk plane. Adjacent magnets attract to each other and magnetostatic energy are much lower. So, much higher areal density can be achieved in perpendicular recording. Another unique feature in perpendicular recording is that a soft magnetic underlayer are incorporated into the recording disk.This underlayer is used to conduct writing magnetic flux so that the writing is more efficient. This will be discussed in writing process. Therefore, a higher anisotropy medium film, such as L10-FePt and rare-earth magnets, can be used.

Older drives read the data on the platter by sensing the rate of change of the magnetism in the head; these heads had small coils, and worked (in principle) much like magnetic-tape playback heads, although not in contact with the recording surface. As data density increased, read heads using magnetoresistance (MR) came into use; the electrical resistance of the head changed according to the strength of the magnetism from the platter. Later development made use of spintronics; in these heads, the magnetoresistive effect was much greater than in earlier types, and was dubbed "giant" magnetoresistance (GMR). This refers to the degree of effect, not the physical size, of the head—the heads themselves are extremely tiny, and are too small to be seen without a microscope. GMR read heads are now commonplace.

HD heads are kept from contacting the platter surface by the air that is extremely close to the platter; that air moves at, or close to, the platter speed. The record and playback head are mounted on a block called a slider, and the surface next to the platter is shaped to keep it just barely out of contact. It's a type of air bearing.

The magnetic surface of each platter is conceptually divided into many small sub-micrometre-sized magnetic regions, each of which is used to encode a single binary unit of information. In today's HDDs, each of these magnetic regions is composed of a few hundred magnetic grains. Each magnetic region forms a magnetic dipole which generates a highly localized magnetic field nearby. The write head magnetizes a region by generating a strong local magnetic field. Early HDDs used an electromagnet both to generate this field and to read the data by using electromagnetic induction. Later versions of inductive heads included metal in Gap (MIG) heads and thin film heads. In today's heads, the read and write elements are separate, but in close proximity, on the head portion of an actuator arm. The read element is typically magneto-resistive while the write element is typically thin-film inductive.

In modern drives, the small size of the magnetic regions creates the danger that their magnetic state might be lost because of thermal effects. To counter this, the platters are coated with two parallel magnetic layers, separated by a 3-atom-thick layer of the non-magnetic element ruthenium, and the two layers are magnetized in opposite orientation, thus reinforcing each other. Another technology used to overcome thermal effects to allow greater recording densities is perpendicular recording, first shipped in 2005, as of 2007 the technology was used in many HDDs.

Modern drives also make extensive use of Error Correcting Codes (ECCs), particularly Reed–Solomon error correction. These techniques store extra bits for each block of data that are determined by mathematical formulas. The extra bits allow many errors to be fixed. While these extra bits take up space on the hard drive, they allow higher recording densities to be employed, resulting in much larger storage capacity for user data.

CD

A Compact Disc (also known as a CD) is an optical disc used to store digital data, originally developed for storing digital audio. The CD, available on the market since October 1982, remains the standard physical medium for sale of commercial audio recordings to the present day.

Standard CDs have a diameter of 120 mm and can hold up to 80 minutes of audio (700 MB of data). The Mini CD has various diameters ranging from 60 to 80 mm; they are sometimes used for CD singles or device drivers, storing up to 24 minutes of audio.

The technology was later adapted and expanded to include data storage CD-ROM, write-once audio and data storage CD-R, rewritable media CD-RW, Super Audio CD (SACD), Video Compact Discs (VCD), Super Video Compact Discs (SVCD), PhotoCD, PictureCD, CD-i, and Enhanced CD.

CD-ROMs and CD-Rs remain widely used technologies in the computer industry. The CD and its extensions are successful: in 2004, worldwide sales of CD audio, CD-ROM, and CD-R reached about 30 billion discs. By 2007, 200 billion CDs had been sold worldwide.

History

The compact disc is a spin-off of the Laserdisc technology. Philips publicly demonstrated a prototype of an optical digital audio disc at a press conference called "Philips Introduce Compact Disc" in Eindhoven, The Netherlands on March 8, 1979. Three years earlier, Sony first publicly demonstrated an optical digital audio disc in September 1976. In September 1978, they demonstrated an optical digital audio disc with a 150 minute playing time, and with specifications of 44,056 Hz sampling rate, 16-bit linear resolution, cross-interleaved error correction code, that were similar to those of the Compact Disc introduced in 1982. Technical details of Sony's digital audio disc were presented during the 62nd AES Convention, held on March 13-16, 1979 in Brussels.

Later that year, Sony and Philips Consumer Electronics (Philips) set up a joint task force of engineers to design a new digital audio disc. The task force, led by prominent members Kees Schouhamer Immink and Toshitada Doi (W•N)Rà_), progressed the research into laser technology and optical discs that had been started independently by Philips and Sony in 1977 and 1975, respectively. After a year of experimentation and discussion, the taskforce produced the *Red Book*, the Compact Disc standard. Philips contributed the general manufacturing process, based on video Laserdisc technology. Philips also contributed Eight-to-Fourteen Modulation (EFM), which offers both a long playing time and a high resilience against disc defects such as scratches and fingerprints, while Sony contributed the error-correction method, CIRC. The *Compact Disc Story*, told by a former member of the taskforce, gives background information on the many technical decisions made, including the choice of the sampling frequency, playing time, and disc diameter. The taskforce consisted of around 8 persons, though according to Philips, the compact disc was thus "invented collectively by a large group of people working as a team."

The first commercially available CD was pressed in Hanover, Germany, by PDO-the Polydor Pressing Operations plant, in 1980. The disc contained a recording of Richard Strauss's Eine Alpensinfonie, played by the Berlin Philharmonic and conducted by Herbert von Karajan. In August 1982 the real pressing was ready to begin in the new factory, not far from the place where Emil Berliner had produced his first gramophone record 93 years earlier. By now, Deutsche Grammophon, Berliner's company and the publisher of the Strauss recording, had become a part of PolyGram. The first CD to be manufactured at the new factory was The Visitors by ABBA. The first album to be *released* on CD was Billy Joel's *52nd Street*, that reached the market alongside Sony's CD player CDP-101 on October 1, 1982 in Japan. Early the following year on March 2, 1983 CD players & Discs (16 titles - CBS Records) were released in the United States and other markets. This event is often seen as the "Big Bang" of the digital audio revolution. The new audio disc was enthusiastically received, especially in the early-adopting classical music and audiophile communities and its handling quality received particular praise.

As the price of players sank rapidly, the CD began to gain popularity in the larger popular and rock music markets. The first artist to sell a million copies on CD was Dire Straits, with its 1985 album *Brothers in Arms*. The first major artist to have his entire catalogue converted to CD was David Bowie, whose 15 studio albums were made available by RCA in February 1985, along with 4 Greatest Hits albums. In 1988, 400 million CDs were manufactured by 50 pressing plants around the world. To date, the biggest selling CD (as opposed to the biggest selling title) is Beatles "1", released in November, 2000, with worldwide sales of 30 million discs.

The CD was planned to be the successor of the gramophone record, rather than primarily as a data storage medium. Only later did the concept of an "audio file" arise, and its generalization to a data file. From its origins as a musical format, CDs have grown to encompass other applications. In June 1985, the CD-ROM (read-only memory) and, in 1990, CD-Recordable were introduced, also developed by both Sony and Philips.

With the advent of the MP3 in the 2000s, the sales of CDs has dropped in seven out of the last eight years. In 2008, large label CD sales dropped 20%., although independent and DIY music sales may be tracking better according to figures released March 30, 2009.

Physical Details

A. A polycarbonate disc layer has the data encoded by using bumps.

B. A reflective layer reflects the laser back.

C. A lacquer layer is used to prevent oxidation

D. Artwork is screen printed on the top of the disc.

E. A laser beam reads the polycarbonate disc, is reflected back, and read by the player.

A CD is made from 1.2 mm thick, almost-pure polycarbonate plastic and weighs approximately 16 grams. From the center outward components are at the center (spindle) hole, the first-transition area (clamping ring), the clamping area (stacking ring), the second-transition area (mirror band), the information (data) area, and the rim. A thin layer of aluminum or, more rarely, gold is applied to the surface to make it reflective, and is protected by a film of lacquer that is normally spin coated directly on top of the reflective layer, upon which the label print is applied. Common printing methods for CDs are screen-printing and offset printing.

CD data are stored as a series of tiny indentations known as "*pits*", encoded in a spiral track molded into the top of the polycarbonate layer. The areas between pits are known as "lands". Each pit is approximately 100 nm deep by 500 nm wide, and varies from 850 nm to 3.5 µm in length.

The distance between the tracks, the pitch, is 1.6 µm. A CD is read by focusing a 780 nm wavelength (near infrared) semiconductor laser through the bottom of the polycarbonate layer. The change in height between pits and lands results in a difference in intensity in the light reflected. By measuring the intensity change with a photodiode, the data can be read from the disc.

The pits and lands themselves do not directly represent the zeros and ones of binary data. Instead, Non-return-to-zero, inverted (NRZI) encoding is used: a change from pit to land or land to pit indicates a one, while no change indicates a zero. This in turn is decoded by reversing the Eight-to-Fourteen Modulation used in mastering the disc, and then reversing the Cross-Interleaved Reed-Solomon Coding, finally revealing the raw data stored on the disc.

CDs are susceptible to damage from both daily use and environmental exposure. Pits are much closer to the label side of a disc, so that defects and dirt on the clear side can be out of focus during playback. Consequently, CDs suffer more scratch damage on the label side whereas scratches on the clear side can be repaired by refilling them with similar refractive plastic, or by careful polishing. Initial music CDs were known to suffer from "CD rot", or "laser rot", in which the internal reflective layer degrades. When this occurs the CD may become unplayable.

Disc Shapes and Diameters

The digital data on a CD begin at the center of the disc and proceeds toward the edge, which allows adaptation to the different size formats available. Standard CDs are available in two sizes. By far the most common is 120 mm in diameter, with a 74- or 80-minute audio capacity and a 650 or 700 MB data capacity. This diameter has also been adopted by later formats, including Super Audio CD, DVD, HD DVD, and Blu-ray Disc. 80 mm discs ("Mini CDs") were originally designed for CD singles and can hold up to 21 minutes of music or 184 MB of data but never really became popular. Today, nearly every single is released on a 120 mm CD, called a Maxi single.

"Shaped CD"

Novelty CDs are also available in numerous shapes and sizes, and are used mostly for marketing. A common variant is a "business card" CD, a single with portions removed at the top and bottom to more closely resemble a business card.

Physical size	Audio Capacity	CD-ROM Data Capacity	Note
12 cm	74–80 min	650–703 MB	Standard size
8 cm	21–24 min	185–210 MB	Mini-CD size
85x54 mm - 86x64 mm	~6 min	10-65 MB	"Business card" size

DVD

DVD, also known as "Digital Versatile Disc" or "Digital Video Disc," is an optical disc storage media format. Its main uses are video and data storage. Most DVDs are of the same dimensions as compact discs (CDs) but store more than six times as much data.

Variations of the term *DVD* often describe the way data is stored on the discs: DVD-ROM (Read Only Memory), has data that can only be read and not written, DVD-R and DVD+R can record data only once and then function as a DVD-ROM. DVD-RW, DVD+RW and DVD-RAM can both record and erase data multiple times. The wavelength used by standard DVD lasers is 650 nm, and thus the light has a red colour.

DVD-Video and DVD-Audio discs respectively refer to properly formatted and structured video and audio content. Other types of DVDs, including those with video content, may be referred to as DVD-Data discs.

As next generation High Definition more advanced optical formats such as Blu-ray Disc also use a disc identical in some aspects, the original DVD is occasionally given the retronym SD DVD (for standard definition). However, the trademarked HD DVD discs have been discontinued since Blu-ray absorbed their market share.

History

In 1993, two high-density optical storage formats were being developed; one was the MultiMedia Compact Disc (MMCD), backed by Philips and Sony, and the other was the Super Density (SD) disc, supported by Toshiba, Time Warner, Matsushita Electric, Hitachi, Mitsubishi Electric, Pioneer, Thomson, and JVC.

Representatives of the SD camp approached IBM, asking for advice on the file system to use for their disk as well as looking for support for their format for storing computer data. A researcher from IBM's Almaden Research Center received that request and also learned of the MMCD development project. Wary of being caught in a repeat of the costly videotape format war between VHS and Betamax of the 1980s, he convened a group of computer industry experts (including representatives from Apple, Microsoft, Sun, Dell, and many others), this group was referred to as the Technical Working Group, or TWG. The TWG voted to boycott both formats unless the two camps agreed on a single, converged standard. Lou Gerstner, president of IBM, was recruited to apply pressure on the executives of the warring factions. Eventually, the computer companies won the day, and a single format, now called DVD, was agreed upon. The TWG also collaborated with the Optical Storage Technology Association (OSTA) on the use of their implementation of the ISO-13346 file system, known as Universal Disk Format (UDF), for use on the new DVDs.

Philips and Sony abandoned their MultiMedia Compact Disc and agreed upon a specification mostly similar to Toshiba and Matsushita's Super Density Disc except for the dual-layer option (MMCD was single-sided and optionally dual-layer whereas SD was single-layer but optionally double-sided) and EFMPlus modulation. EFMPlus was chosen due to its great resilience against disc damage such as scratches and fingerprints. EFMPlus, created by Kees Immink, who also designed EFM, is 6% less efficient than the modulation technique originally used by Toshiba, which resulted in a capacity of 4.7 GB as opposed to the original 5 GB. The result was the DVD specification, finalized for the DVD movie player and DVD-ROM computer applications in December 1995. The DVD-Video format was introduced first, in 1996, in Japan, to the United States in March 1997 (Test Marketed), and mid-late 1998 in Europe, Australia and Brazil. In May 1997, the DVD Consortium was replaced by the DVD Forum, which is open to all other companies.

Etymology

The official DVD specification documents have never defined DVD. Usage in the present day varies, with *DVD*, *Digital Video Disc*, and *Digital Versatile Disc* being the most common.

DVD was originally used as an initialism for the unofficial term *digital videodisk*.

It was reported in 1995, at the time of the specification finalization, that the letters officially stood for *Digital Versatile Disc* (due to non-video applications).

However, the text of the press release announcing the specification finalization only refers to the technology as "DVD," making no mention of what (if anything) the letters stood for.

A newsgroup FAQ written by Jim Taylor (a prominent figure in the industry) claims that four years later, in 1999, the DVD Forum stated that the format name was simply the three letters "DVD" and did not stand for anything. The DVD Forum website has a section called "DVD Primer" in which the answer to the question, "What does DVD mean?" reads, "The keyword is 'versatile.' Digital Versatile Discs provide superb video, audio and data storage and access – all on one disc."

DVD Capacity

Capacity and nomenclature						
Designation		Sides	Layers (total)	Diameter (cm)	Capacity (GB)	(GiB)
DVD-1[12]	SS SL	1	1	8	1.46	1.36
DVD-2	SS DL	1	2	8	2.66	2.47
DVD-3	DS SL	2	2	8	2.92	2.72
DVD-4	DS DL	2	4	8	5.32	4.95
DVD-5	SS SL	1	1	12	4.70	4.38
DVD-9	SS DL	1	2	12	8.54	7.95
DVD-10	DS SL	2	2	12	9.40	8.75
DVD-14	DS DL/SL	2	3	12	13.24	12.33
DVD-18	DS DL	2	4	12	17.08	15.90

SS = Single Sided; DS = Dual Sided; SL = Single Layer; DL = Dual Layer

The basic types of DVD are referred to by a rough approximation of their capacity in gigabytes. In draft versions of the specification, DVD-5 indeed held five gigabytes, but some parameters had to be changed later on to address technical challenges, so the capacity decreased.

The 12 cm type is a standard DVD, and the 8 cm variety is known as a mini-DVD. These are the same sizes as a standard CD and a mini-CD, respectively. The capacity by surface (MiB/cm^2) varies from 6.92MiB/cm^2 in the DVD-1 to 18.0 MiB/cm^2 in the DVD-18.

Note: As with hard disk drives, in the DVD realm gigabyte and the symbol GB are usually used in the SI sense, i.e. 10 (or 1,000,000,000) bytes. For distinction, gibibyte with symbol GiB is used, i.e. 2 (or 1,073,741,824) bytes. Most computer operating systems display file sizes in gibibytes, mebibytes and kibibytes labeled as gigabyte, megabyte and kilobyte respectively.

Each DVD sector contains 2418 bytes of data, 2048 bytes of which are user data.

There is a small difference in storage space between '+' and'-' formats:

Capacity Differences of Writable DVD Formats

Capacity differences of writable DVD formats				
Type	**Sectors**	**Bytes**	**GB**	**GiB**
DVD? R SL	2,298,496	4,707,319,808	4.71	4.384
DVD+R SL	2,295,104	4,700,372,992	4.70	4.378
DVD? R DL	4,171,712	8,543,666,176	8.54	7.957
DVD+R DL	4,173,824	8,547,991,552	8.55	7.961

Pen Drive (USB)

A USB flash drive consists of a NAND-type flash memory data storage device integrated with a USB (universal serial bus) interface. USB flash drives are typically removable and rewritable, much smaller than a floppy disk (1 to 4 inches or 2.5 to 10 cm), and most USB flash drives weigh less than an ounce (28g). Storage capacities typically range from 64 MB to 128 GB with steady improvements in size and price per gigabyte. Some allow 1 million write or erase cycles and have 10-year data retention, connected by USB 1.1 or USB 2.0.

USB flash drives offer potential advantages over other portable storage devices, particularly the floppy disk. They have a more compact shape, operate faster, hold much more data, have a more durable design, and operate more reliably due to their lack of moving parts. Additionally, it has become increasingly common for computers to be sold without floppy disk drives. USB ports, on the other hand, appear on almost every current mainstream PC and laptop. These types of drives use the USB mass storage standard, supported natively by modern operating systems such as Windows, Mac OS X, Linux, and other Unix-like systems. USB drives with USB 2.0 support can also operate faster than an optical disc drive, while storing a larger amount of data in a much smaller space. Nothing actually moves in a flash drive: the term *drive* persists because computers read and write flash-drive data using the same system commands as for a mechanical disk drive, with the storage appearing to the computer operating system and user interface as just another drive.

A flash drive consists of a small printed circuit board protected inside a plastic, metal, or rubberised case, robust enough for carrying with no additional protection—in a pocket or on a key chain, for example. The USB connector is protected by a removable cap or by retracting into the body of the drive, although it is not likely to be damaged if exposed. Most flash drives use a standard type-A USB connection allowing plugging into a port on a personal computer.

Technology

Flash memory combines a number of older technologies, with the low cost, low power consumption and small size made possible by recent advances in microprocessor technology. The memory storage is based on earlier EPROM and EEPROM technologies. These had very limited capacity, were very slow for both reading and writing, required complex high-voltage drive circuitry, and could only be re-written after erasing the entire contents of the chip. Hardware designers later developed EEPROMs with the erasure region broken up into smaller "fields" that could be erased individually without affecting the others. Altering the contents of a particular memory location involved first copying the entire field into an off-chip buffer memory, erasing the field, and then re-writing the data back into the same field, making the necessary alteration to the relevant memory location while doing so. This required considerable computer support, and PC-based EEPROM flash memory systems often carried their own dedicated microprocessor system. Flash drives are more or less a miniaturized version of this.

The development of high-speed serial data interfaces such as USB for the first time made memory systems with serially accessed storage viable, and the simultaneous development of small, high-speed, low-power microprocessor systems allowed this to be incorporated into extremely compact systems. Serial access also greatly reduced the number of electrical connections required for the memory chips, which has allowed the successful manufacture of multi-gigabyte capacities. (Every external electrical connection is a potential source of manufacturing failure, and with traditional manufacturing, a point is rapidly reached where the successful yield approaches zero).

Computers access modern flash memory systems very much like hard disk drives, where the controller system has full control over where information is actually stored. The actual EEPROM writing and erasure processes are, however, still very similar to the earlier systems described above. Many low-cost MP3 players simply add extra software to a standard flash memory control microprocessor so it can also serve as a music playback decoder. Most of these players can also be used as a conventional flash drive, for storing data.

History

First Commercial Product: Trek Technology and IBM began selling the first USB flash drives commercially in 2000. Singaporean company Trek Technology sold a model dubbed the "ThumbDrive," and IBM marketed the first such drives in North America, with its product the "DiskOnKey" (which was manufactured by the Israeli company M-Systems). IBM's USB flash drive became available on December 15, 2000, and had a storage capacity of 8 MB, more than five times the capacity of the commonly used floppy disks (floppy disks having a capacity of 1.44MB).

In 2000 Lexar introduced a Compact Flash (CF) card with a USB connection, and a companion card read/writer and USB cable that eliminated the need for a USB hub. In 2004 Trek Technology brought several lawsuits against other USB flash drive manufacturers and distributors in an attempt to assert its patent rights to the USB flash drive. A court in Singapore ordered competitors to cease selling similar products that would be covered by Trek's patent, but a court in the United Kingdom revoked one of Trek's patents in that country.

UNIT-III

Computers in Education

Computer Application in Educational Institutions

Application Software

Application software is any tool that functions and is operated by means of a computer, with the purpose of supporting or improving the software user's work. In other words, it is the subclass of computer software that employs the capabilities of a computer directly and thoroughly to a task that the user wishes to perform. This should be contrasted with system software (infrastructure) or middleware (computer services/processes integrators), which is involved in integrating a computer's various capabilities, but typically does not directly apply them in the performance of tasks that benefit the user. In this context the term application refers to both the *application software* and its implementation.

A simple, if imperfect analogy in the world of hardware would be the relationship of an electric light bulb (an application) to an electric power generation plant (a system). The power plant merely generates electricity, not itself of any real use until harnessed to an application like the electric light that performs a service that benefits the user.

Typical examples of 'software applications' are word processors, spreadsheets, media players and database applications.

Multiple applications bundled together as a package are sometimes referred to as an application suite. Microsoft Office,

OpenOffice.org, and iWork, which bundle together a word processor, a spreadsheet, and several other discrete applications, are typical examples. The separate applications in a suite usually have a user interface that has some commonality making it easier for the user to learn and use each application. And often they may have some capability to interact with each other in ways beneficial to the user. For example, a spreadsheet may be embedded in a word processor document even though it has been created in a separate spreadsheet application.

User-written software tailors systems to meet the user's specific needs. User-written software include spreadsheet templates, word processor macros, scientific simulations, graphics and animation scripts. Even email filters are a kind of user software. Users create this software themselves and often overlook how important it is.

In some types of embedded systems, the application software and the operating system software may be indistinguishable to the user, as in the case of software used to control a VCR, DVD player or microwave oven.

It is important to note that this definition may exclude some applications that may exist on some computers in large organizations. For an alternative definition of an application: *see Application Portfolio Management.*

Terminology

The exact delineation between system software such as operating systems and application software is not precise, however, and is occasionally subject to controversy. For example, one of the key questions in the United States v. Microsoft antitrust trial was whether Microsoft's Internet Explorer web browser was part of its Windows operating system or a separable piece of application software. As another example, the GNU/ Linux naming controversy is, in part, due to disagreement about the relationship between the Linux kernel and the operating systems built over this kernel.

In computer science, an application is a computer programme designed to help people perform a certain type of work. An application thus differs from an operating system (which runs a computer), a utility (which performs maintenance or general-purpose chores), and a programming language (with which computer programmes are created). Depending on the work for which it was designed, an application can manipulate text, numbers, graphics, or a combination of these elements. Some application packages offer considerable computing power by focusing on a single task, such as word processing; others, called integrated software, offer somewhat less power but include several applications.

Application Software Classification

There are many subtypes of application software:

- *Enterprise software* addresses the needs of organization processes and data flow, often in a large distributed environment. (Examples include Financial, Customer Relationship Management, and Supply Chain Management). Note that Departmental Software is a sub-type of Enterprise Software with a focus on smaller organizations or groups within a large organization. (Examples include Travel Expense Management, and IT Helpdesk)
- *Enterprise infrastructure software* provides common capabilities needed to support Enterprise Software systems. (Examples include Databases, Email servers, and Network and Security Management)
- *Information worker software* addresses the needs of individuals to create and manage information, often for individual projects within a department, in contrast to enterprise management. Examples include time management, resource management, documentation tools, analytical, and collaborative. Word processors, spreadsheets, email and blog clients, personal information system, and individual media editors may aid in multiple information worker tasks.
- *Content access software* is software used primarily to access content without editing, but may include software

that allows for content editing. Such software addresses the needs of individuals and groups to consume digital entertainment and published digital content. (Examples include Media Players, Web Browsers, Help browsers, and Games)

- *Educational software* is related to content access software, but has distinct requirements for delivering evaluations (tests) and tracking progress through material. It is also related to collaboration software in that many Educational Software systems include collaborative capabilities.
- *Simulation software* are computer software for simulation of physical or abstract systems for either research, training or entertainment purposes.
- *Media development software* addresses the needs of individuals who generate print and electronic media for others to consume, most often in a commercial or educational setting. This includes Graphic Art software, Desktop Publishing software, Multimedia Development software, HTML editors, Digital Animation editors, Digital Audio and Video composition, and many others.
- *Product engineering software* is used in developing hardware and software products. This includes computer aided design (CAD), computer aided engineering (CAE), computer language editing and compiling tools, Integrated Development Environments, and Application Programmer Interfaces.

Computer Applications

Dr. Mamta Rani (MCA Ph. D. - Computer Science), Head, department of Computer Applications has teaching experience of more than 8 years. She has presented 13 research papers, published in UK, Korea, Saudi Arabia and India. She has received first prize for best paper presentation in a national conference. She has presented research papers in a number of international and national journals and presently guiding 2 research scholars. As its name implies, this Department emphasizes deployment of computer technology in producing computer applications. The Department offers Masters in Computer Applications and Doctoral programmes.

Doctoral programmes are centered around computer graphics and experimental approaches to the design of fractals. Applications have been developed for the design of patterns in carpet and textile industry. Applications have also been developed in discrete dynamical systems. Currently the department is investigating Fractal Theory in improving performance of Fractal Antennas and for noise mitigation in communication systems.

The Department also works in Computer Networking and Wireless Communication with the objective to improve the Quality of Service (QoS) by reducing congestion in high-speed communication. Currently work is in progress in developing new techniques for fast communication after a disaster has occurred .The department has produced five research papers in the last two years: three in international journals and two in national journals. To keep itself abreast of latest developments in computer applications, the Department makes extensive efforts to develop partnerships with industry. We have partnered with IBM to offer an intensive training programme for teachers on 'IT Infrastructure Management' and DB2. We also have collaboration with Infosys under their Infosys Connect Programme to offer intensive training for our students.

The Teaching Learning Process at the MCA level uses the latest electronic teaching aids and is characterized by a tight coupling between lectures, tutorial and laboratory work. The former contributes to interactive classroom learning where the student is able to discuss with the teacher and peer students. The latter enables planned learning and optimization of student teacher time to maximize learning.

Types of Educational Institutions

Computer-Integrated Surgical Systems and Technology Engineering Research Center: Developing novel computing methods, interfacial technologies, and computer-integrated surgical systems to revolutionize surgical procedures in the 21st century.

The impact of Computer-Integrated Surgical Systems and Technology (cisst) on medical care procedures within the next 20 years will be as significant as the impact of Computer-Integrated Manufacturing (CIM) Systems and Technology has been on manufacturing over the past 20 years. A novel partnership between human surgeons and machines, made possible by advances in computing and engineering technology, will overcome many of the limitations of traditional surgery. By extending human surgeons' ability to plan and carry out surgical interventions more accurately and less invasively, Computer Integrated Surgery (CIS) systems will address a vital national need to greatly reduce costs, improve clinical outcomes, and improve the efficiency of health care delivery. Further, the combination of consistent execution, patient and task models, and logging of intraoperative and outcome data made possible by CIS systems will produce the same sort of process learning advantages for surgery that have been realized in semiconductor CIM systems.

Academic

To support the academic and research activities of the University, an Academic Unix Cluster formed by 6 hosts is maintained on campus:

- General Computing group – consists of hosts HKPU07, HKPU10, HKPU21 and HKPU23 which are for general teaching and learning purposes.
- Research Computing group – consists of hosts HKUP11 and HKPU22 which are dedicated for research projects and pre-registration is required for access. For registration, please complete and return the web-based application form by visiting the "Academic Unix Cluster Services" page at https://mydoc.polyu.edu.hk and then click "Research Account Application". You will be required to provide some basic information of your research projects.

A large variety of software packages on scientific applications, engineering, computer languages, management systems, statistical applications, etc. are installed on these academic computers to support the wide spectrum of disciplines and activities at the University. The list of software packages available on the Academic Unix Cluster can be viewed by clicking the "Software Packages and Utilities" button on the "Academic Unix Cluster Services" page.

Besides serving as computing platform for teaching, learning and research activities, the Academic Unix Cluster also provides "myStore", "myWeb" and "mySurvey" services to enable you to store and manage your files and web pages in a secure way anywhere on the Internet, and to create and conduct Internet-based surveys without programming efforts. Please refer to section 6.3 - 6.5 for details of the services.

Administrative

Computer Use

The computing facilities of the Chabot-Las Positas Community College District are provided for the use of students, faculty, and staff in support of the programmes of the Colleges and District. In order to facilitate proper and responsible use of computers, the following administrative rules and procedures are established for all users. Instructors, managers, departments, or colleges may elect to impose additional requirements or restrictions. Beyond the consequences listed herein, rule violations may have consequences determined by District Board policy and applicable law.

Proper Use

a. Board Policy 2311 specifies that the computer systems of the District are provided solely for the following purposes:
    1) use by authorized employees and agents of the Chabot-Las Positas Community College District for District business;
    2) use by authorized employees of the Chabot-Las Positas Community College District for professional activities related to the employee's job function, or

3) use by registered students or authorized employees of the Chabot-Las Positas Community College District for instructional activities; or
4) public access to approved District or College information resources via the public telephone and data networks.

b. Use of District computer resources for personal or recreational purposes is prohibited. Prohibited activities include, but are not limited to, the following examples:
- storing personal recipes
- balancing your personal checkbook
- preparing a homeowner's association newsletter
- playing any sort of computer games unless the games are a specific component of an instructional activity or assignment.

c. Use of District computer resources for personal gain, profit, or commercial purposes is prohibited. Prohibited activities include, but are not limited to, the following examples:
- consulting for profit
- typing services for profit
- maintaining commercial business records
- developing software for sale, except as permitted in Board Policy pertaining to intellectual property rights
- any activity which is not District business or a professional activity related to the employee's job function.

d. Use of District computer resources for unauthorized activities is prohibited. Unauthorized activities include, but shall not be limited to, the following examples:
- use of passwords or accounts of another user
- attempts to capture or "crack" passwords
- attempts to break encryption protocols
- attempts to use loopholes in computer security or special passwords to gain access to systems, obtain

extra resources, or make unauthorized use of systems

- destruction or unauthorized alteration of data belonging to the District or to another user
- creation or communication of "viruses", "worms", or "Trojan horses"
- acts that restrict access to the system or damage the system
- acts that deliberately misrepresent the identity of the source of a message
- acts that harass, threaten, or defame other persons
- acts that violate any law

Copyrights and Licenses

a. The District acquires a substantial portion of its computer software from vendors under license agreements which restrict the use of the software to specific computer systems and which require the District to limit the use and copying of the software. Board Policy 2311 requires compliance with the terms of these licenses and with copyright law.

Use of District computer resources in violation of copyright restrictions or software license terms is prohibited under Board Policy 2311. Prohibited activities include, but shall not be limited to, the following examples:

- copying District-licensed software in violation of the license terms or copyright law
- installing software on District computers in violation of the license terms or copyright law
- "giving" District software to students or colleagues

b. Each major organization shall be responsible for implementation of this policy: For computer software used on College computers, the College Presidents shall be responsible for establishing implementation procedures.

For computer software used on District-organizational unit computers, the Chief Management Information Officer shall be responsible for establishing implementation procedures.

System Access

a. *Administrative Systems:* The District's administrative systems are operated by MIS. Access to these systems requires MIS approval of a written request prepared by the employee's supervisor or manager. In addition, other administrative review is sometimes required. For example, the Controller will review the need for Finance System access. Usually, requests will be approved for staff who have specific administrative responsibilities requiring system access. Administrative responsibilities that require system access include, but are not limited to, the following examples:

- management or overseeing of department or area budgets
- management of financial records of special projects or grants
- data entry of information pertaining to students, personnel, or finance records
- student information inquiry by counselors or A&R staff

Administrative system users shall access only those system accounts authorized by MIS. All other access to administrative systems is prohibited.

Administrative system users may not, under any circumstances, transfer or confer their system access privileges to another individual or permit use of their assigned system accounts by another individual. Users will be held responsible for all administrative system transactions conducted under their login passwords.

Administrative system users will be granted access privileges only if they agree in writing to adhere to the rules and procedures presented in this section. System access privileges may be revoked without notice in response to violations of these rules and procedures or in response to legitimate requests from the employee's supervisor or manager.

b. *Instructional Systems:* The District's instructional systems are owned and operated by the Colleges. (The sole exception is the instructional Sequent computer, which is operated by MIS.) Access and privileges for these systems are assigned by the systems administrators of specific individual systems. Eligible individuals may become authorized users of a system and be granted appropriate access and privileges by following the approval steps prescribed by the College for that system.

Passwords

a. Passwords are the keys to system security, and they provide the most important defense against unauthorized use of District systems.

Each system user is responsible to:

- follow certain rules when creating passwords
- select passwords that are secure
- change login passwords periodically
- keep passwords secret

Users shall fulfill these responsibilities in conformity with established CLPCCD Password Guidelines.

b. Users of a terminal or PC that is logged in to an administrative system must not leave it unattended. Users will be held responsible for all system transactions conducted under their login passwords.

Ownership

a. The District's computer systems, including hardware, software, and all computerized information and data are owned by the District or are licensed from vendors under license agreements. Except as provided in Board Policy pertaining to intellectual property rights, employees and students have no rights of ownership to these systems or to the information they contain, even if the employee or student entered the information into these systems. Employees may use this information only as directed in the legitimate business of the Colleges and District and only as prescribed by Board Policy 5511.

Electronic Mail Privacy

a. Under Board Policy 2311, the District's electronic mail system and messages are owned by the District and provided for legitimate business use by its employees.

b. The District's E-mail system uses encrypted messages and is relatively secure. It is contrary to MIS department policy for MIS staff to snoop or routinely examine the contents of employee E-mail, and most E-mail messages will enjoy private status.

   Nevertheless, E-mail messages are not guaranteed to be private or confidential, and the District accepts no responsibility for consequences that might arise from disclosure of an E-mail message. Please remember that control over a message is lost once it is sent, and future events may have unanticipated results:

   - The recipient of the message might forward it to others on the system.
   - The recipient of the message might print it and hand it to another reader or might even post it on the wall.
   - The message might accidentally be sent to an unintended recipient, especially when using named Groups for the "TO" address.
   - In unusual circumstances, MIS staff might need to examine mail in order to resolve a system problem.
   - Conceivably, one or more messages might be subpoenaed in a legal proceeding, and then MIS would be required to provide the subpoenaed material.

Etiquette

Users are expected to use the system in a manner that reflects respect for other users.

a. It is a violation of system etiquette to transmit material which is offensive, harassing, or needlessly affects the work of other users.

b. Please carefully consider the appropriateness of any E-mail message being sent to EVERYONE; notification of the arrival of such a message will interrupt every user on the system and consume a portion of their system resources. Such messages are sometimes perceived as the electronic equivalent of "junk mail".

c. Mail messages composed in all capitals are difficult to read and are often perceived as the electronic equivalent of "SHOUTING". Please use such messages sparingly.

Nondiscrimination

a. All users have the right to be free from any conduct associated with the use of District computer systems which discriminates against any person on the basis of race, colour, national origin, gender, or disability. Users of District systems shall refrain from such discriminatory acts.

b. Discriminatory conduct includes, but is not limited to, written or graphic conduct that satisfies both of the following conditions: (a) harasses, denigrates, or shows hostility to or aversion toward an individual or group based on race, colour, national origin, gender, or disability, and (b) has the purpose or effect of creating a hostile, intimidating, or offensive educational environment.

   1) "Harassing conduct" includes, but is not limited to, epithets, slurs, negative stereotyping, or threatening, intimidating, or hostile acts, that relate to race, colour, national origin, gender, or disability. This includes acts that purport to be "jokes" or "pranks" but that are hostile or demeaning.

   2) A "hostile educational environment" is established when harassing conduct is sufficiently severe, pervasive, or persistent so as to interfere with or

limit the ability of an individual to participate in or benefit from District computing systems.

c. Any user who believes he or she has be subject to conduct associated with the use of District computer systems which discriminates on the basis of race, colour, national origin, gender, or disability may report the incident to the College or District Affirmative Action/ Harassment Officer.

Management Rights and Responsibilities

a. Administrative Systems Managers shall make written requests for employees' access to the District's administrative systems. In addition, to maintain system security, managers shall notify MIS in writing immediately when system access is no longer required or authorized for an employee.

   Managers shall be responsible to provide general supervision of departmental employees' adherence to the rules and procedures presented herein, and managers shall have the right to impose additional departmental rules or procedures. In the event of conflict, the rules and procedures presented herein shall take precedence over departmental rules and procedures.

b. *Instructional Systems:* Managers responsible for instructional computing facilities shall be responsible to provide general supervision of staff and students' adherence to the rules and procedures presented herein, and managers shall have the right to impose additional departmental rules or procedures. Under the general direction of College management, the systems administrators of the College instructional systems may develop more detailed guidelines, as needed, concerning administration and daily operation of these systems. In the event of conflict, the rules and procedures presented herein shall take precedence over departmental rules and procedures.

MIS Staff Rights and Responsibilities

a. In the normal course of systems administration, the MIS staff occasionally may need to examine files, electronic mail, and printer output in order to gather sufficient information to diagnose and correct system problems or perform technical maintenance. In the course of this work, the staff reserves the right to inspect, copy, remove, or otherwise alter any data, file, or system resources which may adversely affect the system without notice to the user. In addition, the MIS staff reserves the right to restrict system access of any user who violates the rules/procedures presented in this section.

b. Although MIS staff have the right to examine any system files, they also have a responsibility to maintain users' privacy to the maximum extent possible.

User Rights and Responsibilities

a. As described herein, users of District systems have the right to
   - use District systems as authorized
   - own information stored on District systems solely as provided in Board policy pertaining to intellectual property rights
   - be free of routine intrusions on privacy
   - be free of discrimination in use of District systems.

b. As described herein, users of District systems have the responsibility to:
   - use the systems in compliance with the rules and procedures presented in this section
   - make proper use of District systems
   - comply with copyright law
   - access systems only as authorized
   - keep passwords secret and maintain password security
   - use the system with proper etiquette and respect for other users

- refrain from acts that are discriminatory, defamatory, harassing, or illegal
- agree that the District is not responsible for the content of external networks and for actions by individual users of the systems in violation of these rules.

Research Activities

The research approach of the CISST Engineering Research Center (CISST ERC) will speed CISST research and eventual deployment by reducing the very substantial implementation barriers required to assemble the critical mass of support infrastructure needed for experimental work in this field. Further, by promoting interoperability of components between testbeds, it will promote more rapid dissemination of results between clinical areas. The ERC's research activities are organized into three thrusts.

Thrust 1: Modeling and Analysis

The goal of this thrust is to study fundamental advances in algorithms and methods for modeling patient and surgical procedures, using such models in the planning and execution of surgical procedures, and realizing these advances in robust, supported software libraries suitable for research and application prototyping.

Thrust 2: Interfacial Technologies

The goal of this thrust is development of novel sensing, robotics, and human-machine interface subsystems transcending human sensing and manipulation limitations in performing surgical tasks.

Thrust 3: Systems

The goal of this thrust is integration of subsystems into an evolving family of surgical systems and testbeds addressing realistic and important surgical needs. It involves three closely interrelated activities: 1) integration of core research into modular subsystems and libraries; 2) integration of these subsystems into testbeds; and 3) pre-clinical and clinical validation of these testbeds in specific surgical applications.

Education

The goal of our Education and Outreach Programme is to create new, interdisciplinary undergraduate and graduate engineering programmes that foster teamwork and focus on realistic challenges in computer-integrated surgical systems and technology. We are developing new courses for both engineering and medical students, as well as for practitioners in industry and surgeons; and we are establishing effective links among the ERC's partner institutions to support collaborative education and research programmes through the creation of the "CIS Channel." We are developing new programmes of outreach to K-16 institutions, creating an internship/mentoring programme with industrial sponsors of the ERC, and developing an assessment and tracking process for the education programme.

Industrial Collaboration and Technology Transfer

The CISST ERC's strategic plan calls for collaboration with industry to "create an infrastructure of systems and devices that will permit rapid prototyping and validation of application concepts." To accomplish this goal the ERC has gained the participation of large and small companies in a collaboration that provides opportunities in the areas of research (discovery), product development, education, and commercialization. The industry sectors and companies that are potential collaborators are varied and diversified and include technical areas such as medical imaging, robotics, medical simulation, surgical instrumentation, computing, telecommunications, instrumentation, interventional guidance and innovative therapies, human machine interaction, and ergonomics. We recognize that the industrial sectors include large, medium, and small companies that have different needs, resources, marketing strategies, and strategic goals of their own. Therefore, the collaboration and outreach strategy is to provide for various levels of membership, maximum flexibility, and continuous review and refinement as the Center grows.

Facilities

The CISST ERC is situated on the Homewood Campus of the Johns Hopkins University in Baltimore, MD. The administrative offices of the ERC house the Center Director and Administrative staff. There is 4,450 sq. ft. of ERC laboratory space in the New Engineering Building Basement assigned to the ERC's Director, Dr. Taylor, that houses 3 robotics laboratories as well as space for 25 students, engineers, ERC faculty, and visiting engineers and students from our industrial exchange programmes. Our collaboration with the School of Medicine provides 1,275 sq. ft. of lab and office space under the direction of the ERC's Deputy Director, Dr. Anderson.

Other CISST ERC faculty bring additional important facility resources. The Center for Medical Robotics and Computer Assisted Surgery (MRCAS) at Carnegie Mellon University was formed to foster the application of robotic technologies; Dr. Kanade is co-director of the MRCAS. Dr. DiGioia is an orthopaedic surgeon and serves as the director of Shadyside Hospital's Center for Orthopaedic Research (COR). There are 1,200 sq. ft. of MRCAS lab and 1,300 sq. ft. of Computer Vision lab space available for ERC research.

The Massachusetts Institute of Technology's Artificial Intelligence Laboratory conducts research that is two-fold. Researchers there work to understand human intelligence at all levelsincluding reasoning, perception, language, development, learning, and social levelsand to build useful artifacts based on intelligence. A new 1,500 sq. ft. area is dedicated for work on medical image analysis; it includes dedicated workstations, tracking equipment, and other devices for use in developing segmentation, registration, and tracking algorithms. The Surgical Planning Lab at the Brigham and Women's Hospital is a multidisciplinary, high-tech research institution combining the fields of Computer Science and MRI Radiology towards a goal of real-time 3D imaging of patients during surgery.

The Johns Hopkins Microsurgery Advanced Design Laboratory (MADLAB) is dedicated to the design and development of innovative microsurgical tools and techniques. The MADLAB is located within the Wilmer Eye Institute on the East Baltimore medical campus under the direction of Dr. de Juan. A staff of five engineers, scientists, and artists work closely with clinical personnel to identify potential areas of innovation, generate unique solutions to clinical obstacles, and rapidly develop ideas into near-market-ready products. MADLAB resources include a full machine shop, engineering/ CAD workstations, video editing/animation equipment, a surgical wet lab, and animal OR facilities.

Center Organization and Leadership

The ERC has been established as a special programme within the Whiting School of Engineering and is administered in a manner similar to that of a separate department. As the ERC Director, Dr. Russell Taylor reports directly to the Dean of the School of Engineering on all matters related to ERC research and administration.

The Center's organizational structure has been specifically designed to have advisory input from both industry (through the Industrial Policy Advisory Committee) and the ERC Strategy Board comprised of physicians, scientists, and engineers from all three of the ERC collaborative institutions as well as from outside institutions. Dr. Taylor's primary faculty appointment in the School of Engineering and Deputy Director Dr. James Anderson's in the School of Medicine provide additional assurance of multidisciplinary involvement in decisions regarding ERC administrative and research activities. All three main research thrust areas have leaders representing at least two of the three collaborative institutions, and each has major clinician involvement in research programme development.

Dr. Taylor is Director of the ERC and is primarily responsible for the scientific conduct of the research programme and the overall operation of the ERC. He chairs the leadership committee and co-chairs the Strategy Board. He is responsible for setting the ERC directions and allocates resources with input from the Leadership Committee, Strategy Board, and Industrial Advisory Policy Committee.

Dr. Anderson is the ERC's Deputy Director and acts as the ERC focal point for Medical School Programmes. He assists Dr. Taylor in the overall direction and management of the ERC. He has primary responsibility for executive oversight of the Outreach, Medical Affairs, and Diversity programmes.

Mr. Peter Bouxsein, Director of Outreach Programmes, has primary responsibility for the Industrial Affiliates programme.

Mr. Jeffrey Jarosz is Director of the Education Programme. He is responsible for the implementation and coordination of educational initiatives and develops mentoring and educational outreach programmes.

The ERC is managed by an Executive Director, Dr. Leigh Abts, who has overall administrative and financial responsibility for the function of the center. He reports directly to the Center Director and is supported by an Administrative Assistant.

UNIT-IV

ICTs Pedagogy in Teacher Education

Integrating ICT in Teacher Education

ICTs are one of the major contemporary factors shaping the global economy and producing rapid changes in society. They have fundamentally changed the way people learn, communicate, and do business. They can transform the nature of education–where and how learning takes place and the roles of students and teachers in the learning process.

Education in the East African region faces a number of problems. These problems include the shortage of qualified teachers, very large student populations, high drop-out rates of students and teachers, and weak curricula. All of these negative aspects result in poor delivery of education. The education crisis is worsened by the devastating effects of the HIV/AIDS pandemic, increasing poverty, a brain drain in the teaching community, budgetary constraints, poor communication, and inadequate infrastructure.

While societies in the region undergo rapid changes as a result of increased access to information, the majority of the school-going youth continue to undergo traditional rote learning. Very little is done to take advantage of the wealth of information available on the Internet. Whereas the processing of information to build knowledge is one of the essential literacy skills vital for the workforce in the 21st century, it is often overlooked in current educational practices.

In order to function in the new world economy, students and their teachers have to learn to navigate large amounts of information, to analyse and make decisions, and to master new knowledge and to accomplish complex tasks collaboratively. Overloaded with information, one key outcome of any learning experience should be for learners to critically challenge the material collected in order to decide whether it can be considered useful input in any educational activity. This is the basis for the construction of knowledge. The use of ICTs as part of the learning process can be subdivided into three different forms: as object, aspect, or medium (Plomp, ten Brummelhuis, & Pelgrum, 1997).

- As object, one refers to learning about ICTs as specific courses such as 'computer education.' Learners familiarise themselves with hardware and software including packages such as Microsoft Word, Microsoft Excel, and others. The aim is computer literacy.
- As aspect, one refers to applications of ICTs in education similar to what obtains in industry. The use of ICTs in education, such as in computer-aided design and computer-aided manufacturing, are examples.
- ICTs are considered as a medium whenever they are used to support teaching and learning.

The use of ICT as a medium is rare (Plomp, et al., 1997), in sub-Saharan Africa where the availability of resources is a major obstacle to the widespread integration of ICTs in education.

Technology is not new to education. However, contemporary computer technologies, such as the Internet, allow new types of teaching and learning experiences to flourish. Many new technologies are interactive, making it easier to create environments in which students can learn by doing, receive feedback, and continually refine their understanding and build new knowledge. Access to the Internet gives unprecedented opportunities in terms of the availability of research material and information in general. This availability of research material and information happens to both inspire and threaten teachers.

The computer equipment in the few fortunate schools that have them tends to be underused and lacks appropriate education content. Commonly, the computer equipment is used as objects in computer lessons. A few other subject teachers undertake courses in software packages but are unable to integrate or meaningfully insert this knowledge in their daily teaching work.

A worrying tendency is that boys are the targets rather than girls when investments in ICT hardware and training are made (Kinyanjui, 2002). If not taken seriously, this will increase gender disparities in education in the sub-region.

Respective governments in Eastern Africa recognise that ICTs have a critical role to play in improving education and are engaged in drafting ICT policies or ICT chapters in a number of development plans across economic sectors. The policies tend to clearly link development to a forward-looking educational sector and increased investment in human resources and ICTs.

In the education sector, curriculum review efforts are geared towards modernisation, including the incorporation of important ICT components. However, even the reviewed curricula tend to treat ICT as a subject rather than as an application tool that can be used in all other subjects, in teaching and learning. Very recent discourse indicates that future curriculum reviews may consider a fully fledged ICT mainstreaming process.

Teacher education institutions and programmes have the critical role to provide the necessary leadership in adapting pre-service and in-service teacher education to deal with the current demands of society and economy. They need to model the new pedagogies and tools for learning with the aim of enhancing the teaching-learning process.

Moreover, teacher education institutions and programmes must also give guidance in determining how the new technologies can best be used in the context of the culture, needs, and economic conditions of their country. The case study reported below has tried to do just that.

Integration of ICTs in the Classroom: The Practice

At KTTC more than 100 teacher educators have been trained in ICT, Internet research, modern teaching/learning approaches, and the development and writing of open learning materials. Most of this training takes place during short and regular in-house workshops. Almost 500 pre- and in-service teachers have been offered training on Internet research.

Basic ICT skills training was offered at the beginning of the project. Currently, these skills are being taught/learned with the assistance of self-study CD ROMs. The focus of the capacity building programme has changed. Workshops concentrate on specific education-related themes and tasks, including efficient Internet research, the pedagogical rationale for ICT integration, problem-based learning, innovative instructional methods such as flexible learning and information literacy. Lecturers attend the workshops when they feel ready and are offered almost unlimited access to the computers in order to experiment. It is compulsory for students to attend workshops as part of their curriculum. Most lecturers and students start using the Internet for personal searches. Once they feel somewhat comfortable with the computer, then they start discovering resources for more professional use. The provision of Internet access has triggered interest and enthusiasm in both lecturers and students to undertake training in how to deal with the wealth of information available to them.

Users initiate a search process to access relevant information and for means to integrate this information into learning and teaching practices. This search process promotes the use of higher order thinking and reasoning and problem-solving skills. Lecturers and students are guided through this process which ultimately leads to the efficient and effective handling of information and its incorporation in educational settings. During the first two years of the project, this flexible approach was possible because there was no ready-made training package. The programme was collaboratively constructed by both project advisors and beneficiaries, where both groups built on their respective learning experiences to establish best practices in a real constructivist approach. The approach was built on key principles of adult learning such as flexile and open learning while placing both curriculum and literacy issues higher than those of software and technology.

ICTs in Distance Education

Flexible learning is often taken as synonymous with distance education. Still, Collis and Moonen (2001) identified 19 different flexibility dimensions. Flexibility can involve options in course resources, in types of learning activities, in support for media learning, and many other possibilities. Indeed, flexibility is a characteristic that may satisfy many stakeholders in education (Kirkpatrick & Jakupec, 1999). More flexible offering and delivery of higher education may achieve the desirable social goals of increasing access to education and democratising teaching and the learning process by giving greater control to the learner. By freeing up the space, place, and time constraints of studying, it is possible to attract students who previously may not have been able to attend classes due to various life commitments.

Taylor (1996) suggest that the term 'flexible' refers to 'practices which utilise the capacities for learner-learner and teacher-learner interaction made possible through recent developments in information and communication technology (ICT) to provide increased 'openness' in both on- and off-campus delivery of educational programmes... we use the expression 'flexible modes of delivery' to capture this combination of philosophy and technology and quite explicitly recognise that this combination frees the provision of educational programmes from both geographical and time constraints'. Integrating ICT in distance education is not only a way in which institutions can offer more open and flexible learning opportunities, but ICTs can even support the changes in pedagogy and teacher training as a whole.

It was understood from the very beginning that distance education required special planning and specific techniques for course design and that all depended on what type of delivery system would be chosen. Learning materials for any distance education programme must be developed within a contextual framework involving the learner, the curriculum, and the institution. The learning materials for distance education have to be specially designed according to the principles of self-directive learning. Therefore, the course must be very well structured, with clear objectives and well considered allocation of students' time. And ICTs must be used in innovative and motivating ways. Suitable combinations of media - print, audio, video, and technologies like computers and the Internet - must be selected according to the needs. VVOB Kenya initiated a series of workshops to do exactly that.

New Needs of Teachers

During the Student Committee Meetings at the Annual Conference in Toronto, student members expressed the desire for better communication among fellow ACEI members regarding how to find a teaching job and how to survive the first year of teaching. In response, I scheduled a special session for graduating and first-year teachers at the 2002 Annual ACEI Conference in San Diego, California. This session will address several issues of concern to recently graduated teachers- from how to find a teaching job to day-to-day concerns in the classroom.

I also interviewed a teacher, David Bartkowiak, who recently graduated from the University at Buffalo, and is currently teaching in Georgia. I investigated his application process, and asked him what he found most helpful in finding a teaching job. According to David, the best ways to start your job search are to work with the Career Planning and Placement Center at your college or university and to visit the Teacher Job Fairs. The placement centers can provide information about jobs, writing your resume, and creating your placement file. During the job fairs, students can find representatives of schools from all over the United States and information about teaching positions. Some schools even interview teachers during the fair, so you should be prepared. Being hesitant about taking a job out of state, David started to work as a substitute teacher and a Title I math teacher. He gained valuable experiences working with children in different settings and learned about politics affecting teachers, administrators, and the community. Soon, he felt ready to have his own classroom.

He states: "I think professional contacts are the best things that help get jobs.... Even though the programme I was involved in tried to give us the skills to perform the responsibilities of a teacher, they never really talked about how to get practical experience to add to your resume or get your foot in the door," As ACEI's Student Representative, I want to stress the benefits of joining a professional organization such as ACEI. Membership provides opportunities for networking with other professionals and trying out leadership skills that show future employers that you are able to take leadership positions.

David also recommends that future teachers should learn more about reading: "I can't stress enough that new teachers (especially for elementary education) should find as many courses and resources that they can to become familiar with a variety of strategies for teaching reading." He also suggests that future teachers should visit different schools, observe how teachers handle teaching reading, and make contacts with reading specialists. Student teachers also should be required to take more than one special education class and at least one that deals with how to modify a classroom to meet the needs of all children.

Finally, he recommends: "Everybody should spend some time meeting the staff to see if you get a feeling of a comfortable fit, because they will be the people that can help you through problems with students, families, and just with your personal growth as a teacher." David was lucky to have a supportive faculty and staff, and he feels that he will stay at the same school for years to come. -Judit Szente, Student Representative

Motivation of Teachers Integration in Teacher Education

Background

When barriers to ICT integration in schools are discussed, issues such as access, availability of content, relevance for a subject and computer skills are usually top-of-mind. In this paper, I would like to divert your attention to some intangible factors such as teacher attitude, beliefs and motivation that need to be addressed even before other factors are considered.

In support of my argument, here are some comments made by researchers:

"...ICT integration in education is (therefore) unlikely to succeed unless we understand teachers' personal educational beliefs and their relationship with teaching practices" (Niederhauser & Stoddart, 2001) cited in Tondeur et al. (2008)

Researchers (Scrimshaw, 2004; van Braak et al., 2004) opine that even though the conditions for successful ICT integration finally appear to be in place – such as access to infrastructure, increased computer skills and sufficient computer training – the implementation of educational computer use has not yet reached a critical level, as cited in Tondeur et al. (2008). Ertmer, (2005) also suggests that additional barriers specifically related to teachers' educational beliefs, might be at work, as cited in Tondeur et al (2008).

Ertmer (1999) referred to the barriers caused by teachers' beliefs and attitudes concerning ICT, as second-order barriers. She highlighted that these need to be addressed before other external or first-order barriers are tackled. First-order barriers, such as the lack of access or training are more readily observed and more easily tackled, whereas second-order barriers may require major changes in daily routines and underlying beliefs about effective practice.

Belief in Benefits of ICT in Education

Many teachers themselves need to be convinced that integration of ICT into the classroom brings benefits. A benchmarking study surveying head teachers and class teachers was conducted in 2006 across 27 countries in Europe to benchmark the access and use of ICT in schools. This recent study indicated that 16% of teachers not using computers in the classroom believe that ICT offers "no or unclear benefits" to students. The study further indicates that there is a correlation between this skepticism and a lack of motivation to use ICT in the classroom with age/ no. of years of teaching experience. Further, a small proportion of teachers are just not interested at all in bringing computers into the classroom because of aversion to change.

A study conducted by Tondeur et al. among 574 primary school teachers in Belgium illustrates how the use of ICT is mediated by teachers' beliefs about teaching and learning. The study profiles teachers according to their educational beliefs and links it to the type of computer use in the classroom. Based on the teachers' beliefs, the study defines 4 profiles of teachers: Constructivist & Traditional, Constructivist, Traditional and an "Undefined profile". The traditional teaching style is teacher-centered while constructivist teaching style is student centered allowing frequent and varied use of technology in the classroom. The table below summarizes the relationship between the teacher profile and reported classroom use of computers.

The authors recommend that teacher professional development must not make any overt attempts to change teachers' educational beliefs or pressurize them to integrate ICT. The approach must be to showcase successful ICT integration and provide positive reinforcement and support. Older teachers deserve special attention and an orientation into benefits of ICT integration. Aversion to change has to be specially managed. Some schools have invested specifically in training in change management for teachers and school managers. (e.g. Malaysia's Smart School project).

Teacher Confidence

Further, not all teachers are confident users of ICT and this affects the lesson conducted in the classroom.

The findings of Becta research (2003) of a sample of 170 teachers, listed "lack of confidence" as one of the key barriers to uptake of ICT in the classroom. Over 21% of the responses were related to confidence issues. The Becta literature review on 'Barriers to uptake of ICT by teachers' (2004) illustrates how there are close relationships between the barrier caused by a lack of teacher confidence and several other barriers such as lack of personal access to ICT, lack of competence or technical problems.

Teacher Motivation

The ACM model (Access, Competence and Motivation Model proposed by Viherä and Nurmela, 2001) cited in pan-European benchmarking study can be used to explain the propensity to the use of computers and internet by teachers in classroom situations at schools.

Access to technology and associated resources is clearly a precursor for successful integration of ICT in the classrooms. Among teachers who do not use computers at school, access is the biggest problem. However, among those who do use computers at school, the motivation to use computers in the classroom is a cause for concern.

While access and competence are somewhat correlated, motivation (gauged through the attitude that using computers in classrooms results in significant learning benefits) does not show any correlation with the two other variables. Overall, about 24% of the teachers lacked motivation, though they had either competence or access and competence both.

As in any organization, employee motivation is affected by organizational policies; teacher motivation for ICT integration is affected by the school culture and ICT policy. Cuban et al. (2001) cited in Jones (2004), suggest that the school as an institution may in itself be resistant to the kinds of change needed for the successful integration of ICT.

The school management must encourage teachers to adopt ICT and back it up with adequate support in terms of training, equipment and resources. Training teachers cannot be a one-off event covering issues like how to use a particular software/ hardware. It should be in the form of a longer term professional development programme. Support can be continued through peer groups that may be ICT enabled and in the form of web sites, discussion groups, and e-mail communities.

The school management and senior staff must clearly demonstrate leadership by example and personal involvement in any new and major ICT initiatives. Encouraging experimentation through incentives is important while at the same time, failure should not be looked down upon. All school policies, internal communication, administration, assessments and maybe even extra-curricular activities must reflect their seriousness about ICT. Hayes (2007) highlights how whole-school approaches have positive effects – the entire school benefits instead of a few individuals, involves all stakeholders in the process of ICT integration and provides an opportunity for pooling of skills and resources. Incentives may include certification, professional advancement, financial benefits, paid time off for research or training and formal or informal recognition at the school or local community.

ICTs for Improving Quality of Teacher Training

Improving the quality of education and training is a critical issue, particularly at a time of educational expansion. ICTs can enhance the quality of education in several ways: by increasing learner motivation and engagement, by facilitating the acquisition of basic skills, and by enhancing teacher training.

ICTs are also transformational tools which, when used appropriately, can promote the shift to a learner-centered environment.

Motivating to Learn

ICTs such as videos, television and multimedia computer software that combine text, sound, and colorful, moving images can be used to provide challenging and authentic content that will engage the student in the learning process. Interactive radio likewise makes use of sound effects, songs, dramatisations, comic skits, and other performance conventions to compel the students to listen and become involved in the lessons being delivered.

More so than any other type of ICT, networked computers with Internet connectivity can increase learner motivation as it combines the media richness and interactivity of other ICTs with the opportunity to connect with real people and to participate in real world events.

Facilitating the Acquisition of Basic Skills

The transmission of basic skills and concepts that are the foundation of higher order thinking skills and creativity can be facilitated by ICTs through drill and practice. Educational television programmes can use repetition and reinforcement to teach the alphabet, numbers, colours, shapes and other basic concepts. Most of the early uses of computers were for computer-based learning (also called computer-assisted instruction) that focused on mastery of skills and content through repetition and reinforcement.

Enhancing teacher training. ICTs have also been used to improve access to and the quality of teacher training. For example, institutions like the Cyber Teacher Training Center (CTTC) in South Korea are taking advantage of the Internet to provide better teacher professional development opportunities to in-service teachers. The government-funded CTTC, established in 1997, offers self-directed, self-paced Web-based courses for primary and secondary school teachers. Courses include "Computers in the Information Society," Education Reform," and "Future Society and Education."

Online tutorials are also offered, with some courses requiring occasional face-to-face meetings. In China, large-scale radio- and television-based teacher education has for many years been conducted by the China Central Radio and TV University, the Shanghai Radio and TV University and many other RTVUs in the country. At Indira Gandhi National Open University, satellite-based one-way video- and two-way audio-conferencing was held in 1996, supplemented by print-materials and recorded video, to train 910 primary school teachers and facilitators from 20 district training institutes in Karnataka State. The teachers interacted with remote lecturers by telephone and fax.

Research has shown that the appropriate use of ICTs can catalyse the paradigmatic shift in both content and pedagogy that is at the heart of education reform in the 21st century. If designed and implemented properly, ICT-supported education can promote the acquisition of the knowledge and skills that will empower students for lifelong learning.

When used appropriately, ICTs—especially computers and Internet technologies— enable new ways of teaching and learning rather than simply allow teachers and students to do what they have done before in a better way. These new ways of teaching and learning are underpinned by constructivist theories of learning and constitute a shift from a teacher-centered pedagogy—in its worst form characterized by memorisation and rote learning—to one that is learner-centered.

- *Active Learning:* ICT-enhanced learning mobilises tools for examination, calculation and analysis of information, thus providing a platform for student inquiry, analysis and construction of new information. Learners therefore learn as they do and, whenever appropriate, work on real-life problems in-depth, making learning less abstract and more relevant to the learner's life situation. In this way, and in contrast to memorisation-based or rote learning, ICT-enhanced learning promotes increased learner engagement. ICT-enhanced learning is also "just-in-time" learning in which learners can choose what to learn when they need to learn it.
- *Collaborative Learning:* ICT-supported learning encourages interaction and cooperation among students, teachers, and experts regardless of where they are. Apart from modelling real-world interactions, ICT-supported learning provides learners the opportunity to work with people from different cultures, thereby helping to enhance learners' teaming and communicative skills as well as their global awareness. It models learning done throughout the learner's lifetime by expanding the learning space to include not just peers but also mentors and experts from different fields.
- *Creative Learning:* ICT-supported learning promotes the manipulation of existing information and the creation of real-world products rather than the regurgitation of received information.
- *Integrative Learning:* ICT-enhanced learning promotes a thematic, integrative approach to teaching and

learning. This approach eliminates the artificial separation between the different disciplines and between theory and practice that characterizes the traditional classroom approach.

- *Evaluative :earning:* ICT-enhanced learning is student-directed and diagnostic. Unlike static, text- or print-based educational technologies, ICT-enhanced learning recognises that there are many different learning pathways and many different articulations of knowledge. ICTs allow learners to explore and discover rather than merely listen and remember.

Professional Development and Improving of Teachers

Governments should offer ICT professional development services to subject teachers rather than concentrating on the hiring of ICT teachers only. The focus should not be solely on technology skills.

Enhancing Quality of Training Teaching

The Objective

Teaching is one of the most challenging and crucial professions in the world. Teachers are critical in facilitating learning and in making it more efficient and effective; they hold the key to the success of any educational reform; and they are accountable for successful human development of the nation and for preparing the foundation for social and economic development. Yet, they are usually ill-prepared and left on their own to understand and address the needs of students, parents, administrators, society, the economy, and the past, present, and future.

Modern developments may have eased some teaching burdens, but they certainly have not made life easier for teachers:

- The objectives of education have become more complicated. It is no longer sufficient to teach a certain body of knowledge and skills. Teachers are expected to help students to acquire higher levels of cognitive skills—problem solving, creativity, collaborative learning, synthesis, and, above all, the skill to learn new knowledge and apply that knowledge to new situations.

- Our understanding of the nature of learning has evolved. For learning to take place, learners have to be active, learning has to be meaningful and authentic, and the learning environment should be challenging but not stressful—all easier said than done!
- Knowledge is expanding rapidly, and much of it is available to teachers and students at the same time. This puts an unavoidable burden on teachers to continue updating their knowledge and exposing themselves to modern channels of information.
- The social environment in many countries is making it more difficult for teachers to manage classrooms and learning processes. Teachers' authority is challenged and their knowledge questioned continually. Students, in many instances, are becoming less respectful and more belligerent, and in some extreme cases, teachers must function in the face of physical threats and psychological duress.
- Information and communication technologies have brought new possibilities to the education sector, but, at the same time, they have placed more demands on teachers. They now have to learn how to cope with computers in their classrooms, how to compete with students in accessing the enormous body of information—particularly via the Internet, and how to use the hardware and software to enhance the teaching/learning process.

Obviously, teachers cannot be prepared for these unfolding challenges once and for all. One-shot training, no matter how effective and successful, will not suffice. A new paradigm must emerge that replaces training with lifelong professional preparedness and development of teachers, along the following continuum:

- Initial preparation/training that provides teachers with a solid foundation of knowledge; proficiency in pedagogical, social, and organization skills; deep understanding of the teaching/learning policies and materials they will deal with; and broad familiarity with sources of educational materials and support. It is equally crucial that candidates have a sophisticated grasp of continuous exploration, assessment, and acquisition of new knowledge and competencies, according to future demands.
- Structured opportunities for retraining, upgrading, and acquisition of new knowledge and skills. Many professions require practitioners to renew certification for practice. It is only logical for the critical profession of teaching to demand recertification every two or three years based on evidence of professional upgrading, and it is equally imperative for education authorities to ensure that opportunities and facilities for such upgrading are available.
- Continuous support for teachers as they tackle their day-to-day responsibilities.

The Potential

Implementing the emerging paradigm with conventional measures and techniques faces, in most countries, insurmountable financial, organizational, and institutional obstacles. ICTs may make the difference and can contribute significantly to all three components of the continuum:

- First, ICTs and properly developed multimedia materials can enhance teachers' initial preparation by providing good training materials, facilitating simulations, capturing and analyzing practice teaching, bringing into the training institution world experience, familiarizing trainees with sources of materials and support, and training potential teachers in the use of technologies for teaching/learning.
- Second, ICTs open a whole world of lifelong upgrading and professional development for teachers by providing

courses at a distance, asynchronous learning, and training on demand. ICTs' advantages include ease of revision and introduction of new courses in response to emerging demands.

- Finally, ICTs break the professional isolation from which many teachers suffer. With ICTs, they can connect easily with headquarters, with colleagues and mentors, with universities and centers of expertise, and with sources of teaching materials.

Specific Solutions

The above potential can be translated into a variety of ICT-enhanced interventions. Among them are: 5.4.3 Specific Solutions

Multimedia Training and Support

Videos for Training: Videos can serve an important role in microteaching, demonstration of special instructional techniques, on-demand training and uncorrupted expert instruction - in contrast with the cascade model (whereby, training flows down through levels of less experienced trainers until it reaches the target group; in the process, complex information tends to be lost).

Teacher Development Portal: Teacher development portals provide an integrated teacher development programme using the potential of ICTs. The portal can provide the resources, tools, and platform for all three phases of the teacher development continuum: initial training at teacher training colleges, in-service training opportunities, and continuous teacher support.

More specifically, a portal provides the following resources, tools, and collaborative channels:

- *Simulation and Good Practice:* New technologies, both computer-and Web-based, allow for simulation of specific skills through mini- and micro-lessons that can be watched, manipulated, and tested. Also, demonstrations of real teachers in real classroom settings, representing different subjects, approaches, and methodologies, may be brought into the teacher education center without having to travel to schools. More important, these good practices can be dissected, analyzed, watched again, and assessed over time without disrupting an actual class.

- *Multimedia Modules:* These are teaching/learning activities related to specific pedagogical skills.
- *Resource Materials*, including solutions to common teaching problems, innovations in teaching specific concepts, lesson plans, and links to other portals developed by centers of excellence and professional organizations. The portal site not only finds and links to these other sites, it also provides a special directory or search engine to help users find what they want and avoid the rest.
- *Moderated and unmoderated chat room, bulletin boards, discussion forums, and virtual conferences.*
- *Synchronous and asynchronous online seminars on specific topics*, using Webcasting and audio technology.
- *Free e-mail and personalized Web space.*
- *Free educational software for downloading.*
- *Policies and procedures* can be posted on the portal for easy access by teachers and administrators. This also allows revisions to be made inexpensively and distributed immediately to all schools with Internet access. Furthermore, through the e-mail link, teachers and administrators can provide feedback on the postings to policy makers.
- *Resource teachers*, assigned full-time or part-time, provide, through the portal, advice to classroom teachers about problems and best practices. They can also prepare and provide supplemental lesson plans to capitalize on learning opportunities created by new developments. Furthermore, resource teachers can help design lesson plans and curriculum when textbooks and other

traditional sources are unavailable. The resource teacher can be available by e-mail, portal chat rooms, and bulletin boards. Chat rooms and bulletin boards allow easy archiving and retrieval of earlier queries and answers, which can substantially reduce the number of times the resource teachers have to respond to similar inquiries.

Internet Resources for Teachers

There are thousands of Websites for educators which provide assistance to teachers in a wide range of needs, including lesson plans, instructional tools, student activities, and professional development opportunities. Resource 2.3.3 contains a selective list of Websites that are intended to provide assistance to a wide range of teachers in their day-to-day classroom work. The sites have been selected to illustrate the variety of supports that can be provided to teachers through the Web. Although most of the sites are in English, they serve as models of the types of resources that can be prepared to serve other language groups.

ICTs for Improving Educational Management

The Objective

Compared with any other national activity, the education enterprise is huge and intricate. It involves educational institutions all over the country, teachers and administrators in large numbers, and students of every age, who can account for up to 30% of the population. For instance, the educational system of a middle-income country of about 10 million people can easily encompass more than 11,000 educational institutions, 140,000 teachers, and 3 million students. The budget of this enterprise may reach 20% of the government budget and 3%–5% of the gross national product (GNP). By any measure, this is an enormous enterprise to manage and maintain, and for which to ensure quality of input, process, and output.

Recent reforms within the education enterprise have resulted in observable successes in making educational opportunities more accessible and equitable and the teaching/

learning process more effective. Yet, these successes are making an already unwieldy system even more complicated:

- Expanding educational opportunities means more schools in isolated rural areas and more diversified modes of delivery.
- Aiming for education for all means including students from underserved populations who require special measures to reach and have special needs that must be met.
- The accent on learning requires setting reliable and measurable standards and attending to individual differences.
- Decentralization and devolution of decisions to district and local levels require better information systems and management procedures.
- Involvement of more stakeholders in the education process (parents, employers, unions, political parties, etc.) is resulting in more transparency and accountability. These developments demand a consistent flow of information and force the education enterprise to be managed better and more efficiently.

Any business that is even a fraction of the size and complexity of a country's educational enterprise and uses the management techniques of most educational systems will go out of business in no time. Big businesses have discovered how important management is to keep their companies well run, efficient, and competitive. In so doing, they have used the potential of technology to restructure their procedures and overhaul their production, distribution, training, feedback, maintenance, and administration processes. However, education systems have been slow in exploiting the power of technology.

The Potential

Many educational institutions and systems have introduced simple management and statistical information systems. But this should be only the beginning. Two interrelated measures are needed:

- First, education systems need to undergo structural reengineering of their processes and techniques and to modernize their procedures and applications—at different levels of decision making and administration.
- Second, communication and information technologies must be an integral part of the restructuring design and application.

More specifically, technology for management may enhance reform in two areas:

Management of institutions and systems. The same elements of computing and telecommunications equipment and services that made businesses more efficient and cost effective can be applied to schools and school systems to enable principals and superintendents to streamline operations, monitor performance, and improve use of physical and human resources. Technology also promotes communication among schools, parents, central decision makers, and businesses that fosters greater accountability, public support, and connectivity with the marketplace. At the school/ institution level, technologies are crucial in such areas as admissions, student flow, personnel, staff development, and facilities. At the system-wide level, technologies provide critical support in domains such as school mapping, automated personnel and payroll systems, management information systems, communications, and information gathering, analysis, and use.

Management of policy making. The process of policy analysis and development is a sophisticated and strategic exercise. It is, by necessity, an intricate, nonlinear process in which a variety of people and organizations with diverse perspectives are actively involved in the process through which issues are analyzed and polices are generated, implemented, assessed, adjusted, and redesigned. Here ICTs can be valuable in storing and analyzing data on education indicators, student assessment, educational physical and human infrastructure, cost, and finance. Technology not only can help in diagnosis but, more important, it can also assist in constructing scenarios around different intended policy options to determine requirements and consequences. Each scenario can then be systematically analyzed and evaluated, not only in terms of its educational desirability but also in terms of financial affordability, feasibility, and sustainability over a sufficient period to show results. During policy implementation, technology can facilitate tracer studies and tracking systems as well as summative and formative evaluation.

Specific Solutions

Education Management Information System (EMIS): An Education Management Information System (EMIS) is a comprehensive system that brings together people, process, and technology to provide timely, cost-effective, and user-appropriate information to support educational management at whatever level is needed.

Most educational establishments have some type of management information—even if it is just a blackboard outside a school listing every week's enrollment by grade. Information is being provided to those who might want to use it. But a modern system needs more than this on a supported basis. At a minimum, upgrading, modernizing, and seizing on new approaches to improve education delivery using EMIS requires the following:

1. Determine who the stakeholders are for education information.
2. Assess who needs information for what decisions.
3. Determine which functions need to be supported and at what level.
4. Assess available resources. This means not only financial, but also material, personnel, time, and commitment. More EMIS efforts have failed because of the unavailability of good personnel and commitment than for any other cause.
5. Set priorities (short-, medium-, and long-term), get some knowledgeable review, and set a time frame.

6. Get multiple commitments.
7. Get sufficient resources for people, for the process, and then for the technology.
8. Stay clear about outcomes and monitor them.

EMISs have a technical element, but they are primarily about the use of information. Using information is a highly specific, often personal activity that affects work habits, work style, and work flow. Many old-style information systems have ceased to work, not because they are obsolete, but because the people supporting them failed to maintain them properly. EMIS will involve several elements that are critical to success:

1. Setting standards for information.
2. Setting timing for gathering and processing information. Information will vary simply by being gathered at a different time; if you measure enrollment in January, rather than April, the counts will be different—both accurate, but different.
3. Defining the level of possible accuracy.
4. Defining formats early, so that people get used to and understand how information is presented.
5. Ensuring that the providers of information quickly see the results of their work. The quicker and closer information processing is to the source, the higher its level of accuracy and speed of correction.
6. Measuring the cost of producing information.

The list is indicative and not exhaustive. As you review it, keep in mind that software suitability is highly dependent on the local situation, particularly in terms of functions, support, training and cost.

Simulations for Policy Analysis and Formulation

Simulations offer a means by which to study situations of rapid change and high complexity that conventional empirical research cannot handle. Suppose, for example, that you want to assess the possible impact of new forms of education. A conventional experiment will take years to deliver results, but simulation of critical elements in the new forms may yield valuable insights into problems and promises.

Simulations for policy analysis can be sorted into two categories: structured and unstructured.

- Structured simulations use algorithms to simulate how a system operates. Users' choices and possible outputs are specified in advance. Operation of the simulation points to a "best choice" policy. Early applications constituted single-step, noninteractive simulations to estimate the feasibility of different kinds of policies in the context of a national reform or to estimate the sensitivity of the (assumed) situation to a series of policy decisions.

  Multistep or interactive simulations are most appropriate when more than one decision maker is involved in setting policy, that is, when the policy process is seen as requiring political as well as technical inputs. Because such simulations can be used to generate more than one feasible and likely outcome, they are used primarily to identify alternative policy packages and a range of outcomes rather than to identify a "best answer."

- Unstructured simulations are based on transactions among several actors with competing objectives; constraints become known through action. Policy is the result of negotiation, a product of multiple decisions by several actors. The well-known Delphi technique serves this purpose. The technique was developed originally by the U.S. military to anticipate possible Soviet reactions to an accidental missile launch by the United States. U.S. participants took the roles of Soviet officials and responded within their roles to an extensive set of questions. Answers were collated and presented to participants, and those with deviant responses were asked to justify their position. This process was continued until participants reached a stable set of positions.

Some Latin American countries recently applied the Delphi technique with respect to educational policy alternatives. One study asked experts to comment on the effectiveness, cost, and likelihood of implementation of a wide variety of policies for primary education for which there is insufficient empirical research. Those who varied from the central tendency on a given alternative had to explain their reasoning. The final product is a set of simulated data, based on informed speculation. In this case, the study produced several conclusions that contradict current policy initiatives.

UNIT-V

MS-Windows

Introduction

NextInstallation

Windows is the operating system sold by the Seattle-based company Microsoft. Microsoft, originally christened "Traf-O-Data" in 1972, was renamed "Micro-soft" in November 1975, then "Microsoft" on November 26, 1976.

Microsoft entered the marketplace in August 1981 by releasing version 1.0 of the operating system Microsoft DOS (MS-DOS), a 16-bit command-line operating system

The first version of Microsoft Windows (Microsoft Windows 1.0) came out in November 1985. It had a graphical user interface, inspired by the user interface of the Apple computers of the time. Windows 1.0 was not succesful with the public, and Microsoft Windows 2.0, launched December 9, 1987, did not do much better.

It was on May 22, 1990 that Microsoft Windows became a success, with Windows 3.0, then Windows 3.1 in 1992, and finally Microsoft Windows for Workgroups, later renamed Windows 3.11, which included network capabilities. Windows 3.1 cannot be considered an entirely separate operating system because it was only a graphical user interface running on top of MS-DOS.

On August 24, 1995, Microsoft launched the operating system Microsoft Windows 95. Windows 95 signified Microsoft's willingness to transfer some of MS-DOS's capabilities into Windows, but this new version was based more heavily on 16-bit DOS and retained the limitations of the FAT16 file system, so that it was not possible to use long file names.

After minor revisions of Microsoft Windows 95, named Windows 95A OSR1, Windows 95B OSR2, Windows 95B OSR2.1 and Windows 95C OSR2.5, Microsoft released the next version of Windows on June 25, 1998: Windows 98. Windows 98 natively supported features other than those of MS-DOS but was still based upon it. What's more, Windows 98 suffered from poor memory handling when multiple applications were running, which could cause system malfunctions. A second edition of Windows 98 came out on February 17, 2000; it was named Windows 98 SE (for *"Second Edition"*).

On September 14, 2000, Microsoft released Windows Me (for *Millennium Edition*), also called Windows Millennium. Windows Millennium was based largely on Windows 98 (and therefore on MS-DOS), but added additional multimedia and software capabilities. Furthermore, Windows Millennium included a system-restore mechanism for returning to a previous state in the event of a crash.

Concurrent with these releases, Microsoft had been selling (since 1992) an entirely 32-bit operating system (which therefore was not based on MS-DOS) for professional use, at a time when business primarily used mainframes. It was Windows NT (for *Windows "New Technology"*). Windows NT was not a new version of Windows 95 or an improvement on it, but an entirely different operating system.

On May 24, 1993, the first version of Windows NT was released. It was called Windows NT 3.1, and was followed by Windows NT 3.5 in September 1994 and Windows 3.51 in June 1995. With Windows NT 4.0, launched for sale on August 24, 1996, Windows NT finally became a true success.

In July 1998, Microsoft released Windows NT 4.0 TSE (*Terminal Server Emulation*), the first Windows system that allowed terminals to be plugged into a server, i.e. use thin clients to open a session on the server.

On February 17, 2000, the next version of NT 4.0 was renamed Windows 2000 (instead of *Windows NT 5.0*) in order to highlight the unification of "NT" with the "Windows 9x" systems. Windows 2000 is an entirely 32-bit system with caracteristics of Windows NT, as well as an improved task manager and full compatibility with USB and FireWire peripherals. Then, on October 25, 2001, Windows XP arrived on the scene. This was a merger of the preceding operating systems. Finally, on April 24, 2003, a server operating system was released by Microsoft: Windows Server 2003.

Start, Save, Operate MS-Windows

WFDB Quick Start for MS-Windows 95/98/NT/2000/ME/XP

1. Install Cygwin *in a location that does not have any spaces in its pathname*. The default and preferred location is c:\cygwin. Do not use locations under Programme Files, Documents and Settings, or any other directory containing a space in its name. Be sure to leave the "Default Text File Type" as "Unix" (not "DOS"), and be sure to select and install the curl-devel, diffutils, gcc, gcc-mingw, make, openssl-devel, sunrpc, and xorg-x11-devel packages (these are not installed by default in a minimal Cygwin installation).
2. Install an HTTP client library (optional). If you installed curl-devel together with Cygwin as specified above, you may go on to step 3. Otherwise, install libcurl or libwww now.
   - o You will be able to use the WFDB software to read files on local disk drives and CD-ROMs whether or not you install one of these libraries.
   - o Direct access from WFDB applications to data files on remote web and FTP servers (NETFILES) is possible *only* if you install libcurl or libwww.
   - o Direct access from WFDB applications to password-protected data files on remote web and FTP servers requires libcurl 7.12.0 or later.

- o If you skip this step now, you may install libcurl or libwww and recompile the WFDB library later to enable NETFILES access for all of your WFDB applications. It will not be necessary to recompile the applications themselves.

3. Install XView (optional).
   - o You will not be able to compile or use WAVE unless you have installed xorg-x11-devel (in step 1 above) and XView, but none of the other WFDB applications require these packages. Other components of PhysioToolkit, such as plt and SEMIA, require X11 and XView.
   - o Add /usr/openwin/bin (or the directory containing textedit, if you have a non-standard installation of XView) to your PATH *before attempting to compile WAVE*. (See the instructions here.)
4. Download the current version of the WFDB software package as sources or binaries. Binary packages are provided as a convenience and may not be up-to-date; we strongly recommend following the procedure described below for compiling the software from the sources instead. If you plan to compile WFDB applications that are not included in the binary package, please start with the sources, and read the note below.

If you download the sources (recommended):

- o Choose a working directory for the installation. This directory must not have any spaces in its pathname. If your Windows username has no spaces, you can use your Cygwin home directory (c:\cygwin\home*username*); otherwise, create a directory beneath c:\cygwin (for example, c:\cygwin\home\wfdb) and use that as your working directory. Save the archive of sources (wfdb.tar.gz) in this working directory.
- o Open a Cygwin terminal emulator window. To open a Cygwin window, either click on the Cygwin desktop icon, or find and run c:\cygwin\cygwin.bat. By default,

the current directory within the Cygwin window will be c:\cygwin\home*username* initially. If you chose a different working directory, enter that directory by typing a command such as:

- o cd /home/wfdb

(Omit c:\cygwin\ from this cd command, and use a forward slash (/) rather than a backslash (\) as a directory separator where needed.) Perform the remainder of the installation by typing the commands as shown below into this Cygwin window. Do not use an MS-DOS window for this purpose.

- o Unpack the archive of sources (using tar, included with Cygwin):
- o tar xfvz wfdb.tar.gz

If your browser decompressed the archive during the download, you will need to use this command instead:

tar xfv wfdb.tar

This creates a directory with a name of the form wfdb-10.*m.n* within your working directory. Look at the list of files printed by the tar command to determine the name of the directory for the next step.

- o Enter this directory, configure, and install the package:
- o cd wfdb-10.*m.n*
- o ./configure
- o make install

(In the cd command, replace wfdb-10.*m.n* with the name of the directory as printed by tar in the previous step.)

- o The binaries will be installed in /usr/bin (accessible from outside the Cygwin environment as c:\cygwin\usr\bin). Be sure that this bin directory is in your PATH.
- *o (Optional)* Check that the WFDB library and applications have been correctly compiled and installed:
- o make check

This step compiles a short programme that exercises the WFDB library, prints a summary of test results, and prompts you to press <Enter>. After you have done so, the WFDB applications are tested. The tests are very short (typically less than a second each), except that the last one (xform using NETFILES) may take up to a minute if you have a slow or inoperative Internet connection. If any application test fails, its output can be found in the checkpkg subdirectory of the WFDB source tree; compare this output with the files of the same names that can be found in the checkpkg/expected subdirectory.

If you download the binaries (not recommended):

- o Copy cygwfdb dll and all of the .exe files from the directory of MS-Windows binaries into a directory in your PATH. If you have not installed Cygwin (especially not recommended), also copy the other cyg. dll files from the directory of MS-Windows binaries into the same directory as the.exe files. Note: you *must* install Cygwin and Xview in order to use WAVE.

5. If XView is installed, test WAVE by starting the Cygwin X server and then running (in the xterm window) the command:
6. wave-r mitdb/200 -a atr

Note that WAVE's menus (marked with a) are opened using a right click. Annotation editing requires the use of the middle button; if your mouse has only two buttons, you may be able to simulate a middle button click by "chording" (press both buttons at the same time, then release them; see this note for details if necessary).

If you have not used WAVE before, you may want to follow through the tutorial material in the beginning of the WAVE User's Guide.

7. *Read the Manuals:* Really! :-) If you want to write your own software to work with PhysioBank data, begin with the WFDB Programmer's Guide. To learn about the wide variety of existing software that can be used to study PhysioBank data, read the WFDB Applications Guide and the WAVE User's Guide.

How to Set Custom Shortcuts in the Windows XP "Save As" dialog box

This tutorial will guide you in setting custom "shortcuts" in the Windows XP "Save As" dialog box. *note:* this also works in Windows Vista Ultimate Edition - but I'm not sure about the other versions of Vista.

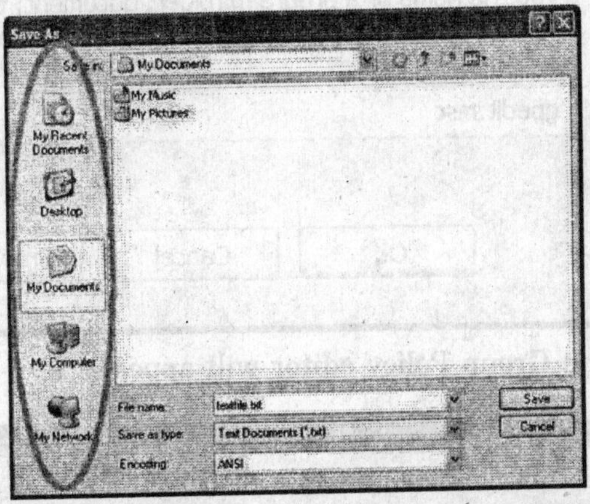

1. Below you'll find a screenshot of the default "Save As" dialog box in Windows XP. Make note of the shortcuts that you actually use, so you can make sure to keep them.

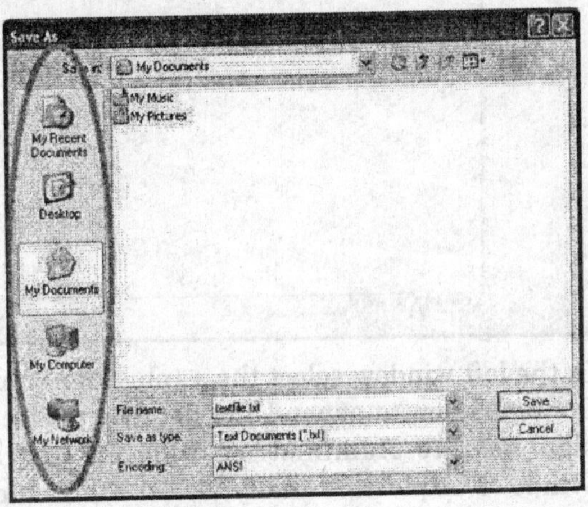

click to enlarge

2. Click Start and select Run. In the Run window enter gpedit.msc and click OK.

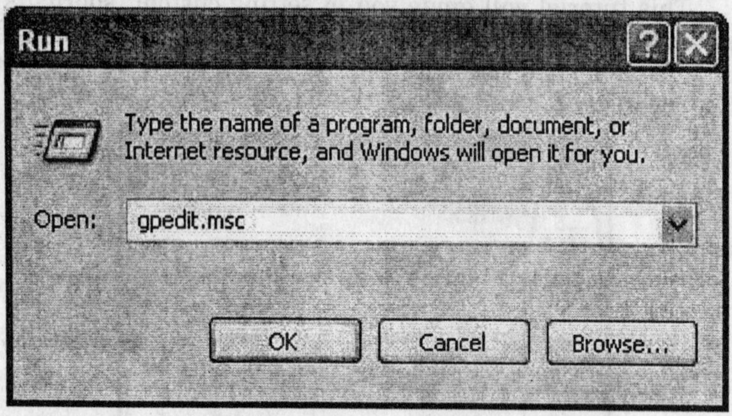

3. The Group Policy editor will appear.

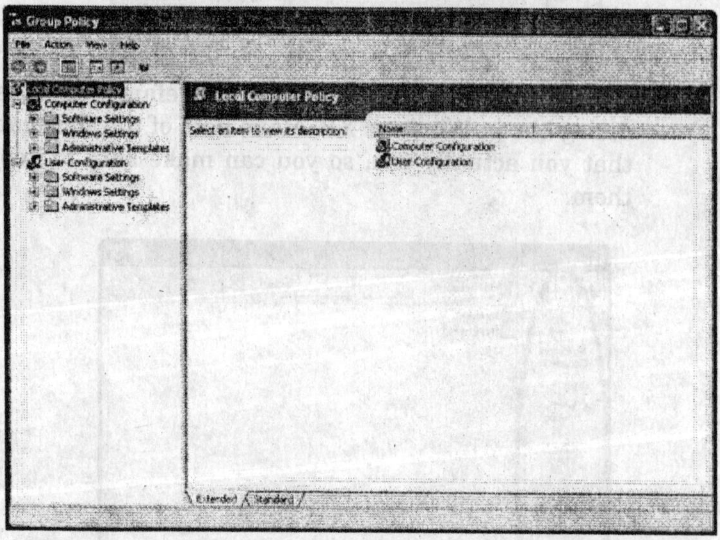

4. In the left window select the + (plus sign) next to User Configuration to expand the list. Next select the plus sign next to Administrative Templates and then Windows Explorer. Finally, select the Common Open File Dialog entry.

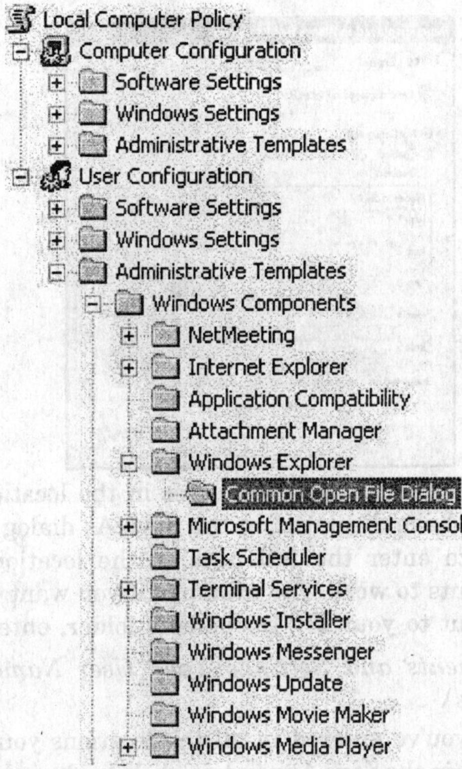

5. Double-click the Items displayed in Places Bar entry in the main Group Policy window.

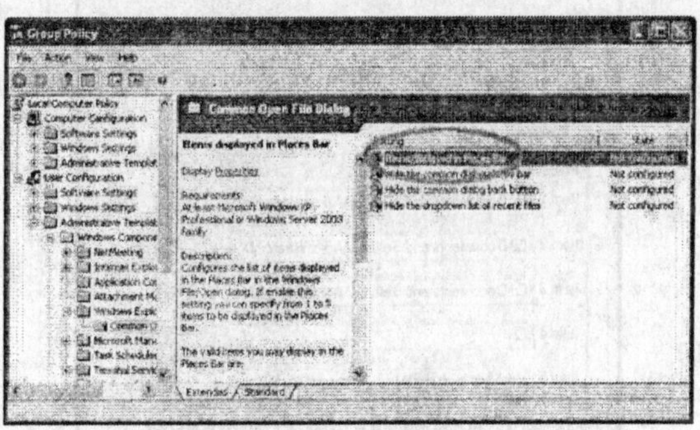

6. The Items displayed in Places Bar Properties window will open.

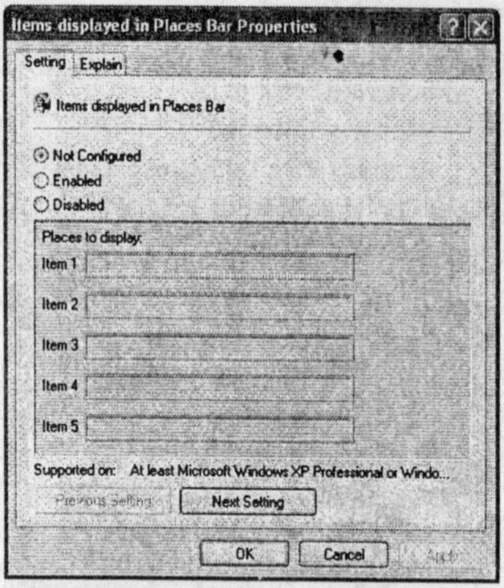

7. Select Enabled and then enter in the locations you'd like to have displayed in the Save As dialog box. You need to enter the full path to the location for the shortcuts to work. For example, if you want to have a shortcut to your My Documents folder, enter in:

C:\Documents and Settings\Your User Name\My Documents

Once you've entered in all the locations you'd like to appear in the Save As window, click Apply and then`OK.

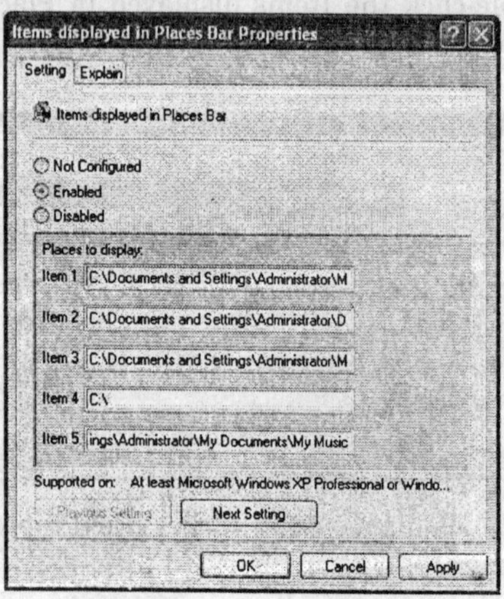

8. Back in the Group Policy editor, you should see that the Items displayed in Places Bar is now Enabled. Close the Group Policy editor.

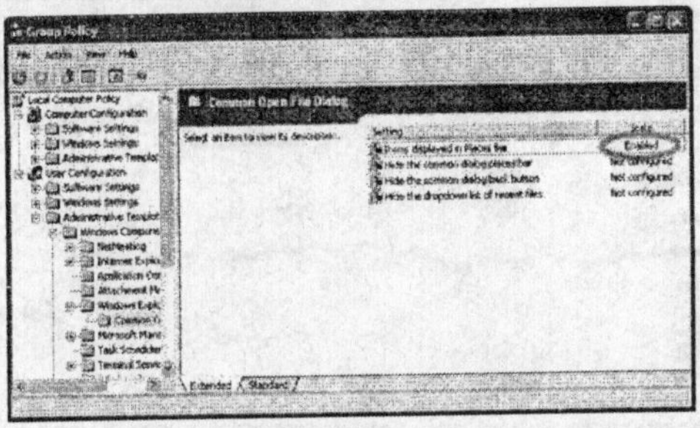

9. Test it out by saving a file - you should now have the new shortcuts displayed.

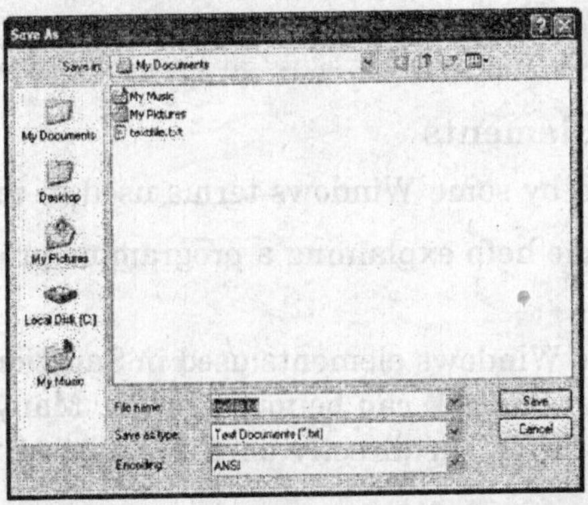

10. The same shortcuts will be used in the Open dialog box - not just the Save As box.

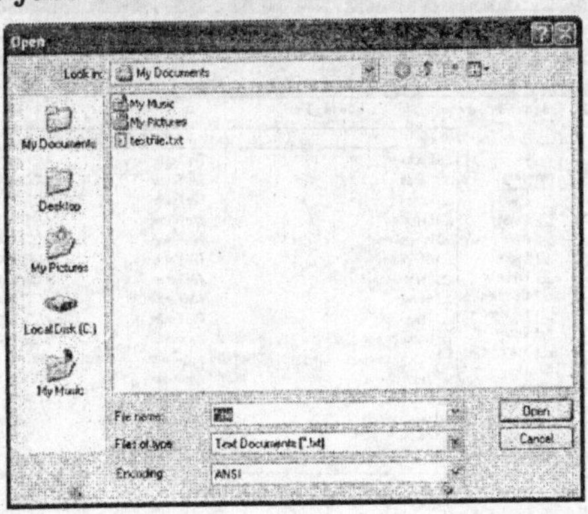

11. This will also work in Windows Vista - though I've only confirmed that it works in Vista Ultimate edition.

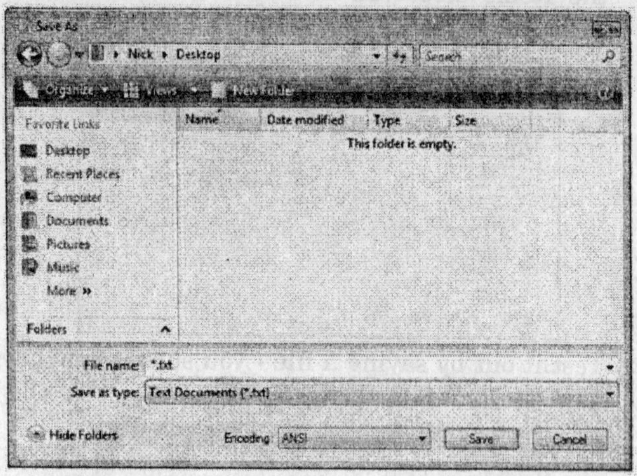

Windows Elements

Confused by some Windows terms used in the Help files?

Need some help explaining a programme problem to Tech Support?

All of the Windows elements used in Sanction II (and lot's of other programmes!) can be found below. Many of the items can be seen in action directly on the image of the Windows Explorer!

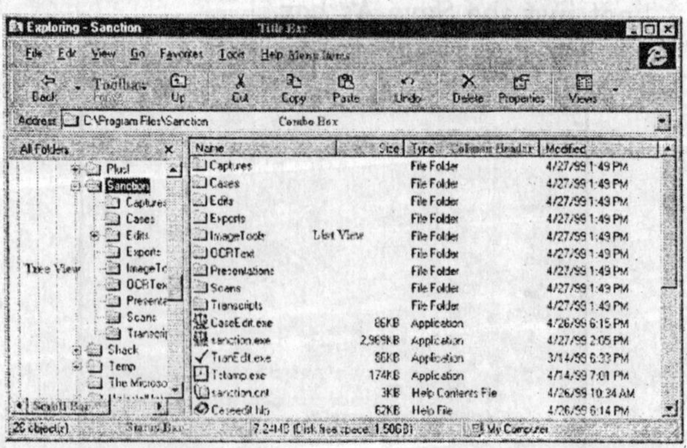

Tree View : A graphic "tree" where "branches" are displayed or hidden by a mouse click or the keyboard arrows. You cannot multi select (see below) from a Tree View control, you can only select one branch at a time. When a branch is "open", it is "expanded". When the branch is hidden, it is "collapsed". In Sanction II, the Tree View is the left most portion of the main screen which displays the group elements in the case database.

List View : A list of items with column headers describing what's in each column. Multiple list view items can be selected using either the SHIFT key or holding down the Control key. This is sometimes referred to as "multi-selecting". The center portion of the Sanction II main screen is the List View.

The Windows Explorer is a combination of the Tree View and List Views.

Tool Bar : Tool bars are the icon buttons typically located at the top of the screen directly under the menu items (although tool bars can also be at the left, right, bottom or even "floating").

Sanction II uses Tool bars in various parts of the programme including the Main screen, Presentation Mode and Annotation Tool Windows.

Scroll Bar : Scroll bars are the up/down, right/left arrows that help you view screens that are larger than the current window. Sanction II uses scroll bars for long lists of items in Tree and List views.

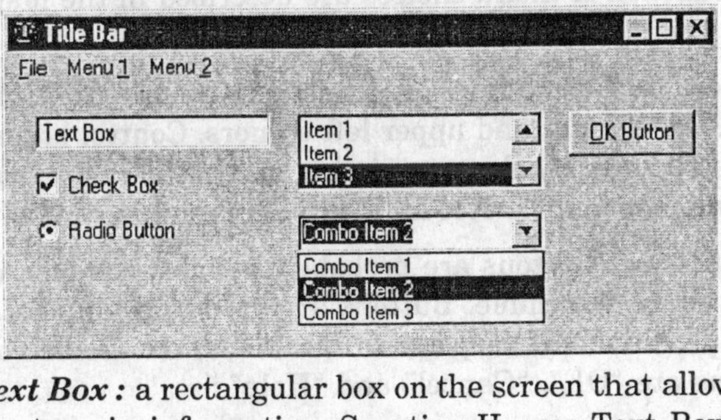

Text Box : a rectangular box on the screen that allows the user to type in information. Sanction II uses Text Boxes for adding items, finding items, setting options, etc.

List Box : a list of items in a rectangular window that allows the user to select individual or multiple items.

Combo Box : similar to a List Box except items in a combo box are not visible until you click on the box. Clicking on a combo box displays a scrollable list of items that can be selected with either the mouse or the arrow keys. Depending on the location of the combo box, the list may either drop down or up. Sanction II's Presentation Mode uses a combo box to access Presentation items.

Check Box : small square boxes on the screen that toggle between a "checked" and "unchecked" state. Check boxes are typically used for setting options. Sanction II uses check boxes for setting Print, Scan and Find options and various other settings in the programme.

Radio Button : like a check box, radio buttons are used for setting options but typically allow only one choice to be selected. Selecting one radio button disables the unselected choices.

Title Bar : the title bar is the colored rectangular region at the top of a programme window. Double clicking on the title bar maximizes/restores the on screen window.

Menu Items : menus are usually found at the top of a window directly beneath the Title Bar. Selecting a menu item causes an event to occur such as closing a file or creating a new one. Sanction II menu choices are described in the main help file.

Control Box : many Title Bars also contain Control Boxes in the upper right and upper left corners. Control boxes allow the user to quickly close, minimize, maximize, resize, etc. with a single mouse click. Not all menu bars contain control boxes.

Buttons : buttons are probably the most common control found in a programme. Buttons are used to begin operations, close programmes, respond to questions, etc. Some common buttons are "OK", "Cancel" and "Help".

Function Keys : Function keys are the keys marked F1-F12 on your keyboard. These keys perform actions which vary from programme to programme, and not all Function keys always perform an action. The F1 key is most commonly used for launching a program's Help file, however there is no standard applied to what each Function key should do. See the Sanction II main help file for a description Sanction II's Function key commands.

Hot Keys : Hot keys are similar to Function keys except they usually require a combination of keys. Menu items often have hot key combinations that can be recognized by the "_" character beneath one of the menu item's text. An underscore means that the menu item can be accessed by hitting the ALT key and the underscored letter. In multiple menus, you do not need to hold down the ALT key after the first selection.

Right Click : a term used to describe clicking on a mouse– different actions may occur when clicking with the right mouse button as opposed to the left. The most common use of the right mouse click is to pop up a list of selectable menu choices. In general, you "select" with the left mouse button and choose options with the right mouse button. Sanction II uses right clicks extensively throughout the programme.

Pop Up Menu : a pop up menu is a list of menu items that "pops up" on screen after some event. Typically pop up menus come up on screen after a right mouse click. Sanction II makes extensive use of pop up menus throughout the programme.

Drag and Drop : not a programme element, but rather an action. To drag and drop, you select items (with a left mouse click) and then drag the items from their location to their destination. Note, to drag items you must depress the left mouse button and HOLD IT DOWN during the drag. You must also click on a highlighted area of the selection, or else all items will be de-selected. When you release the button the "drop" occurs. Sanction II uses drag and drop to add and manipulate items in the Tree and List Views.

Multi Select : multi selecting is clicking on multiple items (commonly as part of a drag and drop). There are two ways to multi-select with the mouse. To select an entire range of consecutive items, hold down the SHIFT key and highlight the range of items. When all items have been highlighted, release the left mouse button and SHIFT key. To select multiple items that are not consecutive, Click on the items with the left mouse button while simultaneously holding down the Control key (Ctrl).

Some Advanced Terms

Here's a few terms that will make you a Window's expert when it comes time to explain what's happening on screen.

Modal Window : A modal window is one that appears on screen and forces the user to make some action before the window goes away. When a modal window is displayed, only items on that window can be accessed. Attempting to click outside the window causes the familiar "stop" error sound. The most common modal window is a Warning or Question box - The user must select OK, or Yes or No before returning control to the actual programme. If a modal window becomes "trapped" behind another window, it may appear that your programme has locked up. In reality, the modal window is just waiting for a response before releasing control. If you suspect a modal window is hidden, try hitting the Escape key or the Enter key. In most cases this will provide a response to close the modal window.

Focus : focus is the term used to describe what part of the programme is currently active. When a user clicks on a Tree View item for example, the Tree View has "focus". Any keystrokes you make are intercepted by the tree and acted on (such as the up/down arrow keys). When a cursor flashes in a Text Box, the text box has "focus". Any keystrokes you type appear in the text box.

Always on Top : An always on top window is similar to a modal window, however it does not prohibit the user from using other programme functions. When an Always on Top window is on screen, no matter where you click or what has focus, the Window remains "on top". The most common use of an always on top window is to display "tools" that a programme may use (such as an image editor's lines, pens, erasers, etc.). This Help file is an always on top window.

Sanction II uses always on top windows for the magnify feature in Presentation Mode.

Control Menu

- New type of pop-up menu
  - o visually similar to a marking menu
- Combines choice and control
  - o single continuous reversible action
  - o no focus switches
  - o immediate feedback
- We propose a new type of pop-up menu that is circular and visually similar to marking menu.
- A control menu is shown here.
- As this menu is a pop-up it is contextual. The mouse click used to pop-up the menu indicates where the action chosen by the menu is to be applied.
- The gesture used to pop-up the menu continues so as to select an operation from the menu and to then control this operation.

Programme Manager

Programme manager is the main window of Microsoft Windows 3.x that allows users to execute all the programmes on their computer. Users familiar with later versions of Microsoft Windows such as Windows 98 can think of programme manager as the desktop of Windows 3.x. Programme manager is still available in all versions of Microsoft Windows. Users running Windows 95, 98, NT, 2000, or XP can open programme manager by clicking Start / Run and typing progman and clicking ok. The file is known as progman.exe and is located in the root directory of Windows, deleting this file will cause problems with your computer.

Menus

Because there are various assignments you can perform on the computer, the operating system also provides many categories of objects. These objects allow you to perform available actions. The actions you can perform on the computer may depend on the object on which the action is performed and various other options. One of the objects the computer provides is called a menu.

In the previous lesson, we saw that when you right-click on the desktop, you see a series of words. This series of words is called a menu. A program's menu, simply referred to as a menu, is a series of words usually aligned on a (vertical) column, each line of words indicating a particular action. Like everything else you will use on the computer, a menu depends simply on the person who created it.

To use a menu, you must first know whether and where it is available. We also saw that the menu that appears depended on what you had right-clicked: the Taskbar, an empty area on the desktop, or a picture on the desktop. The menus available on the programmes are as varied as the programmes themselves are.

Practical Learning: Opening a Menu

1. Start the computer
2. Click an empty area on the desktop and notice that nothing happens and nothing displays
3. On the Taskbar, click Start:

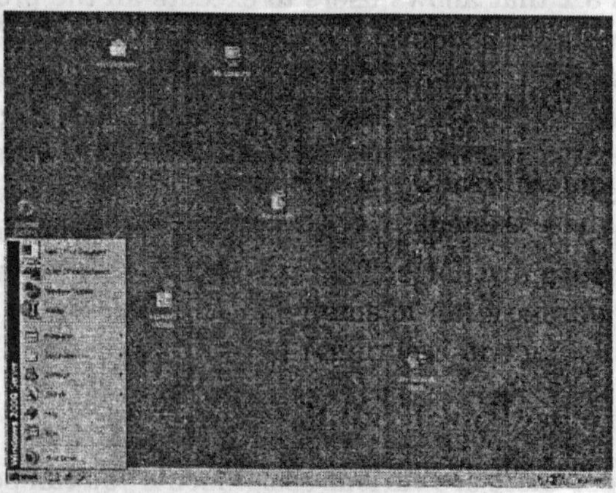

4. Notice that a menu appears

5. Right-click an empty area on the desktop. Notice that a different menu appears
6. Right-click an empty area on the Taskbar and notice the menu that appears

7. Right-click the clock on the right section of the Taskbar and notice the menu that appears:

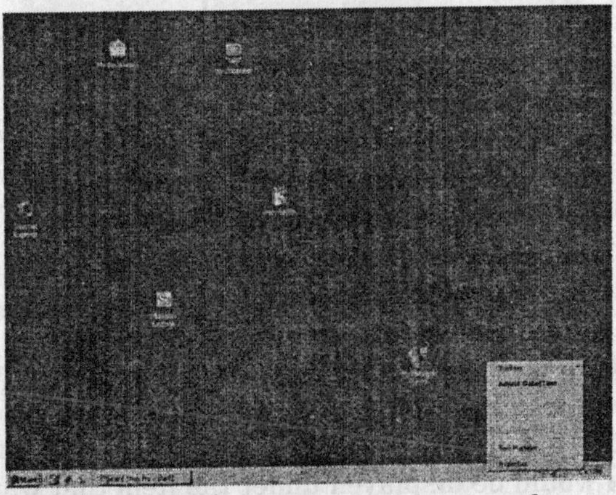

8. Right-click Recycle Bin and notice the menu that appears
8. Right-click Recycle Bin and notice the menu that appears
9. Click an empty area on the desktop. Notice that this dismisses any menu that was opened.

The following descriptions and rules apply to all menu items of all programmes of the Microsoft Windows computer, regardless of the below screenshots.

Main Menu Display

We have just seen that, when you know where a menu is available, to access it, you can just click or right-click the item that holds the menu. How a menu appears can be influenced by the available room. The operating system decides on the availability of room to display the menu. Observe how the same menu is displayed in the following two illustrations:

If a menu is accessed from the middle to top section of a window, the operating system would display it under the item that was clicked.

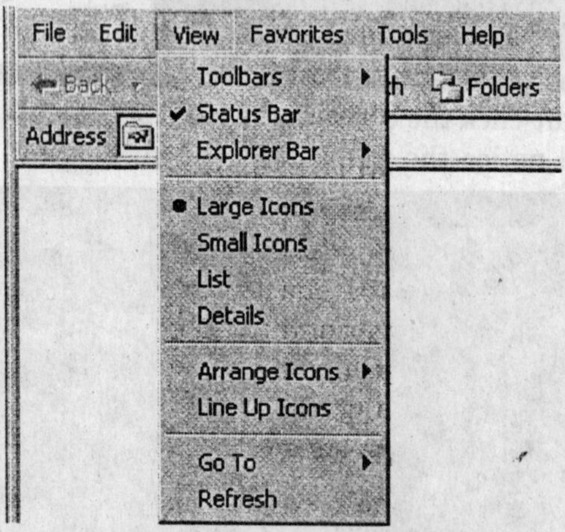

If the menu is being accessed from the bottom section of the screen, the operating system would calculate the available room under the item that was clicked. If there is enough room, the menu would be displayed under the item that was clicked. If there is not enough room, then the operating system would decide to display the menu above the item that was clicked:

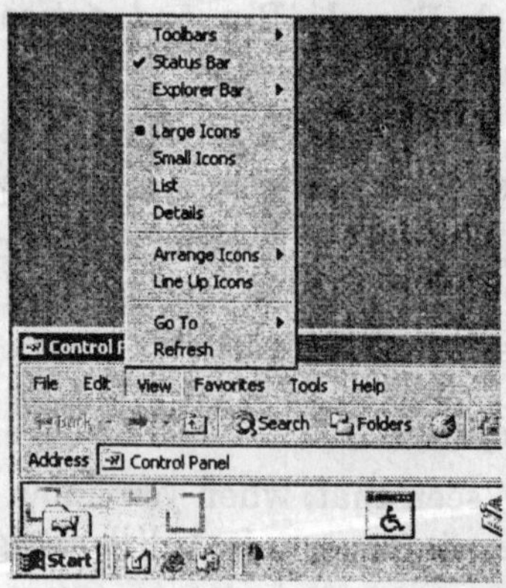

To Run Programme from Programme Manager

Programme management or programme management is the process of managing multiple interdependent projects that lead towards an improvement in an organization's performance.

Projects deliver outputs; programmes create outcomes. A project might deliver a new factory, hospital or IT system. By combining these project with other deliverables and changes, their programmes might deliver increased income from a new product, shorter waiting lists at the hospital or reduced operating costs due to improved technology.

Programme management is concerned with doing the right projects, whereas project management is about doing projects right. Successful projects deliver on time, to budget and to specification. Successful programmes deliver long term improvements to an organisation. Improvements are usually idenitified through benefits. An organization should select the group of programmes that most take it towards its strategic aims whilst remaining within its capacity to deliver the changes.

For example, a programme designed to launch a new product is likely to contain a whole portfolio of projects including:

- design of the new product - this delivers a design specification
- modifications to the production line or factory - delivers a manufacturing capability
- marketing - delivers advertisements, brochures and pamphlets
- staff training - delivers staff trained to sell and support the new product

Typically a programme is broken down into projects that reflect the organization's structure. The design project will be run by the design team, the factory will manage the modifications to the production line, and so on.

Whilst each of these projects is designed to deliver some 'thing', known as a 'deliverable' or an 'output', the overall programme is designed to deliver benefits that will improve the organization. Benefits in this example will include extra sales income from the new product. Benefits will normally be enjoyed long after the end of the programme and all of its component projects.

It should be recognised that programmes deliver a capability to change. Only when that capability is transferred to the line management and utilised by the host organanisation will the benefits actually be delivered. Therefore a programme team cannot, on their own, deliver benefits. Benefits can only be delivered through the utilisation of a new capability.

Programmes are normally designed to deliver the organization's strategy, such as an ambition to be the fourth biggest supermarket in a regio by 2015 or reduce wastage by 5% in two year's time. Programme management also emphasises the coordinating and prioritizing of resources across projects, managing links between the projects and the overall costs and risks of the programme.

Programme management provides a layer above the management of projects and focuses on selecting the best group of projects, defining them in terms of their objectives and providing an environment where projects can be run successfully. Programme managers should not micromanage, but should leave project management to the project managers.

The UK government, through the Office of Government Commerce, has invested heavily in programme management. In Europe, the term normally refers to multiple change projects: projects that are designed to deliver benefits to the host organization. Many organizations only run one programme at a time, a programme containing all their projects. Some larger organizations may have multiple programmes each designed to deliver a range of improvements.

Key Factors

Governance

The structure, process, and procedure to control operations and changes to performance objectives.

Alignment

The programme must support a higher level vision, goals and objectives.

Assurance

Verify and validate the programme, ensuring adherence to standards and alignment with the vision.

Management

Ensure there are regular reviews, there is accountability, and that management of projects, stakeholders and suppliers is in place.

File Manager

1. In general, refers to a software programme that is often a portion of the operating system that helps a user manage all the files on their computer. For example, all file managers allow the user to view, edit, copy, and delete the files on their computer.
2. When referring to Microsoft Windows 3.x, File Manager is programme included with Windows 3.x that enabled users to manage their files on the computer. File Manager was replaced with Explorer and My Computer with the introduction of Windows 95. Although Windows 95 and Windows 98 users still have the ability to run these programmes.
   - See document CH000122 for additional information about accessing these programmes in Windows 95 and 98.

Working with Files

In addition to performing common file manipulation tasks, such as moving, copying, and deleting, you'll also want to download files from the Internet, search for files in your directories, and FTP files. Some of these functions are built into Emacs, while some of these tasks require additional applications that can be downloaded.

Downloading Files

Once you know the URL of the file to download, you can use the wget command from within the Emacs shell to retrieve the file. If you do not know the URL of the file to download, use the W3 application to browse the web and find the URL of the file (refer to Section 6.1 for information on using the W3 application). Then use the command wget to download it. For more information on the wget command, refer to the wget man page.

To download a file:

1. From inside Emacs, type M-x shell to start the shell.
2. Since the wget command places the downloaded file into your current directory, change directories to the desired directory.
3. When you are in the appropriate directory, type wget [url], then press Enter. Remember that you can copy and paste the URL of the file to download from the W3 web browser application.

As the file is being downloaded, one dot appears on the screen for each kilobyte of data received. The wget command lets you know when the download is complete. Another option for downloading (or uploading) a file is via FTP. Refer to Section 5.3 on FTPing a file for more information.

Finding a File

There are several ways you can find a file. This section discusses two options. If you know the name of the file, or at least remember part of it, you can use the find-file command:

1. In Emacs, type M-x find-file.

   Result: You will be prompted for the name of the file in the default working directory.

2. Type the name of the file (or use wildcards) you wish to find.

Alternatively, you may want to browse your directories to look for a file. You can do this using the Emacs directory editor, dired. To start dired:

1. In Emacs, type C-x d or M-x dired. You will be prompted for the name of the file. You can type the name (or part of the name) of the file to find, using the Tab key to complete the file name. dired will list any files that match the name you entered. Alternatively, you can view a full listing of the directory by providing a directory name (or pressing Return to view the current directory) when prompted.

FTPing a File

Emacs contains a built-in file transfer protocol, or FTP, application. The FTP application can be used to upload and download files to and from other machines. In order to use FTP, you will need to know the hostname of the machine to contact.

To invoke the FTP application:

1. Within Emacs, type M-x ftp.

Result: You will be prompted for an ftp hostname.

Alternatively, you can start an Emacs shell using M-x shell and use FTP from the command line. There is a short tutorial on using the command line FTP.

Manipulating Files

This section contains information on moving, copying, and deleting files from within Emacs. In general, there are two ways you can go about these tasks. One option is to use the command line from an Emacs shell, and the other is to use dired. Both methods are discussed in this section.

Using the Command Line

If you are familiar with Unix command-line arguments, you may prefer to use the command line to manipulate files. To use the command line, open an Emacs command shell using M-x shell. The following list shows some basic file manipulation commands and what they do:

cp file1 file2

Copies file1 to a new file named file2.

mv source target

Moves a file from the source directory to the target directory.

rm file

Deletes a file.

mkdir directoryname

Creates a directory with the name directoryname.

rmdir directoryname

Deletes the directory directoryname if it is empty.

ls

Lists all the files in the current directory.

You can find more information on any of these commands (most can be run with various options that allow for more user control) by looking them up in the online man pages. Since the list presented here covers only the most basic commands, you may want to consult the Linux user's guide.

Using the Directory Editor

Although many Linux users use the command line to manipulate files, Emacs provides a powerful alternative, called dired. Dired is the Emacs directory editor, and is great for manipulating files if you'd rather not use the command line or aren't familiar with it. To start dired:

1. In Emacs, type M-x dired. You will be prompted for the directory to open.
2. Type in the directory to display, or press Return to open the default directory.

Once you've started dired, you can move around in the Emacs buffer to have the file names, permissions, owners, sizes, and dates created/edited read aloud.

In dired, some commands mark files for manipulation (for example, you can mark several files, then delete them all), and some commands (such as the copy command) are executed immediately. Note that, in dired, case does make a difference for many commands. Some of the more common dired commands and what they do are listed below:

press the Returnkey

Pressing Return when the focus is on a particular file opens that file in the appropriate major mode.

d : Marks a single file for deletion, but doesn't actually delete the file. You can mark multiple files for deletion, then delete them all simultaneously.

u : If a file is marked for deletion, this option unmarks it.

x : Deletes all files marked for deletion. You will be prompted to make sure you want to delete the files in question; type **yes** or **no** as appropriate.

C : Copies a file. You will be asked for the name of the new file to create when you copy the old file.

R : Renames a file. You will be prompted for the name of the new file to create when you rename the file.

Disk Menu

How many times have you found yourself wishing for an easier way to load and run programmes? The process of calling up a disk catalog, looking for the desired pathname, then typing (or mistyping) it can be a frustrating experience—especially if the pathname is something cryptic like FNINPT.BAO.2. Perhaps a better alternative is to select the programme from a menu taken from the disk directory.

That's exactly what you can do with "ProDOS Disk Menu." To use it, create a startup disk by saving both ProDOS and BASIC.SYSTEM on a disk. Then save Disk Menu with the filename STARTUP.

When you boot this disk, a menu containing the first 16 programmes in the directory appears on the 40-column screen. If more than 16 programmes are on the disk, press P to view the next page. Pressing P on the last page returns you to the first page (Disk Menu accepts both uppercase and lowercase commands.)

If you don't find the programme you want, press C. A screen prompt asks you to switch disks, then Disk Menu reruns itself.

To select a programme, press the up/down arrow keys to position the cursor over the desired file-name, then press RETURN. A screen prompt offers three choices: (R)UN, (L)OAD, OR (U)NDO. If you made a mistake and selected the wrong programme, press U to return to the menu.

Loading Multiple Programmes

There are three ways to exit Disk Menu: run any programme, load a BASIC programme, or press Q to quit. Notice that loading a machine language programme *does not* exit Disk Menu. Therefore, if you have a BASIC programme that utilizes several ML subroutines, you could load the ML routines into memory one after the other, then exit DISK MENU by running the BASIC programme.

The programming techniques used in Disk Menu are quite simple. The programme retrieves the volume name from the disk and opens the volume directory. It reads the directory into an array, skipping all non-programme files (except the type mentioned below). Then, depending on the current page, the programme reads the filenames into the page array for display and selection.

A few parts of the programme may need some explanation. For example, line 325 skips past the first few records on the volume directory, which do not contain information essential to the menu.

Disk Menu does not list any file types other than BASIC and binary files (.BAS and .BIN). Although data is sometimes stored in binary files, it is usually considered good practice to store data and programmes on separate disks.

When writing Disk Menu, I was tempted to make it include files contained in subdirectories, but refrained because in my experience such files are usually chained to other programmes, and would therefore only clutter up the menu. However, if you use subdirectories differently, the necessary alterations should be fairly simple.

View Menu

The View Menu contains commands that display or hide windows. The commands on the menu are:

- **Project Manager**—Displays the Project Manager dialog.
- **Editor**—Displays the Editor workbook.
- **Debug Window**—Displays the Debug window.
- **Clipboard**—Displays the Clipboard dialog showing the contents of the clipboard.
- **Processes**—Displays the Process dialog.
- **Console**—Displays the Console window.
- **Package List**—Displays the Package List dialog.
- **Window List**—Displays the Window List dialog.
- **Manage Windows**—Displays a submenu of window-management choices, mostly affecting the currently-selected window. Among the choices are
  - o *Iconize:* Turns the currently selected IDE window into an icon. This may be useful for getting an IDE window out of the way temporarily without actually closing it. See state.
  - o *Restore:* If the selected IDE window is maximized, unmaximizes that window. Otherwise returns an iconized IDE window (if any) to its previous state (normal or maximized). See state.
  - o *Maximize:* Resizes the selected window so that it fills the screen, or to some other area as determined by a track-limits method. See state.
  - o *Destroy:* Closes the selected window. This command calls **close** to guarantee that the window is closed, whereas File | Close Window calls user-close, where

particular user-close methods may instead decide to merely hide the window or do nothing.

- o *Bury:* Moves the frontmost IDE window to the back. This may be useful for getting a window out of the way without actually closing it.
- o *Unbury:* Moves the backmost IDE window to the front. This may be useful for retrieving a window shortly after burying it.
- o *Show Second:* Moves the IDE window that is just behind the frontmost window to the front. The keyboard shortcut (Ctrl-Alt-J) is handy for quickly switching back and forth between two IDE windows.
- o *Show Third:* Moves the third-frontmost IDE window to the front. The keyboard shortcut (Ctrl-Alt-K) is handy for quickly switching between three IDE windows.
- o *Show Fourth:* Moves the fourth-frontmost IDE window to the front. The keyboard shortcut (Ctrl-Alt-L) is handy for quickly switching between four IDE windows.
- o *Scroll IDE Down:* scrolls the entire IDE interior downward by a portion of one page. Scrolling the IDE may be useful for placing various groups of windows in different areas of the scrollable IDE canvas. Using another menu command to select an IDE tool window will also scroll the IDE interior to fully show the selected window. This command and the following three are present only when the use-ide-parent-window option is enabled (as it is by default).
- o *Scroll IDE Up:* scrolls the IDE interior upward.
- o *Scroll IDE Left:* scrolls the IDE interior leftward.
- o *Scroll IDE Right:* scrolls the IDE interior rightward.

- *New Listener :* Opens a listener as an additional pane in the Debug window. The new listener will run in a separate thread, named Listener *X* where *X* is a number.

You can close the new listener with the File | Close Pane while the listener is the selected window, or by clicking on the close box (the control labelled with an X in the upper right).

- *New Editor* : Opens a new editor workbook (a tabbed collection of text-edit buffers). Current editors are unaffected.
- *New Inspector* : Opens a new Inspector window, leaving any current Inspector windows in place.
- *Extended Toolbar* : Displays the extended (floating) toolbar. See Ide User Guide, chapter 2, section 2.3 for information on how to move items from the extended toolbar to the standard toolbar already on the Project Window.
- *Toolbars* : Toggles between displaying and hiding the toolbars on the Project Window. Checked if they are currently displayed.
- *Status Bar* : Toggles displaying and hiding the status bar on the Project Window. Command is checked if the status bar is currently visible.
- *Background Window* : This command (which will appear only if the use-ide-parent-window configuration option is nil) displays a background window below IDE windows to prevent displays from other applications from showing through. Clicking right over the background window displays a menu showing other visible IDE windows and allowing the background window to be maximized (to cover the screen) or unmaximized (just big enough to be a background for windows other than the Project Window). Also on that menu is a Save All command with the same effect as the Save All command on the File menu. On GTK, the background window is always there.
- ***Maximize IDE*** : This command (on GTK only) will maximize the IDE parent window by calling (setf maximize-ide).

Options and Windows Menu

This document gives step by step instructions for customizing the options that appear on the right-click menu for various file types. I have found this particularly useful for designing and testing web pages.

Typically, before uploading a HTML page, you will want to view it in both Netscape and Internet Explorer, and you may wish to make quick edits using, say, WordPad. To make this easier for myself I have added a "Netscape" and an "Edit" option to the right-click menu for all HTML files, (IE is my default browser). This means I can open HTML files in Internet Explorer, Netscape or WordPad with two clicks, instead of dragging files all over the desktop, or opening applications and doing a "File Open".

For GIFs and JPEGS, I have also added the Netscape option, and I've linked the "Edit" option to my favorite graphics editing programme.

Warning

This document discusses editing the Windows Registry. This gives you complete control over the configuration of your menus, but you should be extremely careful not to change Registry values that are used by other applications. The author accepts no responsibility for any problems that may arise as a result of any changes to the Registry, even for those changes outlined in this example.

If you want to avoid modifying the registry directly, many of the changes described here can also be made in Windows Explorer's "Folder Options" menu. To use this approach, double click "My Computer", select the "Tools" menu, then "Folder Options", then the "File Types" tab. From here, you can highlight the file type you wish to change, then click the "Advanced" button to change the menu options that appear for the file type. This won't give you complete control of every option, but it is probably sufficient for most needs, and it is much less likely to cause problems as a result of accidental changes to the wrong registry keys.

Some Common Questions

Before tackling how to add menu options, here are a few interesting or common questions I've received.

Note: I stopped using Windows a few years ago, (I switched to Linux), so I'm afraid I no longer offer help with Windows Registry problems. Please accept this apology if I don't reply to Windows-related questions.

Modifying the Right-Click Menu

Now on with the show...

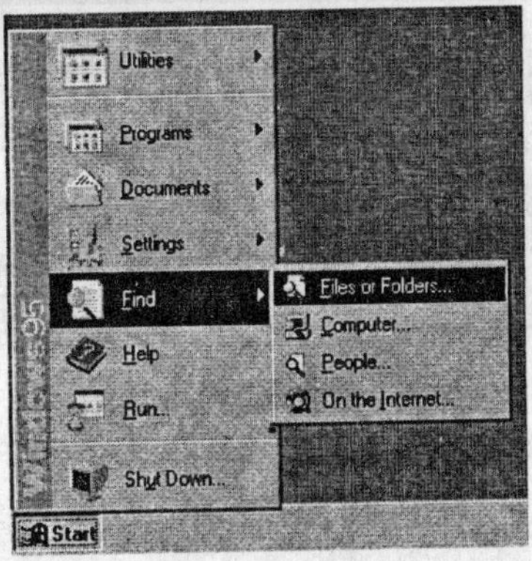

- First we need to find the location of the programme we want to use
- (Note: You can also get this information from the "Properties" box if you have a shortcut to the programme on your desktop. Otherwise...)
- Click on "Find Files or Folders" in the Start Menu
- Search for the programme you want to add to the right-click menu
- Make a note of the folder where the programme is found
- Some common programmes you might like to use are:
- Netscape.exe - Netscape Communicator
- IExplore.exe - Internet Explorer
- WordPad.exe - WordPad

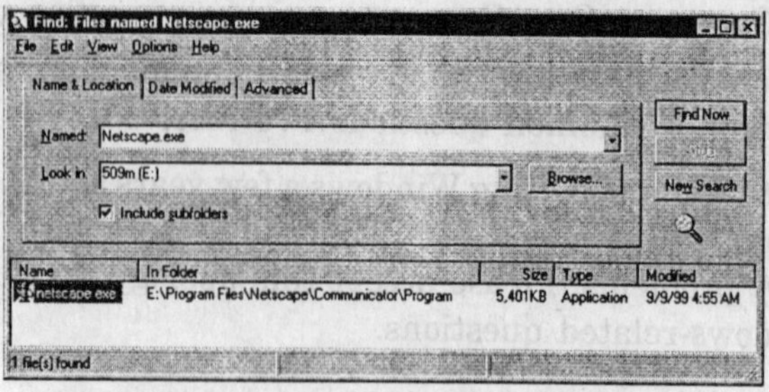

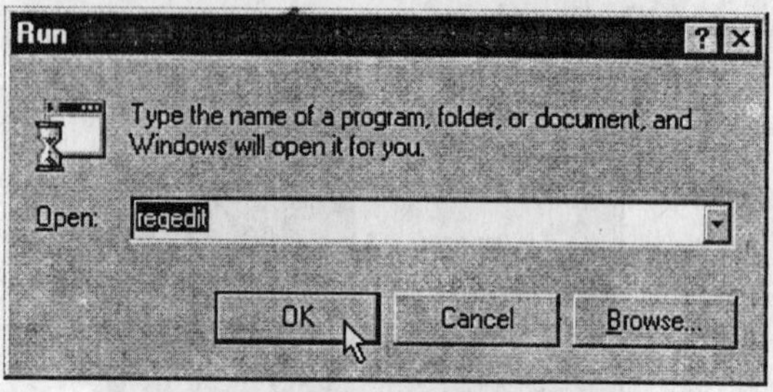

- From the Start Menu select "Run"
- Enter "regedit"
- This runs the Registry Editor

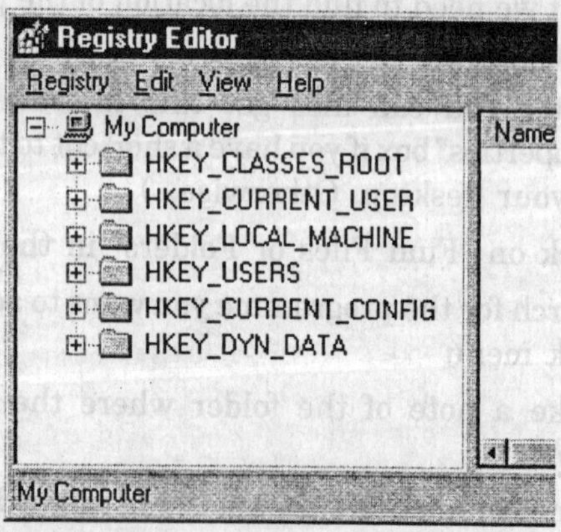

- Open the HKEY_CLASSES_ROOT "folder"
- This opens a long list of file extensions, (.exe, .html, .ini, etc)

- Following the extension list, extension groups are listed, (for example "htmlfile" refers to all files with ".htm" and ".html" extensions, "jpegfile" refers to .jpg and .jpeg files, "giffile" refers to .png files)
- Note: To find the extension group associated with a particular extension, click on the extension and note the value in the "Data" field, (on the right side), for the value named "(Default)"

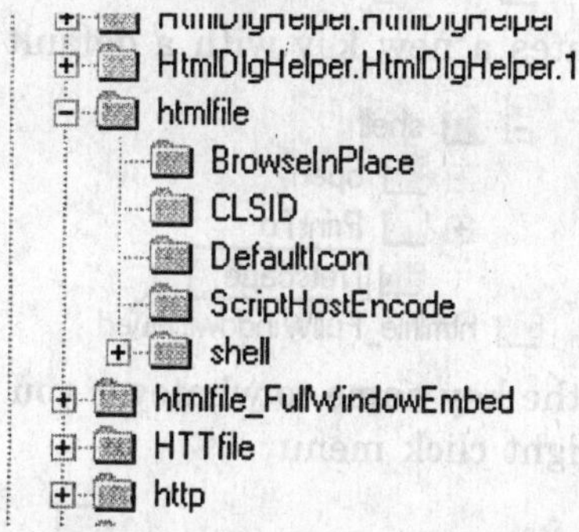

- Select the extension, or extension group you wish to modify - typically, you will want to modify an extension group, rather than an individual extension
- In this example we want to add a "Netscape" option to all .html and .htm files, so we open the "htmlfile" extension group
- Note: we could modify each extension separately if we wished

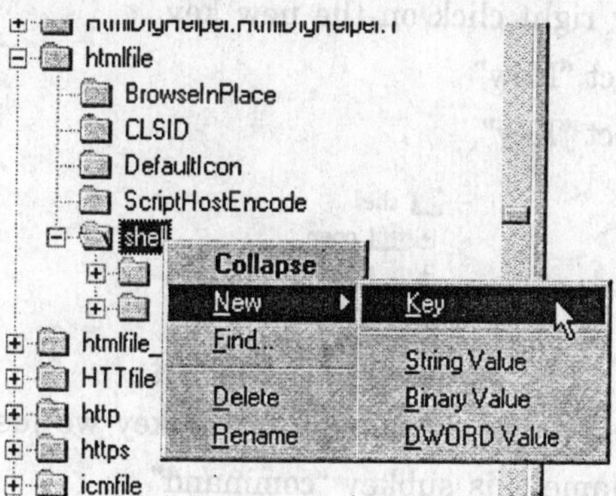

- Right click on the "shell" option
- Select "New"
- Select "Key"

- This creates a new key with a default name

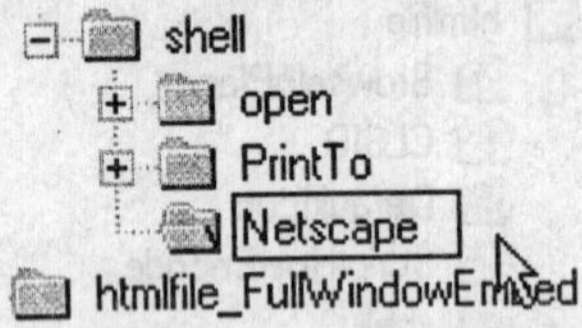

- Change the key name to whatever you wish to appear on the right click menu

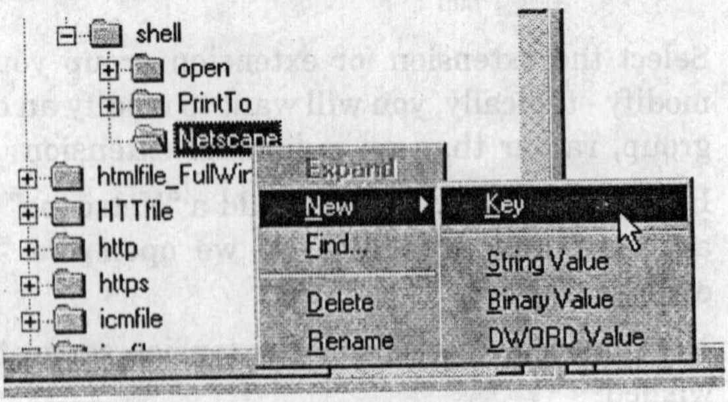

- Now right click on the new key
- Select "New"
- Select "Key"

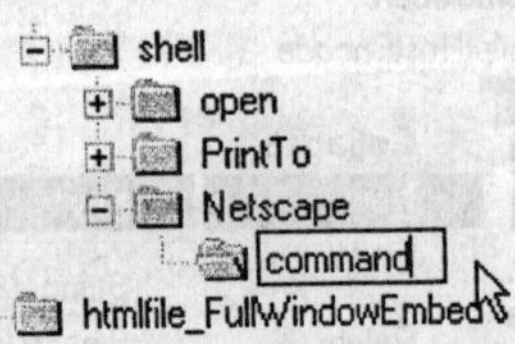

- This creates a "subkey" of the key we just created
- Rename this subkey "command"

- Note that in the right hand window the name "Default" and "value not set" appear
- Double click on the "Default", (or the small "ab" icon to the left)
- This brings up an Edit window which is used to set the default value

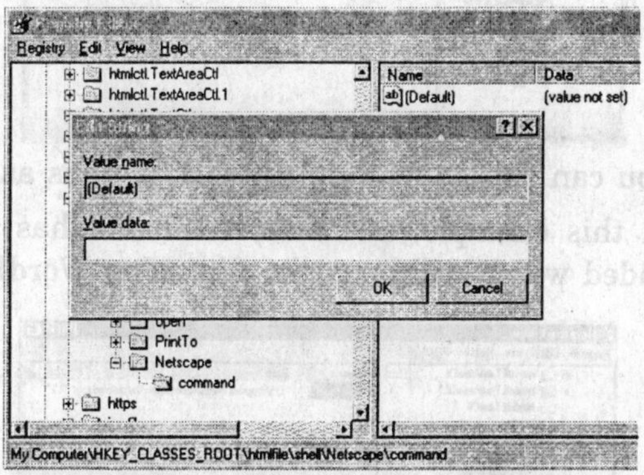

- The "value" to enter is the name of the programme to run
- The format of the value field is:
- FOLDERNAME\PROGRAMNAME "%1"
- In this example its:
- E:\Programme Files\Netscape\ Communicator\ Programme\Netscape.exe "%1"
- Note: When we use the new menu option, "%1" is replaced with the name of the file we clicked on. This tells Netscape which file to open
- Click "OK" to set the default value

- This completes the process-Right clicking on any "htmlfile" will now have a "Netscape" option that opens the selected file in Netscape

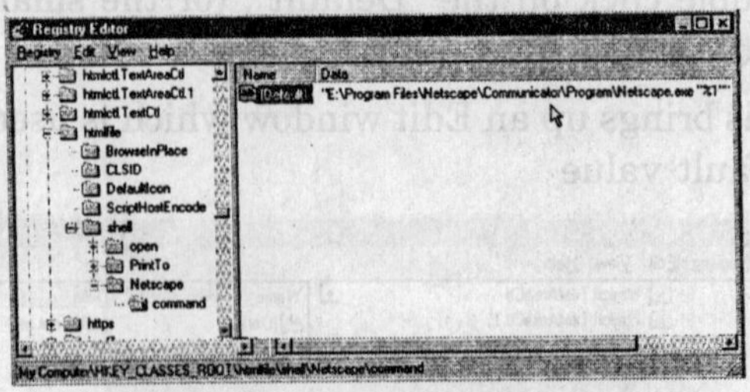

- You can add as many right click options as you wish
- In this example, an "Edit" command has also been added which will open the file using WordPad

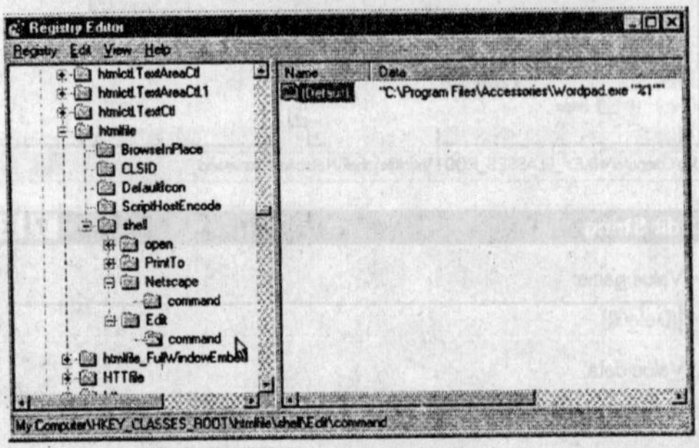

- Note that the menu options are listed in the order in which they were created
- The simplest way to reorder the options is to rename the option that you want to appear at the end of the list

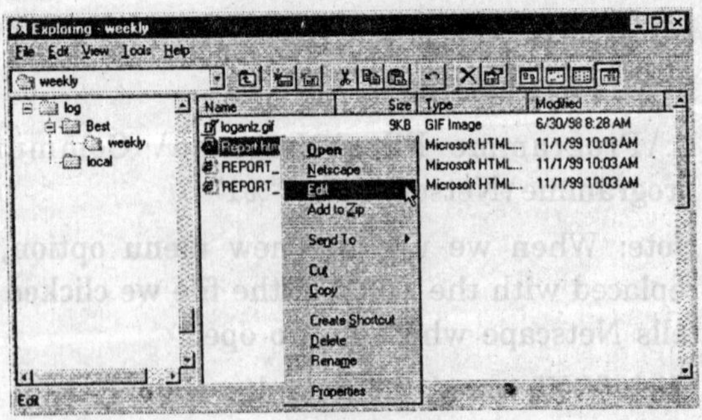

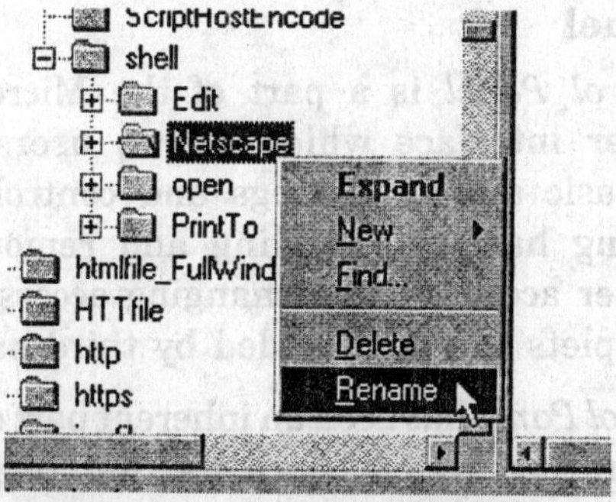

- **To rename a menu option, right click on the key in the Registry Editor and select "Rename"**

- **Rename the key to a temporary name, then rename it back to its original**
- **In the above case, we renamed the "Netscape" option and it now appears below the "Edit" option**
- **Note that you can remove the menu item by deleting the key in the Registry Editor**
- **The "Delete" option is directly above the "Rename" option**
- **Note that to delete the "Netscape" key, you must first delete its "command" subkey**

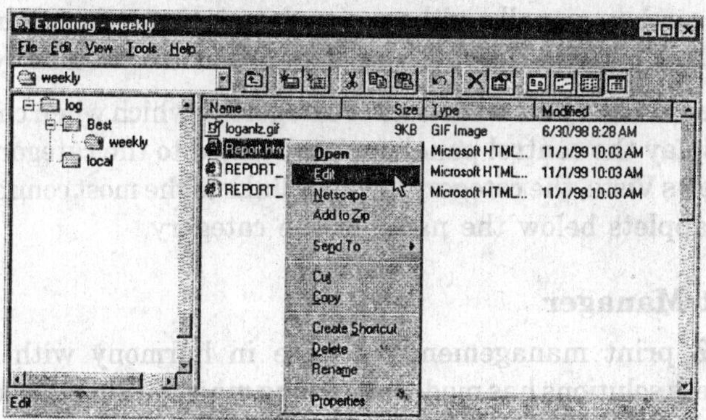

Control Panel

The *Control Panel* is a part of the Microsoft Windows graphical user interface which allows users to view and manipulate basic system settings and controls via applets, such as adding hardware, adding and removing software, controlling user accounts, and changing accessibility options. Additional applets can be provided by third party software.

The *Control Panel* has been an inherent part of the Microsoft Windows operating system since its first release (Windows 1.0), with many of the current applets being added in later versions. Beginning with Windows 95, the *Control Panel* is implemented as a special folder, i.e. the folder does not physically exist, but only contains shortcuts to various applets such as *Add or Remove Programmes* and *Internet Options*. Physically, these applets are stored as *.cpl* files. For example, the *Add or Remove Programmes* applet is stored under the name *appwiz.cpl* in the *SYSTEM32* folder.

In recent versions of Windows, the *Control Panel* has two views, *Classic View* and *Category View*, and it is possible to switch between these through an option that appears on the left side of the window.

Many of the individual *Control Panel* applets can be accessed in other ways. For instance, *Display Properties* can be accessed by right-clicking on an empty area of the desktop and choosing *Properties*.

The classic view consists of shortcuts to the various control panel applets, usually without any description (other than the name). The categories are seen if the user use "Details" view.

The category view consists of categories, which when clicked on display the control panel applets related to the category. In Windows Vista, the category displays links to the most commonly used applets below the name of the category.

Print Manager

CZ print management software in harmony with your business solutions has made everything magical! Small, medium and large companies are embarking on print management software. Printer monitor no longer remains a questionable issue; our print management software controls printing by providing different rules and proper quota management. We provide holistic print control solutions at every level of enterprise, our print management software manage printing - print count, prints logs, print quotes, print accounting and print audit. Before actual printing of the document, user may be required to enter user name and PIN number; pint documents may be associated with client billing code / project code/ shared # etc. Print server management has added extra level of security and better printer usage. Our print management software support domain and workgroup network architecture.

CZ Print Job Tracker 4.0

CZ Print Job Tracker 4.0 print management software has simplified and automated print administration for print server and non-print server environment i.e. direct IP printing atmosphere. The software provides centralized control of print manager that helps to administer printer monitor and counter. This software is printer brand independent, can be used with any / all brands of printer. Since, the print management software has centralized print control, all printers located in an enterprise and print jobs are controlled easily from one server station and it has also made easy to send email alert. Our print management software solution suits all enterprise, academic, professional services and consulting solutions.

Starting from print request generated at each workstation the process steps are well authenticated, securing all your print information to final elimination of wasted papers. Companies can use this software to keep count of print jobs, to monitor the printers, also to allow the end-user to attach client billing code to the print job so that they can bill the client later. Finally billing report is generated and sent in your desired language (the reports can be created in any language), this report can also be seen from your web browser. Printer accounting software helps to track - jobs in queue, deleted print jobs and actually printed jobs. Waiting jobs are streamlined and moved to other printer that is free and automated notification mail is sent to job owner. CZ Print Job Tracker 4.0 can be used with workstations supporting different OS (Windows/Unix/Linux/Mac) to bill the print jobs by entering client codes / project codes or to enter user name and PIN number before actual printing of the document. This software helps to reduce printing cost and print control easily by having quota and account balance checkpoints, if account balance is low or quota goes to zero, print job automatically stops. The software helps to increase over all efficiency of the print network, improves throughput of printers in the network, well authenticated print jobs, synchronizing and integrating various printers in the network, cost curtailment and quality enhancement remains the bottom line of this print management software.

CZ Print Release Station 3.0

CZ Print Release Station 3.0 is print management software, best-suited paragon print solution for libraries, schools, colleges and universities of low budget, where print jobs hold and release is centralized and unwanted print is restricted. Printing expenditure is brought down by charging for their patrons / students printing; best management of resources, reducing accidental paper wastage and abusive printing. Print jobs are kept on hold until released manually by student, patron staff or employee. When a print job is submitted, a dialog window can popup to allow the user to change the print job name on the user's workstation for privacy, and / or create a password that the user will use to release that print job on the print release station. This software tool has proved fruitful for many organizations to save unwanted printing cost.

CZ Print Job Report 3.0

CZ Print Job Report 3.0 is a part of print management tool for generating reports especially for analysis of print cost and client billing. The print management software reporting tool is designed to provide with myriad options to manage reports. Not only you can view but also generate 100 reports - 64 reports are default ones with option to customize 36 reports. These reports are compatible with CZ print management software and by remotely connecting this software tool to your database you can view reports from any computer in your network running on Windows platform. Creating email reports, generating emails and mailing reports all these processes are automated when using with our CZ Print Job Tracker print management software. The software provides the capability to export these reports to Adobe-PDF, MS-Excel, MS-Word and Rich Text formats for advanced reporting. The most magical feature the reports can be easily and quickly created in any language available in the world. The software tool is best fit to generate automatic e-mail reports and automatic web-reports.

CZ Print Job Report 3.0 can be used with any other third party print management software to view and generate reports; all you need is that the other print management software should fulfill the minimum requirement of the sample database. For any print management software Print job tracking and client billing is easy by billing print usage to clients and making them pay for print. The first step is selection of database for generating report, next time frame is defined, if time frame is not defined default time frame remains selected, then based on the defined time frame report is generated, user can also select from 100 reports (64 default and 36 customized) to view for cost analysis.

CZ Print Polisher 1.0

Discover the power of your printer with our virtual print driver and manage various print tasks. CZ Print Polisher 1.0 print control software that helps you to capture the printer power. Printing and print management services can be optimized to save customization time. User can set page boarder, define margins, define header and footer rules, paper size, page layout for the pages to be printed, page can be previewed and then print command options can be set, to manage overall printing. User can control and acquire the print page content by exporting to BMP, JPG, TIFF, EMF, TGAPCX, JP2, JPC, PGX, PCX, RAS, PNM images on mouse click events. You gain full control on printer resources i.e. toner, ink, paper and so you can save a good deal of resources for further use. Header, footer can be easily incorporated with user and computer name to the paper(s). You can view normal page, zoom-in and zoom-out print preview. You can set various options for printing, for output you can print multiple pages per sheet; also scale/poster/fit-to-page printing can be set. Print order can be set to normal or you can skip (odd or even number) pages at the time of printing also. User can change graphics resolution and altitude right at printing time. User can also create overlays and add multi-line watermarks and watermark texts on each paper sheet.

CZ Print Polish Marker 1.0

CZ Print Polish Marker 1.0 print control software that helps you to capture the printer power. Header, footer can be easily incorporated with user and computer name to the paper(s). User can also create overlays and add multi-line watermarks and watermark texts on each paper sheet.

Clipboard Viewer

For some reason, Windows XP messed up the Clipboard Viewer. It's barely listed on the Help menus, and it isn't installed automatically when you upgrade to Windows XP. Even when you tell Windows to install it from its CD, it doesn't put a Clipboard Viewer icon appear on the menu.

And that's a shame, as the viewer is a handy way to see exactly what's on your clipboard.

Windows XP's Clipboard Viewer is called the "Clipbook Viewer," and although flawed, it lets you see what's on your Clipboard. Here's how to put Windows XP's Clipbook Viewer onto your Start menu.

1. Click the Start menu button and open My Computer.
2. Open your C drive. (It's listed in the Hard Disk Drives section.)
3. Double-click on the Windows folder. (You might have to tell it to let you see what's inside.)
4. Double-click on the System32 folder. (Again, you might have to tell it to let you see what's inside.)

5. Scroll down the page until you locate a file named Clipbrd.
6. Drag and drop the Clipbrd file onto your Start button.

Just let go of your mouse button when it's pointing at the Start button; that drops a shortcut to the Clipbook Viewer onto your Start menu. When you open your Start menu, the Clipbrd program's icon will appear near the top.

To put a shortcut to that file on your Desktop, right-click the Clipbrd file, choose SendTo, and choose Desktop (Create Shortcut). Whenever you want to see exactly what's being stored on your Clipboard, double-click on that icon. The Clipbook Viewer will appear, letting you peer inside its contents.

Note: Microsoft seems to have stripped the Clipbook Viewer of the advanced features found in older versions. You can't "stockpile" multiple clips, for instance, or swap clips with networked computers. (The program's Help menu still says you *can* do things things, oddly enough.) But if you just want to see what's on your Clipboard, the stripped-down Clipbook Viewer works fine.

Paintbrush

Paint (formerly Paintbrush for Windows) is a simple graphics painting programme that has been included with almost all versions of Microsoft Windows since its first release. It is often referred to as MS Paint or Microsoft Paint. The programme opens and saves files as Windows bitmap (24-bit, 256 colour, 16 colour, and monochrome, all with the .bmp extension), JPEG, GIF (without animation or transparency, although the Windows 98 version, a Windows 95 upgrade, and the Windows NT4 version did support the latter), PNG (without alpha channel), and TIFF (without the multiple pages). The programme can be in colour mode or two-colour black-and-white, but there is no grayscale mode. For its simplicity, it rapidly became one of the most used applications in the early versions of Windows—introducing many to painting on a computer for the first time—and still has strong associations with the immediate usability of the old Windows workspace.

History

The first version of Paint was introduced with the first version of Windows, Windows 1.0. It was later renamed to Paintbrush in Windows 3.0, but the name was changed back to Paint in Windows 95 and later. This version only supported the MSP and BMP file formats. The former is no longer supported by newer versions of Paint, along with PCX and RLE. Older versions cannot open or edit PNG files, and can only open GIF, JPEG, and TIFF files with a graphics filter for the specific file type.

In Windows 95, a new version of Paint was introduced. The same icons and colour palette continued to be used through Windows XP. The version of Paint included in Windows 95 and Windows NT 4.0 allowed saving and loading a custom set of colour wells as colour palette files (*.PAL) using *Save colours* and *Get colours* functions from the *Colours* menu. This functionality worked correctly only if the colour depth of images was 16-bits per pixel (bpp) or higher (65,536 (64k) colours [High Colour]).

In the Windows 98, Windows 2000 or Windows Me versions of Paint, images could be saved in JPEG and GIF formats if the necessary Microsoft graphics filters were installed, usually by another Microsoft application such as Microsoft Office or Microsoft PhotoDraw. In Windows Me onwards, the canvas size expands automatically when larger images are opened or pasted.

In Windows XP and later versions, Paint is based on GDI+ and therefore, images can be natively saved as JPEG, GIF, TIFF and PNG without requiring additional graphics filters (in addition to BMP). However, alpha channel transparency is still not supported because the GDI+ version of Paint can only handle up to 24-bit depth images. Also, since another accessory, Imaging for Windows, was discontinued in Windows XP, support for acquiring images from a scanner or a digital camera was also added to Paint. However, the tertiary colour function, used for creating GIF files with a transparent background, was removed. Also, the ability to save and load palette colours to and from .pal files was removed.

In Windows Vista, the toolbar icons and default colour palette have been changed. Also, an increased number of undo levels, a zoom slider, and a crop function have been added.

Recent images from a Windows 7 build show the use of the Ribbon UI.

Features

Recent versions of Paint allow the user to pick up to three colours at a time: the primary colour (left mouse click), secondary colour (right mouse click), and tertiary colour (control key + any mouse click).

The programme comes with the following options in its *Tool Box* (from left to right in image):

- Free-Form Select
- Select
- Eraser/Colour Eraser
- Fill With Colour
- Pick Colour
- Magnifier
- Pencil
- Brush
- Airbrush
- Text
- Line
- Curve
- Rectangle
- Polygon
- Ellipse
- Rounded Rectangle

The *Image* menu offers the following options: Flip/Rotate, Stretch/Skew, Invert Colours, Image Attributes, Clear Image, and Draw Opaque. The "Colours" menu allows the user to Edit Colours (only menu option under Colours). The Edit Colours dialog box shows the standard Windows colour picker which includes a 48-colour palette and 12 custom colour slots that can be edited. Clicking "Define Custom Colours" displays a square version of the colour wheel that can select a custom colour either with a crosshair cursor (like a "+"), by Hue/Saturation/ Luminance, or by Red/Green/Blue values.

There are 28 colour wells in the workspace. The default colours in the *Colour Box* are the following: Black, White, Gray, Silver, Maroon, Red, Olive, Yellow, Dark Green, Green, Teal, Cyan, Navy blue, Blue, Purple, Magenta, Old Gold, Lemon Yellow, Slate gray, Kelly green, Dark Carolina blue, Aquamarine, Midnight blue, Periwinkle, Violet-blue, Coral, Brown, and Pumpkin orange. A colour palette is also available.

Paint also has a few hidden functions not mentioned in the help file: a *stamp mode*, *trail mode*, *regular shapes*, moving pictures, and a strange brush. For the stamp mode, the user can select part of the image, hold the control key, and move it to another part of the canvas. This, instead of cutting the piece out, creates a copy of it. The process can be repeated as many times as desired, as long as the control key is held down. The trail mode works exactly the same, but it uses the shift key instead of the control key.

A 10x magnification is available by clicking just below to 8x selector. The user may also draw straight horizontal, vertical, or diagonal lines with the pencil tool, without the need of the straight line tool, by holding the shift key and dragging the tool. Moreover, it is also possible to thicken (control key + +) or thin (control key + ") a line simultaneously while it is being drawn. To crop whitespace or eliminate parts of a graphic, the blue handle in the lower right corner can be clicked and dragged to increase canvas size or crop a graphic. The colours in the image can be inverted by pressing control key + I. Users can also draw perfect shapes (which have width equal to height) using the Rounded Rectangle, the Circle, and the Rectangle Tool by holding down the Shift key while dragging.

Older versions of Paint, such as the one bundled with Windows 3.1, allowed controlling the drawing cursor with the use of arrow keys as well as a colour-replace brush, which replaced a single colour underneath the brush with another without affecting the rest of the image. In later versions of Paint, the colour erase brush may be simulated by selecting the colour to be replaced as the primary colour, and the one it will be replaced with as the secondary colour, and then right-click dragging the erase tool. The drawing cursor can also be controlled with arrow keys in current versions of Paint if *Mouse keys* under *Accessibility options* is enabled and configured appropriately.

Paint's exclusive availability on the Windows platform has led to the creation of clones by users of other operating systems, such as Kolourpaint for users of Linux, BSD and Solaris.

The new version of Paint found in Windows 7 offers many new features, namely a selection of brushes including Oil, Watercolor, and Calligraphic.

Support for Indexed Palettes

By default, almost all versions of Paint create 24-bit images and are generally unable to properly downgrade them to indexed palettes using less than 24 bits per pixel. This means that when saving images in any of the supported formats specifying a format that uses indexed palettes with less than 24 bits per pixel instead of true colour formats, a warning message is displayed about possible loss of quality. In fact, Paint does not normally utilize binary, colour or gray scale dithering or palette optimization, and the image will be saved with usually irreversibly scrambled colours, potentially ruining one's work. For example, a typical Windows screen will change the buttons and menu bar from grey to khaki green when saved as an 8-bit BMP format. Saving to a monochrome BMP or a GIF format does invoke dithering processes; however, even these use a fixed black-and-white (in the case of monochrome BMP) or standard 256-colour (in the case of GIF) palette.

Paint is nonetheless able to correctly load and save indexed palettes in any of the supported formats if an image is opened as an 8-bit or otherwise indexed palette image. In that case, the image's palette will be preserved when saving. However, there is no way to see the actual palette, and colour choices for brushes, text and erasers as well as user-defined colours will be limited to the closest available colour in the indexed palette.

Write

Windows Write was a simple word processor that came with Microsoft Windows 1.0, Windows 2.0, and the Windows 3.x series. Throughout its lifespan it was minimally updated, and is comparable to early versions of MacWrite. Early versions of Write only worked with Write (.wri) files, but with the modernization of Microsoft Word for Windows in 1989, and the introduction of Windows 3.0 the following year, Write became capable of reading and composing early Word (.doc) documents. With Windows 3.1, Write became OLE capable.

Windows Write is similar to the modern WordPad, which was introduced in Windows 95, and like WordPad, Write was more advanced than Notepad (though Notepad's simplicity is an intentional feature to make basic text operations faster and easier) and was considered a modern word processor. However, Write did not have the many features of software such as Microsoft Word. Write had automatic pagination which WordPad lacks.

As its default programme icon was a pen having just finished writing a capital letter A, the programme was referred to by some users as 'A-Write'.

In Windows 95 and later versions of Windows, the Windows Write executable (write.exe) simply executes WordPad.

Terminal

A terminal emulator, terminal application, term, or tty for short, is a programme that emulates a "dumb" video terminal within some other display architecture. Though typically synonymous with a command line shell or text terminal, the term *terminal* covers all remote terminals, including graphical interfaces. A terminal emulator inside a graphical user interface is often called a terminal window.

A terminal window allows the user access to a text terminal and all its applications such as command line interfaces (CLI) and text user interface applications. These may be running either on the same machine or on a different one via telnet, ssh, or dial-up. On Unix-like operating systems it is common to have one or more terminal windows connected to the local machine.

Terminals usually support a set of escape sequences for controlling colour, cursor position, etc. Examples include the family of terminal control sequence standards known as ECMA-48, ANSI X3.64 or ISO/IEC 6429.

Early adopters of computer technology, such as banks, insurance companies, and governments, still make frequent use of terminal emulators. They typically have decades old applications running on mainframe computers. The old "dumb" video terminals used to access the mainframe are long since obsolete; however, applications on the mainframe are still in use. Quite often, terminal emulators are the only way a user can access applications running on these older machines.

Raw and Cooked input/output

On Unix-like systems, for an individual keypress received by the terminal or terminal emulator, it sends an individual code from the character set in use. Also, carriage return and line feed are distinct operations. In raw mode, text passes directly from the terminal or PTY (a device node that a programme wishing to emulate a terminal binds to) to the TTY device. In cooked mode a number of changes are made as the data pass between the terminal or PTY and the TTY: The application gets complete lines of input at once neatly terminated with a line feed and can send just a linefeed when it wants a new line. Also, text typed is echoed back to the user. When a programme is started, terminal is generally in cooked mode which allows easy input and output of text, but applications that want more control will often put the terminal into raw mode, or a slightly more processed rare mode. The individual characteristics of cooked mode can be turned on and off individually which may be needed for certain applications.

Synchronous Terminals

In asychronous terminals data can flow in any direction at any time. In synchronous terminals a protocol controls who may send data when. The IBM 3270-based terminals used with IBM mainframe computers are an example of synchronous terminals. They operate in an essentially "screen-at-a-time" mode (also known as block mode). Users can make numerous changes to a page, before submitting the updated screen to the remote machine as a single action. This paradigm can be surprising to those used to the more common asynchronous terminal behaviour, though in fact it is conceptually quite similar to the submission of HTTP forms on the Web.

Terminal emulators that simulate the original 3270 hardware terminal are available for most operating systems, for use both by those administering systems such as the z9, as well as those using the corresponding applications such as CICS.

Other examples of synchronous terminals include the IBM 5250, and the ICL 7561. The Honeywell Bull VIP7800 and Hewlett-Packard 700/92 terminals also had a block mode.

Examples of Terminal Emulators

Many terminal emulators have been developed, for terminals such as VT100, VT220, VT320, IBM 3270/8/9/E, IBM 5250, IBM 3179G, Data General D211, Hewlett Packard HP700/92, Sperry/Unisys 2000-series UTS60, Burroughs/Unisys A-series T27/TD830/ET1100, ADDS ViewPoint, Sun console, QNX, AT386, SCO-ANSI, SNI 97801, Televideo, and Wyse 50/60. Additionally, programmes have been developed to emulate terminals which are themselves programmes, such as xterm and assorted console terminals (e.g., for Linux). Finally, some emulations simply refer to a standard, such as ANSI. These programmes are available on many platforms ranging from DOS and Unix to GUI operating systems such as Windows and Macs, to embedded operating systems found in cellphones and industrial hardware.

Under Microsoft Windows, programmes that provide the remote-access form of terminal emulation include the built-in programmes HyperTerminal (not included in Windows Vista) and Microsoft's telnet client, as well as third-party programmes like PuTTY, AlphaCom, HostAccess by Rogue Wave, Poderosa, Terminator, TigerTerm, TN3270 Plus, Ericom Software PowerTerm InterConnect, z/Scope Express VT, Tera Term, SwitchTermJ, SecureCRT, Access*One, DynaComm, TinyTERM by Century Software and Attachmate Reflection [Indigo Terminal Emulator by Shadeblue Software]. For Windows CE and Windows Mobile there are products like MochaSoft, MobileVT, Access*One and NaurTech. MS-DOS examples include ProComm, Qmodem, Telemate, and Telix. A programme called Crosstalk ran on both MS-DOS and CP/M.

A so-called "DOS box" or "Command prompt" is the Windows equivalent of a locally-connected terminal window (in fact, it is a Win32 console).

Mac OS X includes Terminal as its default terminal emulator for local access. There are a number of third-party terminal emulators for local access on Mac OS X, such as GLTerm, iTerm, MacTelnet, dataComet, and MacWise. ZTerm is a remote-access terminal for the Mac.

For the X Window System, there are many different terminal emulators for local access, such as xterm, dtterm, Eterm, GNOME Terminal, Konsole, rxvt, mrxvt, wterm, SwitchTerm, TeemTalk, and aterm.

Notepad

Notepad is a simple text editor included in all versions of Microsoft Windows since Windows 1.0 in 1985.

Overview

Notepad is a common text-only (plain text) editor. The resulting files–typically saved with the .txt extension–have no format tags or styles, making the programme suitable for editing system files that are to be used in a DOS environment.

One notable feature of Notepad is that it does not support formatting of any kind - if text/**rich text** is copied from a web page and pasted into a word processor, the formatting and embedded metadata comes along with the text, and can be difficult to remove. However, if text is copied from a formatted web site, pasted into Notepad, then copied again from Notepad before being pasted into a destination programme, Notepad will have stripped all of the formatting. An alternative of this use is, however, provided in many word processors through the possibility to paste unformatted text, which may be easier to use with a little initial effort.

As an interesting aside, Notepad does support both left-to-right and right-to-left based languages, and one can alternate between these viewing formats by pressing and releasing the arrow key followed by Ctrl+Shift, using the right or left arrow and shift keys to go to right-to-left format or left-to-right format, respectively. Notepad can edit files of almost any format; however, it does not treat Unix- or Mac-style text files correctly (*see newline*). Wordpad however does.

Early versions of Notepad offered only the most basic functions, such as finding text. Newer versions of Windows include an updated version of Notepad with a search and replace function (Ctrl + *H*), as well as Ctrl + *F* for search and similar keyboard shortcuts. In older versions such as those included with Windows 95, Windows 98, Windows Me and Windows 3.1, there is a 64k limit on the size of the file being edited, an operating system limit of the *EDIT* class.

Up to Windows 95, Fixedsys was the only available font for Notepad. Windows NT 4.0 and 98 introduced the ability to change this font. In Windows 2000 and XP the default font was changed to Lucida Console.

Up to Windows Me, there were almost no keyboard shortcuts and no line-counting feature. Starting with Windows 2000, shortcuts for common tasks like new, open and save were added, as well as a status-bar with a line counter (available only when word-wrap is disabled).

In the Windows NT-based versions of Windows, Notepad can edit traditional 8-bit text files as well as Unicode text files (both UTF-8 and UTF-16, and in case of UTF-16, both little-endian and big-endian; see Endianness.)

Notepad makes use of a built-in window class named "EDIT".

Notepad also has a built-in simple logging function, which simply inserts a new timestamp each time the file is opened. To activate this feature, the first line of the text file must be ".LOG", without the quotes.

Notepad may be used as a text-based HTML editor for its pure simplicity and more control over WYSIWYG editors. However, because it lacks many features, such as syntax highlighting, web developers may favor more specialized editors for this purpose.

Unicode Detection

The Windows NT version of Notepad, installed by default on Windows 2000 and Windows XP, has the ability to detect Unicode files even when they are missing a byte order mark. To do this, it utilizes a Windows API function called IsTextUnicode(). However, this function is imperfect, incorrectly identifying some all-lowercase ASCII text as UTF-16. As a result, Notepad interprets a file containing a phrase like "aaaa aaa aaa aaaaa" as two-byte Unicode text file and attempts to display it as such. If a font with support for Chinese is installed, Chinese characters are displayed.

A few people misinterpreted this issue for an easter egg. Many phrases which fit the pattern (including "this app can break" and "bush hid the facts") appeared on the web as hoaxes. Experts correctly attributed it to the Unicode detection algorithm. This issue has been resolved in Windows Vista version of Notepad.

Competing Software

Notepad does not require a lock on the file it opens, so it can open files already opened by other processes, users or computers, whereas WordPad cannot. Also, since Notepad lacks advanced formatting functionality, many people find its simple interface faster and easier to use for basic text operations. The DOS EDIT text editor, especially as updated in Windows 95, where it became an MDI application, also provides many features never offered by Notepad.

There are many third-party replacements for Notepad with additional functionality, including both free software (e.g. Notepad++ and Notepad2) and freeware (e.g. TED Notepad).

Notepad lacks many features available in other text editors, such as regular expressions, macros, block-select, and MDI.

Calendar

This feature is included in the following editions of Windows Vista:

Windows Calendar is a flexible, easy-to-use tool for planning and managing all of your activities and coordinating your schedule with other people's. As the pace of life accelerates at work and at home, many people find it helpful to use a PC-based calendar to manage their time and coordinate their schedule with family, friends, and colleagues. Windows Calendar also includes a feature you can use to create a personal task list and to receive automatic notifications and reminders about specific tasks or upcoming appointments.

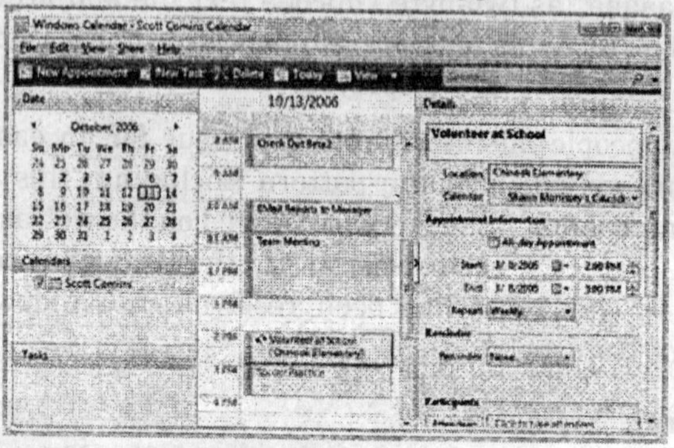

Manage your life and time better with Windows Calendar.

Personal Time Management

Creating Appointments

With Windows Calendar you can easily create appointments. After an appointment is on your calendar, you can set up an alert to remind you when the appointment is approaching. You can set Windows Calendar to alert you minutes, hours, or even days ahead of time, depending on how much advance notice you want. You can also set up recurring appointments. Perhaps you attend a weekly book club meeting, have a standing haircut appointment every six weeks, or pay your mortgage on the same day each month. With Windows Calendar, you can create one appointment and then instruct the calendar to set up a series of similar appointments at the intervals you choose.

Managing Tasks

Windows Calendar includes a personal task list, which makes it easy to organize and manage the things you need to do. For each task on your list, you can describe what you need to do, set a deadline for completion, choose a priority ranking so you tackle the most important tasks first, and keep track of your progress. You can also set reminders to let you know when a task is nearly due. And as you complete each task, you can simply check it off your list and have the satisfaction of watching it disappear.

Shared Calendars

Windows Calendar enables you to set up individual calendars for multiple people. This is especially helpful for families or other groups who share a single PC. Windows Calendar makes it easy for people who use the same computer to coordinate their personal schedules by letting them compare information from any or all personal calendars, side-by-side in a single view.

Imagine a busy family with two parents and three children ages 10, 12, and 15. Because everyone in the family has access to a shared PC running Windows Vista, each person can use Windows Calendar to set up and manage his or her own personal schedule. Windows Calendar enables each family member to view the others' calendars, either selectively or all at once.

As the parents plan for the week ahead, they can overlay their children's calendars and spouse's calendar onto their own to see what everyone in the family has planned and to make sure no one overlooks any important activities. After reviewing all of the schedules together, they might notice that they need to schedule time to attend one child's soccer game, another's school play, and a parent-teacher conference for the third child. Or they might choose to compare their schedule only with their spouse's calendar to make sure at least one parent will be home by a certain time each evening. Appointments from each calendar are displayed in a different colour, making it easy to tell whose schedule each item belongs to.

Calendar Subscriptions and Publishing

Windows Calendar is fully compatible with the popular iCalendar format, so you can import and export calendar information to and from other applications and websites.

Using Windows Calendar, you can subscribe to calendars hosted on websites in the iCalendar format and then view those calendars alongside your own. For example, you can subscribe to the season schedule of your favorite professional baseball team, the activities calendar for your child's middle school, or the annual schedule of a civic organization whose meetings you attend-and automatically stay up to date with any changes in those events.

The iCalendar compatibility of Windows Calendar also makes it easy to publish your own calendar on the Internet through a web host. If, for example, you chair a committee, organize a carpool, or coach your child's basketball team, you can use one of the calendar views in Windows Calendar to create a schedule and then publish it to the Web so others can see and share that information. If you want, you can publish your personal schedule with password protection, so only designated friends and family members can access and view your calendar.

Calculator

Microsoft Calculator, commonly known as Calculator from the application's title bar, is a calculation application included in all versions of the Microsoft Windows operating system. It can be reached by running the command "calc" on most Windows systems.

History

It was first shipped with Windows 1.0 as a simple arithmetic calculator.

In Windows 3.0, a Scientific mode is added, which includes exponents and roots, logarithms, factorial-based functions, trigonometry (supports radian, degree and gradians angles), base conversions (2, 8, 10, 16), logic operations, Statistic functions such as single variable statistics and linear regression. In Windows 3.0 and Windows 3.1 its interface had a white background with 2D buttons.

In Windows 95 and later, it uses an arbitrary-precision arithmetic library, replacing the standard IEEE floating point library. It offers bignum precision for basic operations (addition, subtraction, multiplication, division) and 32 digits of precision for advanced operations (square root, transcendental operators). Other changes include the use of 3d buttons.

In Windows ME, digit grouping is added. Degree and base settings are added to menu bar.

Windows 7

In Windows 7, separate Programmer, Statistics, Unit Conversion, Date Calculation, Templates modes were added. Tooltips were removed.

In every mode (except Statistics) one can see the history of calculations.

The applet was redesigned to accommodate multitouch.

In Scientific mode, the base conversion functions were moved to Programmer mode, and Statistics functions were moved to Statistics mode.

On the right of the main Calculator panel one can add the panel with *Date Calculations*, *Unit Conversion*, and *Templates*.

In Templates mode, one calculate a result on a chosen field based on the values on other fields. Pre-defined templates include gas mileages, estimate leases, mortgages, an more. In pre-beta versions of Windows 7, Calculator also provided a Wages template.

Features

Calculator has a simplified interface, small size, and can perform all of the functions of most four-function or scientific calculators. By default, the application is in the "Standard" mode, and functions as a four-function calculator. More advanced functions are available in "Scientific" mode, including logarithms, numerical base conversions, some logical operators, radian, degree and gradians support as well as simple single-variable statistical functions.

It does not provide support for user-defined functions, complex numbers, storage variables for intermediate results (other than the classic accumulator memory of pocket calculators), automated polar-cartesian coordinates conversion, or support two-variables statistics, making it impractical to use with many engineering, physics or high school mathematics tasks.

Calculator is not able to do "constant calculations". When a user wants to apply the same constant and operation many times, the second and following calculations can be done without retyping the operation and constant. So one can type: 2*7=[14] 3=[21] 4=[28] etc. Calculator ignores the number typed before the equal sign.

Some versions of Calculator have a way to automate long calculations. Writing a text file in Notepad or another text editor containing a number on the first row, then operators followed by numbers on the next row and pasting this content to calculator's textbox will result in it performing the described calculations. Most of Calculator's functions can be accessed with a specific letter or symbol — A full list can be found in Calculator's help file. This may not work correctly with all versions of Calculator, and depends on precise text formatting.

Many specialized keyboards have a "calculator" key, which launches Microsoft Calculator by default.

Microsoft Calculator Plus

It is a separate application for Windows XP and Windows Server 2003 users, which adds a 'Conversion' mode over

Windows XP version of Microsoft Calculator. 'Conversion' mode supports unit conversion and currency conversion.

Currency exchange rates can be updated using the built-in update feature, which downloads exchange rates from the European Central Bank.

Clock

- Totally free meaning you can use it anywhere without paying
- Use 12 hour or 24 hour time displays
- The clock can be minimized while keeping the clock going
- Supports multiple monitors!
- The digit sizes are auto adjusted to maximally fit the screen
- A desktop shortcut can be created to start the clock
- The digits and message colours can be changed
- The background images can change to a new picture on a regular basis
- FULL SCREEN size for large easy to read digits

This software is great for churches or places needing to display the current time in full screen mode. Can be used in conjunction with the countdown clocks we also offer.

Works great in Windows Vista, XP as well as 95/98/ME/2K.

Alarm-Free Digital Clock

Alarm is a digital clock that you can set to display a message and play a sound at a time of your choice.

It is meant to be of help when you want to be warned while you are working (and chances are big you are going to forget you have to do this very important thing later on)...

A quite humorous quote from a user on newfreeware.com:

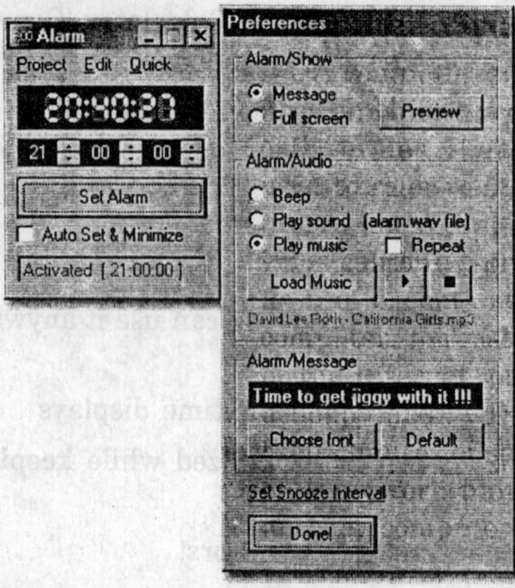

Alarm.exe

Type of File: Application

Description: Alarm clock

Size: 208 KB (212.992 bytes)

File Version: 2.0.0.4

Language: English (United States)

Compatibility: Windows 9*/ME/NT/2*/XP/Vista

Options/Features:

- Shows the current time in Configurable LED's
- Beeps or plays a sound (you can replace the default alarm siren)
- Plays music (you can use your own mp3, mid, wav and so on music files)
- Shows a small dialog or alarms you with a Full Screen Alert with your text
- Option to Preview your alarm
- Customizable Snooze function with Interval Setting
- Runs on Windows 95/98/ME/NT4/2000/2003/XP/Vista

Computer Virus

A computer virus is a computer programme that can copy itself and infect a computer without the permission or knowledge of the owner. The term "virus" is also commonly but erroneously used to refer to other types of malware, adware, and spyware programmes that do not have the reproductive ability. A true virus can only spread from one computer to another (in some form of executable code) when its host is taken to the target computer; for instance because a user sent it over a network or the Internet, or carried it on a removable medium such as a floppy disk, CD, DVD, or USB drive. Viruses can increase their chances of spreading to other computers by infecting files on a network file system or a file system that is accessed by another computer.

The term "computer virus" is sometimes used as a catch-all phrase to include all types of malware. Malware includes computer viruses, worms, trojan horses, most rootkits, spyware, dishonest adware, crimeware, and other malicious and unwanted software), including true viruses. Viruses are sometimes confused with computer worms and Trojan horses, which are technically different. A worm can exploit security vulnerabilities to spread itself to other computers without needing to be transferred as part of a host, and a Trojan horse is a programme that appears harmless but has a hidden agenda. Worms and Trojans, like viruses, may cause harm to either a computer system's hosted data, functional performance, or networking throughput, when they are executed. Some viruses and other malware have symptoms noticeable to the computer user, but many are surreptitious.

Most personal computers are now connected to the Internet and to local area networks, facilitating the spread of malicious code. Today's viruses may also take advantage of network services such as the World Wide Web, e-mail, Instant Messaging, and file sharing systems to spread.

History

The Creeper virus was first detected on ARPANET, the forerunner of the Internet in the early 1970s. Creeper was an experimental self-replicating programme written by Bob Thomas at BBN in 1971. Creeper used the ARPANET to infect DEC PDP-10 computers running the TENEX operating system. Creeper gained access via the ARPANET and copied itself to the remote system where the message, "I'm the creeper, catch me if you can!" was displayed. The *Reaper* programme was created to delete Creeper.

A programme called "Rother J" was the first computer virus to appear "in the wild"—that is, outside the single computer or lab where it was created. Written in 1981 by Richard Skrenta, it attached itself to the Apple DOS 3.3 operating system and spread via floppy disk. This virus was created as a practical joke when Richard Skrenta was still in high school. It was injected in a game on a floppy disk. On its 50th use the Elk Cloner virus would be activated, infecting the computer and displaying a short poem beginning "Elk Cloner: The programme with a personality."

The first PC virus in the wild was a boot sector virus dubbed (c)Brain, created in 1986 by the Farooq Alvi Brothers, operating out of Lahore, Pakistan. The brothers reportedly created the virus to deter pirated copies of software they had written. However, analysts have claimed that the Ashar virus, a variant of Brain, possibly predated it based on code within the virus. Before computer networks became widespread, most viruses spread on removable media, particularly floppy disks. In the early days of the personal computer, many users regularly exchanged information and programmes on floppies. Some viruses spread by infecting programmes stored on these disks, while others installed themselves into the disk boot sector, ensuring that they would be run when the user booted the computer from the disk, usually inadvertently. PCs of the era would attempt to boot first from a floppy if one had been left in the drive. Until floppy disks fell out of use, this was the most successful infection strategy and boot sector viruses were the most common in the wild for many years.

Traditional computer viruses emerged in the 1980s, driven by the spread of personal computers and the resultant increase in BBS, modem use, and software sharing. Bulletin board-driven software sharing contributed directly to the spread of Trojan horse programmes, and viruses were written to infect popularly traded software. Shareware and bootleg software were equally common vectors for viruses on BBS's. Within the "pirate scene" of hobbyists trading illicit copies of retail software, traders in a hurry to obtain the latest applications were easy targets for viruses.

Macro viruses have become common since the mid-1990s. Most of these viruses are written in the scripting languages for Microsoft programmes such as Word and Excel and spread throughout Microsoft Office by infecting documents and spreadsheets. Since Word and Excel were also available for Mac OS, most could also spread to Macintosh computers. Although most of these viruses did not have the ability to send infected e-mail, those viruses which did took advantage of the Microsoft Outlook COM interface.

Some old versions of Microsoft Word allow macros to replicate themselves with additional blank lines. If two macro viruses simultaneously infect a document, the combination of the two, if also self-replicating, can appear as a "mating" of the two and would likely be detected as a virus unique from the "parents." A virus may also send a web address link as an instant message to all the contacts on an infected machine. If the recipient, thinking the link is from a friend (a trusted source) follows the link to the website, the virus hosted at the site may be able to infect this new computer and continue propagating.

Cross-site scripting viruses emerged recently, and were academically demonstrated in 2005. Since 2005 there have been multiple instances of the cross-site scripting viruses in the wild, exploiting websites such as MySpace and Yahoo.

Infection

In order to replicate itself, a virus must be permitted to execute code and write to memory. For this reason, many viruses attach themselves to executable files that may be part of legitimate programmes. If a user attempts to launch an infected programme, the virus' code may be executed simultaneously. Viruses can be divided into two types based on their behavior when they are executed. Nonresident viruses immediately search for other hosts that can be infected, infect those targets, and finally transfer control to the application programme they infected. Resident viruses do not search for hosts when they are started. Instead, a resident virus loads itself into memory on execution and transfers control to the host programme. The virus stays active in the background and infects new hosts when those files are accessed by other programmes or the operating system itself.

Non-resident Viruses

Nonresident viruses can be thought of as consisting of a *finder module* and a *replication module*. The finder module is responsible for finding new files to infect. For each new executable file the finder module encounters, it calls the replication module to infect that file.

Resident Viruses

Resident viruses contain a replication module that is similar to the one that is employed by nonresident viruses. This module, however, is not called by a finder module. The virus loads the replication module into memory when it is executed instead and ensures that this module is executed each time the operating system is called to perform a certain operation. the replication module can be called, for example, each time the operating system executes a file. In this case the virus infects every suitable programme that is executed on the computer.

Resident viruses are sometimes subdivided into a category of *fast infectors* and a category of *slow infectors*. Fast infectors are designed to infect as many files as possible. A fast infector, for instance, can infect every potential host file that is accessed. This poses a special problem when using anti-virus software, since a virus scanner will access every potential host file on a computer when it performs a system-wide scan. If the virus scanner fails to notice that such a virus is present in memory the virus can "piggy-back" on the virus scanner and in this way infect all files that are scanned. Fast infectors rely on their fast infection rate to spread.

The disadvantage of this method is that infecting many files may make detection more likely, because the virus may slow down a computer or perform many suspicious actions that can be noticed by anti-virus software. Slow infectors, on the other hand, are designed to infect hosts infrequently. Some slow infectors, for instance, only infect files when they are copied. Slow infectors are designed to avoid detection by limiting their actions: they are less likely to slow down a computer noticeably and will, at most, infrequently trigger anti-virus software that detects suspicious behavior by programmes. The slow infector approach, however, does not seem very successful.

Causes

Computer viruses are caused and are not unintentional. These computer viruses are programmes that play havoc on home computers and on networks connected with shared computers as well. Because these computer viruses are programmes once they get into the system it becomes an auto pilot machine that can do anything and exploit the most secure aspects of the system. How can you protect yourself from these computer viruses?By one thing is to be diligent in keeping your antivirus software up to date as much as possible and running at least quick scans daily. Comprehensive scans need to be implemented at least once a week to be safe.

These little computer viruses can cause much harm to your computer by exploiting sensitive information that you have stored, such as passwords and personal information that contains your life history. One thing to remember as well on how easy it is to contract a computer virus is by a simple to a website that is off limits. Well off limits to the majority of people surfing the net. But porn sites are notorious for having malicious scripts on their sites that once you visit them you contract a cookie, a foreign script that sometimes you never get rid of.

Sometimes you get directed to these websites unintentionally by the keywords you put into your search engine.

No fault of yours but just the way the search engine works when defined by the use of keywords. So if you find yourself on a taboo site, get out quick and run your quick scan to insure that you didn't pick up anything you didn't want.

Remedies

Viruses

A computer virus is software that is malicious in nature and can copy and distribute itself. It usually infects a computer without the knowledge of the user. Spam, adware, or spyware is not a computer virus, since they do not have the ability to reproduce. Computer Viruses, Worms, Trojan Horses and other "mal-ware" (collectively referred to as viruses) are not your friends! If you are unfortunate enough to "catch" a computer virus, your life's energy can be diverted to computer recovery for days. Some viruses will target and invade your email address book and might send itself to individuals or the whole list. It may show up on your friends computer in an email "sent by you" or any other name in your address list. This masquerade technique makes it very hard to stop and can cause more than a few ruffled feathers!

Some viruses may show up as nothing more than a simple "gotcha" message but the nastiest type of this abusive software can destroy all of the contents of a hard drive; requiring complete reinstallation of all software. In the 1990's, computer viruses started spreading at an alarming rate. Hundreds of new viruses appear every year at an average of one per day. If you are connected to the internet, you MUST have a current updated Anti-Virus software product. If you don't, the chance of you being visited by a computer virus is huge! Not only is Anti-Virus software a must, but all current Windows updates must be installed as they are released by Microsoft. Overlooking this crucial bit of maintenance can be disastrous.

What can PC Direct Care do about viruses?

If you "catch" a virus, we will find it, remove it, and repair the damage it has done. Some particularly ill-intended viruses are designed to destroy files. If you are the unfortunate recipient of such a virus, we will recover what is recoverable and will concentrate on making your computer healthy again. We will also scan your system for Trojans that can send personal or corporate data out to marketers, hackers and criminals with intent to gain access via stolen login information, including passwords. Once found, we will remove them.

We will help you to choose the correct Anti-Virus and Anti-Spyware solutions for your system, and install them for you.

And finally, we will teach you how to avoid contracting viruses in the future and will show you how to reduce the amount of dangerous software that you receive; by vigilance and basic safe practices.

Malware and Spyware

Malware is short for “malicious software”, and includes all software designed to infiltrate or damage a computer system without the users consent. It is the main cause of computer trouble for home PC users today!

The terms spyware and malware are often used interchangeably to describe unwanted and uninvited programmes that are inadvertently downloaded and installed into your system. Sometimes this happens simply by just visiting certain a web sites. There has been such an incredible proliferation of these malicious programmes as they spread over the Internet; it’s a rare computer user indeed that hasn't had a run-in with these nasty little troublemakers! The impact can range from 'mildly irritating' to a complete disruption of computer performance. The usual intent of these programmes is to place advertising on your screen via pop-ups, or by browser hijacking (redirecting your browser to a specific page). Other malware can be much more insidious and dangerous; by capturing keystrokes to steal login and password information, or turning your computer into a "spam zombie" or "spam gateway", to use your system as a hub for the distribution of thousands of spam messages to other unsuspecting internet users. The performance hit on your machine can be enormous.

UNIT-VI

MS-Word

Introduction

Let us consider an office scene. Many letters are typed in the office. The officer dictates a letter. The typist first types a draft copy of the letter. The officer goes through it to check mistakes regarding spelling errors, missing words, etc. and suggests corrections. The typist changes the letter as suggested by the officer. This is a simple example of word processing.

There are many software packages to do the job of word processing. Some of them work in DOS environment. Example are WordStar, Word Perfect and Professional Write. But in these days working in WINDOWS is becoming more and more popular. So let us consider software for word processing which works in WINDOWS. Our choice is MS-WORD because it is the most popular software in these days.

MS-WORD is a part of the bigger package called MS OFFICE, which can do much more than word processing. In fact when you open up MS OFFICE you will find four main components in it. They are MS-WORD (for word processing), MS EXCEL (for spreadsheet), MS ACCESS (for database management) and MS POWERPOINT (for presentation purposes). However, we will limit ourselves to MS-WORD only in this lesson.

Objectives

After going through this lesson you should be in a position to:

- start the MS-WORD package
- be familiar with the MS-WORD screen
- advantages and Features of Word Processing
- some common Word Processing Packages
- how to invoke Ms-Word
- learn the capabilities of Ms-Word

Concept of Word-processing

Word Processor is a Software package that enables you to create, edit, print and save documents for future retrieval and reference. Creating a document involves typing by using a keyboard and saving it. Editing a document involves correcting the spelling mistakes, if any, deleting or moving words sentences or paragraphs.

(a) Advantages of Word Processing: One of the main advantages of a word processor over a conventional typewriter is that a word processor enables you to make changes to a document without retyping the entire document.

(b) Features of Word Processing: Most Word Processor available today allows more than just creating and editing documents. They have wide range of other tools and functions, which are used in formatting the documents. The following are the main features of a Word Processor

i. Text is typing into the computer, which allows alterations to be made easily.

ii. Words and sentences can be inserted, amended or deleted.

iii. Paragraphs or text can be copied /moved throughout the document.

iv. Margins and page length can be adjusted as desired.

v. Spelling can be checked and modified through the spell check facility.

vi. Multiple document/files can be merged.

vii. Multiple copies of letters can be generated with different addresses through the mail-merge facility.

(c) Some Common Word Processing Packages: The followings are examples of some popular word processor available

- Softword
- WordStar
- Word perfect
- Microsoft word

Entering Text

For this lesson you will create a one page document which includes the use of a bulleted list. Suggested possibilities include:

- A note to parents listing things to bring for a field trip
- A lesson/unit plan which lists technology integration

Note: Purple text is to be copied to Paste into the document you create

Step 1. Open Microsoft Word. Remember to leave your browser window open until this lesson is finished.

Step 2. Open a new blank document using keyboard commands

- IBM - Use Ctrl+N (Hold down the Ctrl key and tap the N key one time)
- Macintosh - Use Command+N (Hold down the Command key and tap the N key one time)

Step 3. Enter the following line at the top of the page:

Internet Based Lesson Plan

- Do not use all caps anywhere on the page. The eye has difficulty scanning text in an all caps format, even including headlines.

Step 4. Highlight the line of text and perform the following actions using toolbar buttons, menu items or keyboard combinations:

- Format the text to Bold

- Increase the side to 18 pt.
- Center the text
- Press Return/Enter two times
- Click Bold button to remove Bold
- Return text size to default
- Note: all of these actions can be performed using the Formatting toolbar.

Step 5. Copy the following paragraph and paste it into your document two lines below the headline using toolbar buttons, menu items or keyboard combinations:

Students will work in teams of four to gather information for a report on a chosen topic. Each team will have two weeks to gather the information and one week to prepare a multimedia report, which will be given to the class. The report may be produced as a HyperStudio stack, a PowerPoint slide show, or a Claris HomePage web page. Five Internet sites will be listed as resources where information can be gathered. If a group can not find enough information, searches will be allowed on only the search engine Yahooligans. If any group is going to do a search, the search must be cleared with the teacher first. Below is a list of the classroom stations which will be setup for this unit:

**Click and drag to highlight the paragraph you see above. With the text selected use the toolbar button, menu item or keyboard combination to copy text. Go to the new Word document and paste what you copied using the toolbar button (it looks like a clipboard), menu item (it is in the Edit menu) or keyboard combination (IBM=Ctrl+V, Mac=Command+V).*

Step 6. Enter a list of stations in the form of a bulleted list. That can be done in two ways.

1. Select the bulleted list button, copy the list, paste it into the document. (be sure your cursor is at the bullet)
2. Copy and paste the entire list, highlight the list, select the bulleted list button

or

1. Select the items one at a time
2. Copy and paste into the Word document
3. Select the bulleted list button

List of stations

Internet connected student workstation Encyclopedia CD in a student workstation Books and/or magazines related to the subject Printed copies of web pages related to the project topic Videotape or Laser Disk on the subject.

After all bulleted points have been entered hit the Return/ Enter key one time. Another bullet will be displayed at the cursor.

Step 7. Remove the last bullet produced. The most simple way to do that is to deselect the bullet button in the formatting toolbar.

Step 8. Highlight the five bulleted points. Go to the Format menu, select Bullets and Numbering and change the style of the bullet.

Step 9. Add one final paragraph. describing what the report should look like. You may generate your own text or copy the paragraph below:

Instructions to students - Your group is to present a report to the class regarding your selected topic. Each person should participate. Remember, you are to include pictures which you copied from the Internet. You should also remember to give credit for each source you quote. Your report can be in the form of a HyperStudio stack, a PowerPoint slide show, or a Claris HomePage web page.

Selecting and Inserting Text

There are many methods of selecting text and entire paragraphs using Word. Here you will learn various techniques of selecting text using both your keyboard and mouse.

Inserting a Text Box

Text boxes will give you control over the position of a block of text in your document. You can place text boxes anywhere in the document and format them with shading and borders.

Additionally, you can link text boxes so that the contents flow between the boxes automatically.

Click Insert>>Text Box to insert a text box. Click and drag your mouse where you would like to position the text box. It appears with a border that you can use to resize or reposition the text box.

Making Paragraph

Some formatting options can be applied to whole paragraphs regardless of the size of the paragraph.

A new paragraph is created everytime you press Enter

Paragraph formatting options include the following:

Alignment -

Line Spacing -

Indents - These are paragraph specific

Tabs - These are line specific

Bulleted Lists -

Numbered Lists -

Borders -

Shading -

There are two ways you can apply paragraph formatting.

You can either define the formatting and then enter the text or enter the text and then apply the formatting.

The default paragraph formatting options give you a left aligned paragraph with single spacing.

If you want to apply paragraph formatting to an existing paragraph just position the insertion point anywhere in the paragraph before applying your formatting.

Word automatically applies this to the whole paragraph.

You can change the formatting for consecutive paragraphs by selecting them first. The quickest way to delete text is to select it and press Delete. To select a word click on it twice. To select a sentence click at the start and drag the mouse over the text, To select a paragraph click on it three times.

Text can be easily dragged and dropped. Select the text hold down the right mouse button and drop. Always include the paragraph mark in your selection.

You can select an area of specific text by using the Alt key. Click the area to begin your selection and hold down Alt while dragging with the right mouse button.

You can insert line numbers next to your paragraphs if you want to restrict the number of lines. Highlight the text (File > Page Setup)(Layout tab), click line numbers and select "Add Line Numbering".

It is possible to insert a vertical text header down the left hand side of a page.

If you are printing envelopes and labels it is possible to change the label font and font size (Tools > Envelopes and Labels) right click.

You can let Word format your text automatically as you type using the AutoFormat feature.

You can cut and paste multiple selection in one go by using what is called a "spike", pressing (Ctrl + F3) will add an entry to the spike and (Ctrl + Shift + F3) will paste the multiple selections entries on the spike.

You can easily insert right flush, centre tabs & decimal number tabs by togglying the choice in the top right corner by using the ruler.

To move selected text between windows drag it to another window, to copy it hold down Ctrl as you drag.

Text can be hidden and this will appear with red dotted lines underneath it in Page Layout view.

You can have fonts as large as 1,600+ points although not is all fonts. In order to format fonts that are this big you must use the (Format > Font) dialog box.

To see all the attributes associated with a paragraph choose (Format>Paragraph) and remember that these attributes apply to the whole paragraph and not just a selection.

Widow/Orphan Control?

If you choose your line spacing to "single" then the line spacing is based on the size of the larget character.

If you have your line spacing set to "Exactly" then any characters, pictures, graphics etc that are too tall to fit into this space will be truncated to fit.

If you are writing text to fit on one page and one or two sentences full on to the next page you can use the "Shrink to fit" feature to fit it onto one page. Always save a backup copy before doing this as there is no easy way to undo.

You can easily select the paragraph mark along with the paragraph by pressing Ctrl while you double click the paragraph.

To insert some sample text into a document type "=rand(4,5)" then Enter. The first number is the number of paragraphs and the second number is the number of sentences.

If you need to apply the same formatting to more than one item just double click the Format Painter button on the Formatting toolbar and click the text you want to format.

If you think Word is behaving strangely when you select, drag and drop text it is worth checking your settings (Tools > Options) (Edit tab). For more information on the individual settings see the General section at the front.

If you type a lot of Two Initial Capitals words then it is worth ensuring that whenever you change and correct the second letter of a word to back to a lowercase the word is added to the exceptions list. Make sure the check box is selected (Tools > AutoCorrect) (AutoCorrect tab) click Exceptions, "Automatically add words to list "is checked.

You can have animated text (Format > Font)(Text Effects tab). Text animation is purely for on screen use.

The highlight button on the Formatting toolbar can be used to make text or graphics stand out from the rest of your document.

Aligning

Text can be centred, right justified, left justified or fully justified (ie on both sides).

If you want to change the alignment of a paragraph, highlight the paragraph, then click on the desired button on the Formatting toolbar.

Left -

Right -

Centre -

Justify

Step 1-The Paragraph Mark at the end of Your Paragraphs Contains All the Attributes for the Entire Paragraph

Paragraphs can have space before and after a paragraph. (Format > Paragraph)(Indents and Spacing tab "Before" and "After". Spacing is altered in increments of 6 points by default, which is considered to be half a line. You can type in other values though. Never use the Enter key to insert blank paragraphs although it is very quick.

To vertically space text you should always use the paragraph spacing associated with each paragraph. Generally there is more space before heading than before a paragraph, and there is less space between a heading and its following paragraph than between two adjacent paragraphs.

What is the Insertion Point?

There is no need to add extra carriage returns before or after your pargraphs inorder to space out your paragraphs

Adjust the paragraph spacing above and below (Format > Paragraph)(Indents and Spacing tab)

Pressing Enter creates a paragraph with exactly the same paragraph formatting as the one before it.

When you press Enter, the new paragraph inherits all the formatting from the previous paragraph.

Step 4-Things to Remember

- Everytime you press Enter you are creating a new paragraph.
- A paragraph contains one or more characters including a paragraph mark.

Getting Help

We have already told you that for working in Ms-Word you should be familiar with WINDOWS. If you have not covered WINDOWS so far then read that first and then go through MS-WORD. By now you must be aware of the fact that a software package is improved from time to time. These improvements are sold in the market as new *versions* of the same software. Thus you will find many versions of MS-WORD being used in different offices.

In this lesson we will cover the version MS-WORD 97, which is latest in the market and contain many improvements over the older versions. However, you do not have to worry if you have an older version such as WORD 6.0 or WORD 95. All the commands available in these older versions are also available in WORD 97 and they are compatible.

While working in MS-WORD you have to work with a mouse. Also one can work, to some extent, through the keyboard. The use of mouse is simpler as it is fully menu driven. In MS-WORD every command is available in the form of 'icons'.

You can go inside MS-WORD by the following way

1. Take the mouse pointer to START button on the task bar. Click the left mouse button. The monitor will show like as follows:

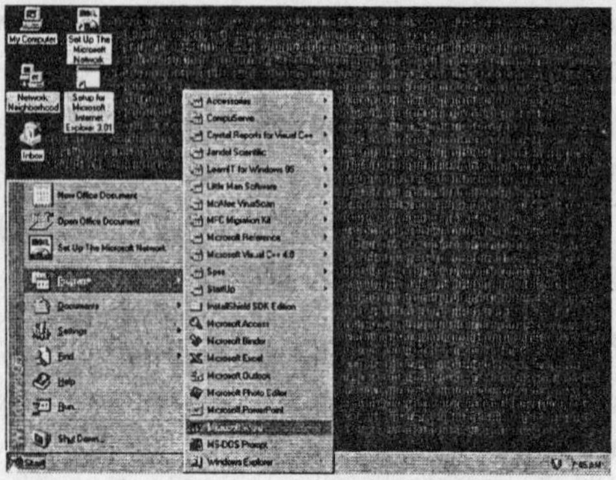

2. Move the pointer to programmes. You will notice another menu coming up to the right.
3. In that menu identify where Microsoft word is placed. Move the cursor horizontally to come out of programmes.
4. Move into the rectangular area meant for Microsoft word. Click the left mouse button there. The computer will start MS-WORD. You will find the screen as follows.

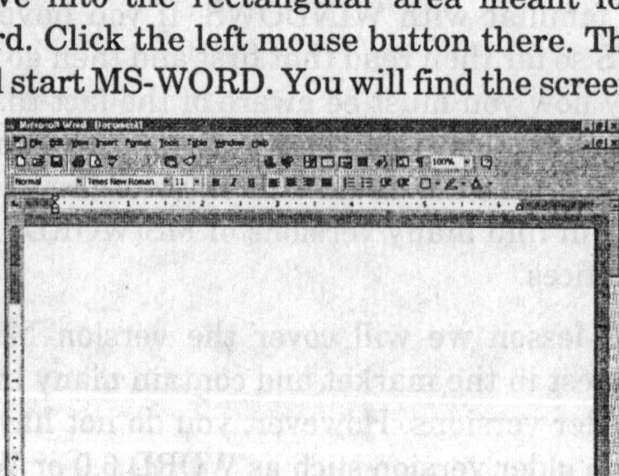

Let us discuss the important components of the screen.

a. *Title Bar:* The title bar displays the name of the currently active word document. Like other WINDOWS applications, it can be used to alter the size and location of the word window.

b. *Tool Bars:* Word has a number of tool bars that help you perform task faster and with great ease. Two of the most commonly tool bars are the formatting tool bar and the standard tool bar. These two toolbars are displayed just below the title bar. At any point of time any tool bar can be made ON or OFF through the tool bar option of View Menu.

c. *Ruler Bar:* The Ruler Bar allows you to format the vertical alignment of text in a document.

d. *Status Bar:* The Status Bar displays information about the currently active document. This includes the page number that you are working, the column and line number of the cursor position and so on.

e. *Scroll Bar:* The Scroll Bar helps you scroll the content or body of document. You can do so by moving the elevator button along the scroll bar, or by click in on the buttons with the arrow marked on them to move up and down and left and right of a page.

f. *Workspace:* The Workspace is the area in the document window were you enter/type the text of your document.

g. *Main Menu:* The Word main menu is displayed at the top of the screen as shown in the Fig. 9.1. The main menu further displays a sub menu. Some of the options are highlighted options and some of them appear as faded options. At any time, only highlighted options can be executed, faded options are not applicable. Infect if the option is faded you will not be able to choose it. You may not that any option faded under present situation may become highlighted under different situations.

Moving and Copying

It is easy to copy and move text or objects in your Word document by using the cut, copy, and paste shortcut keys or commands, but recent versions of Word offer a more intuitive and faster way of moving and copying text and objects by using the mouse.

To Move Text or objects Using the Mouse:

1. Highlight the portion of the document you wish to move

2. Click on the highlighted text and, holding the mouse key, drag it to the new place in your document
3. Release the mouse key

To Copy Text Using the Mouse:

1. Highlight the portion of the document you wish to copy
2. Click on the highlighted text with the right mouse key and hold it as you drag the text to the new place in your document
3. When you release the mouse key, select Copy from the pop up menu

While Word is quite good at fixing the spacing when you copy and move using this method, it is still a good idea to check both locations in your document to make sure the spacing is correct.

Searching and Replacing

If you need to find a particular word or phrase in your document, you can use the Find command. This command is especially useful when you are working with large files. If you want to search the entire document, simply execute the Find command. If you want to limit your search to a selected area, select that area and then execute the Find command.

After you find the word or phrase you are searching for, you can replace it with new text by executing the Replace command.

Exercise-7

Use Find with the Ribbon

1. Type the following:

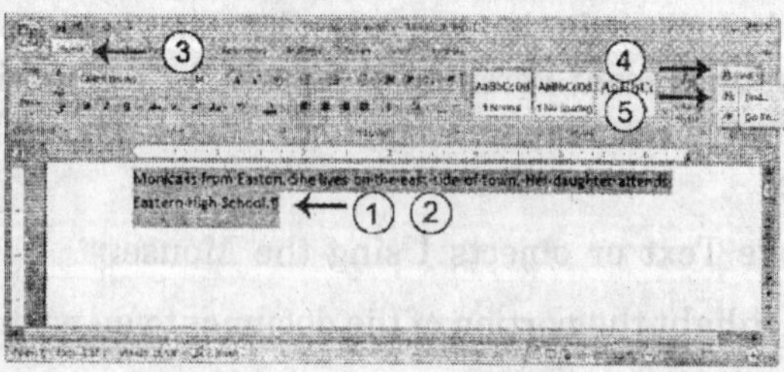

Monica is from Easton. She lives on the east side of town. Her daughter attends Eastern High School.

2. Select: "Monica is from Easton. She lives on the east side of town. Her daughter attends Eastern High School."
3. Choose the Home tab.
4. Click Find in the Editing group. A menu appears.
5. Click the Find option on the menu. The Find and Replace dialog box appears.

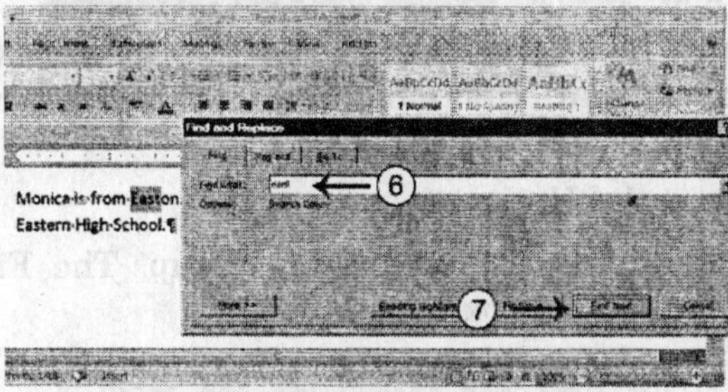

6. Type east in the Find What field.
7. Click Find Next.

   Note that the "East" in Easton is highlighted.
8. Click Find Next again.

   Note that "east" is highlighted.
9. Click Find Next again.

   Note that the "East" in Eastern is highlighted.
10. Click Find Next. The following message should appear: "Word has finished searching the selection. Do you want to search the remainder of the document?"
11. Click No.
12. Click Cancel.

Alternate Method—Find with Keys

1. *Select:* "Monica is from Easton. She lives on the east side of town. Her daughter attends Eastern High School."

2. Press Ctrl+f.
3. Follow steps 6 through 12 in the preceding section.

Use Replace with the Ribbon

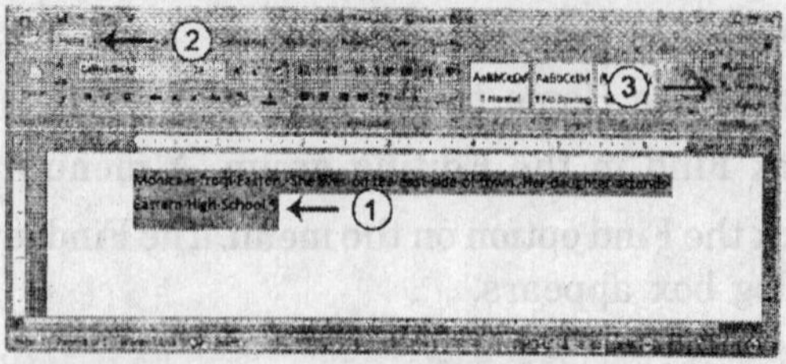

1. Select "Monica is from Easton. She lives on the east side of town. Her daughter attends Eastern High School."
2. Choose the Home tab.
3. Click Replace in the Editing group. The Find and Replace dialog box appears.

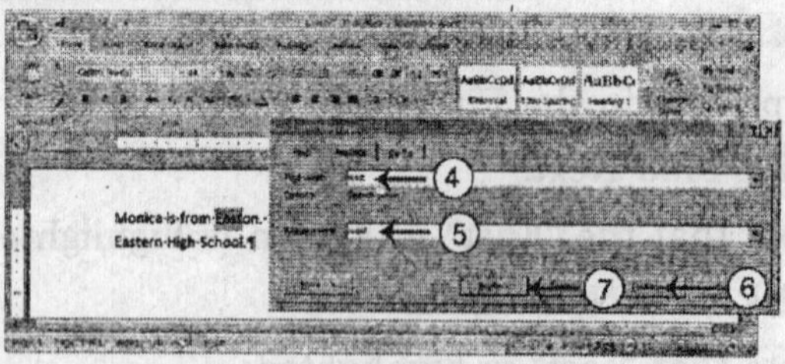

4. Type east in the Find What box.
5. Type west in the Replace With box.
6. Click Find Next. The East in Easton is highlighted.
7. Click Replace. Word replaces the "East" in "Easton" with "West" and then highlights the word "east."
8. Click Replace. Word replaces the word "east" with "west" and then highlights the word "Eastern."
9. Click Close. Do not replace the "East" in "Eastern" with "West."
10. Your text should now read,

    "Monica is from Weston. She lives on the west side of town. Her daughter attends Eastern High School."

Alternate Method—Replace with Keys

1. Select "Monica is from Easton. She lives on the west side of town. Her daughter attends Western High School."
2. Press Ctrl+h.
3. Follow steps 4 through 11 in the preceding section.

Formatting Character and Paragraph

When you type information into Microsoft Word, each time you press the Enter key Word creates a new paragraph. You can format paragraphs. For example, you can indent the first line of a paragraph, you can set the amount of space that separates paragraphs, and you can align a paragraph left, right, center, or flush with both margins. Styles are a set of formats you can quickly apply to a paragraph. For example, by applying a style, you can set the font, set the font size, and align a paragraph all at once. In this lesson, you will learn about the various formats you can apply to a paragraph and about styles.

When you are formatting a paragraph, you do not need to select the entire paragraph. Placing the cursor anywhere in the paragraph enables you to format it. After you format a paragraph, pressing the Enter key creates a new paragraph in the same format.

Open a Blank Document

To begin a new Word project, you start by opening a new document.To begin this lesson, open a blank document in Microsoft Word.

Using a Document

1. Click on File
2. Select New

   *To create a blank document, simply select Blank Document. To create a document based on one of the templates provided in Microsoft Word, select which one you would like to create and select OK

Data Entry and Editing

You can easily make and view tracked changes and comments while you work in a document. By default, Microsoft Office Word 2007 uses balloons to display deletions, comments, formatting changes, and content that has moved. If you want to see all of your changes inline, you can change settings so that tracked changes and comments display the way you want.

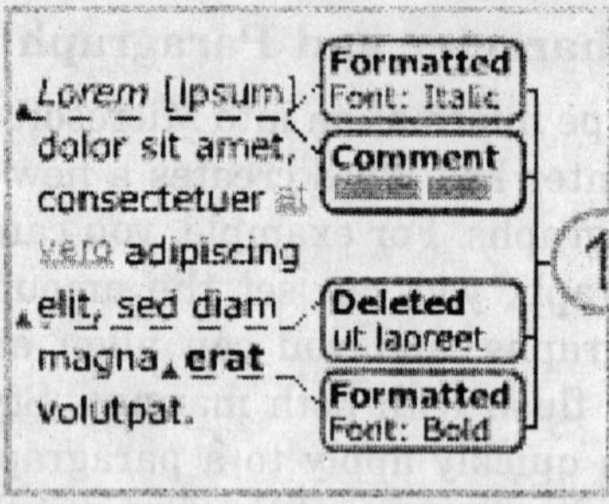

1. Balloons show formatting changes, comments, and deletions.

Note: To prevent you from inadvertently distributing documents that contain tracked changes and comments, Word displays tracked changes and comments by default. Final Showing Markup is the default option in the Display for Review box.

In this article:

- Track changes while you edit
- Turn off change tracking
- Change the way that markup is displayed

Track Changes While you Edit

1. Open the document that you want to revise.
2. On the Review tab, in the Tracking group, click the Track Changes image.

   To add a track changes indicator to the status bar, right-click the status bar and click Track Changes. Click the Track Changes indicator on the status bar to turn track changes on or off.

3. Make the changes that you want by inserting, deleting, moving, or formatting text or graphics. You can also add comments.

Note: If you use change tracking and then save your document as a Web page (.htm or .html), tracked changes will appear on your Web page.

Turn off Change Tracking

- On the Review tab, in the Tracking group, click the Track Changes image.

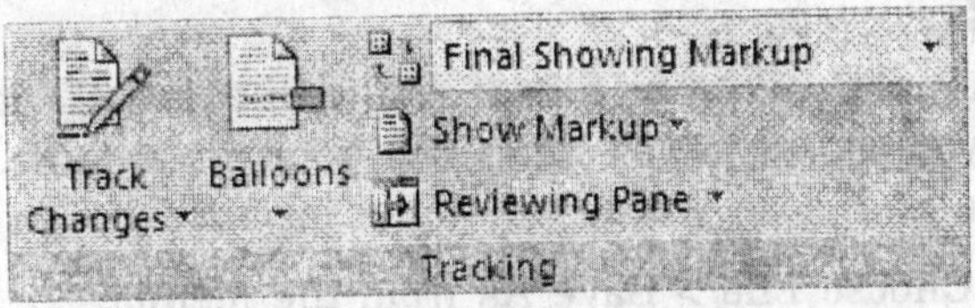

If you customized the status bar to include a track changes indicator, clicking Track Changes in the Tracking group will also turn off the indicator in the status bar.

Note: Turning off change tracking does not eliminate the tracked changes in your document. To ensure that there are no more tracked changes in your document, be sure that all changes are showing, and then use the Accept or Reject commands for each change in the document.

Change the Way that Markup is Displayed

Do any of the following:

- You can change the colour and other formatting that Word uses to mark changed text and graphics by clicking the arrow next to Track Changes and then clicking Change Tracking Options.

Note: While you can't assign specific colours for changes made by different reviewers, each reviewer's changes appear as a different colour in the document so that you can track multiple reviewers.

- You can view all changes, including deletions, inline instead of inside balloons that appear in the margins of your document. To show changes inline, in the Tracking group, click Balloons, and then click Show all revisions inline.

When you click Show all revisions inline, all of the revisions and comments in the document appear inline.

- To highlight the margin area where all balloons appear, click Markup Area Highlight under Show Markup.

Saving

You must save your files if you wish to recall them later. Before you can save, you must give your file a name. To save your file and close Word, follow the instructions given here:

1. Choose File > Save As from the menu.
2. Specify the correct folder in the Look In box.
3. Name your file by typing lesson3.doc in the File Name box.
4. Click Save.
5. Choose File > Exit from the menu.

Retrieval of Data

Data retrieval is possible only from the HTML-format output document. Spectra may be retrieved individually or in groups, and multiple retrieval of concatenated, high resolution spectra can be restricted to a specific wavelength interval. Spectra are delivered as FITS files, and are easily imported into standard image processing packages such as IDL, IRAF (via the external TABLES package) or MIDAS.

Single Spectrum Retrieval

The concatenated high resolution spectra and low resolution SILO images, grey-shaded columns of the output table, are stored at the Principal Centre in Vilspa and a mirror site, CADC in Canada, and the low resolution spectra and rebinned high resolution spectra are stored at your National Host. To fetch a single spectrum, click on the link (Low, Rebin, High or SILO) in the output table Fetch column corresponding to that spectrum.

Single spectra are retrieved uncompressed and, depending on the characteristics of your browser, you will be prompted to give the local filename either before or after download. It is recommended that you use the same naming convention as that under which the data are stored on the servers:

- CameraImageDispersionAperture.FITS for 1D extracted spectra
- CameraImage.SILO for 2D line-by-line low resolution images where Camera is SWP, LWP or LWR, Image is the 5-digit image number, Dispersion is L,H or R (rebinned) and Aperture is L or S.

The sizes of these data products are:

- Low - low resolution 1D spectra: ~18 KBytes
- Rebin - high resolution 1D spectra, rebinned onto low resolution wavelength scale: ~18 KBytes
- High - high resolution 1D spectra, orders concatenated: ~300-350 KBytes
- SILO - low resolution line-by-line images: ~240-250 KBytes

Multiple Spectrum Retrieval

Spectrum Selection: You may include/exclude *all* files of a particular type for multiple retrieval, e.g. *Mark:* High, will mark/unmark all high resolution spectra, and to fine-tune your selection further you may include/exclude *individual* spectra by checking/unchecking them in the Mark column corresponding to their location (National Host or Principal Centre/Mirror [shaded grey]).

Wavelength Selection: For faster retrieval from the Principal Centre/Mirror, you may restrict multiple download of high resolution spectra to a specific wavelength interval. By default, the full camera range is assumed (and displayed for reference), but if you request a wavelength cut (in Ångstroms) for a camera, that interval rounded to the nearest Ångstrom, is applied to *all* selected high resolution spectra for that camera.

In this case, the naming convention adopted for the retrieved spectra is **C**amera**I**mage**D**ispersion **A**perture_*lambda1*_*lambda2*.FITS, where *lambda1*_*lambda2* is the wavelength cut in Ångstroms, e.g. SWP45467_1400_1750.FITS. For a given camera, if one or both input wavelengths is blank, non-numeric or lies out of camera range, the *full* camera range is assumed. Clicking **Reset Wavelengths** resets the input wavelengths to the default full-camera values.

Note: Compared with retrieval of the full camera range, wavelength selection imposes a server processing *overhead* of ~0.3sec/spectrum, but *reduces* download time by ~100(1-r)%, where r is the fraction of the camera range selected. For current network bandwidths, this results in a considerable *net* saving of retrieval time for all but the largest wavelength cuts.

Retrieval Format

Multiple spectrum retrieval generates a packed file in either tar or ZIP format. Compression of packed files is recommended for network efficiency, in particular when downloading large data sets.

ZIP files are compressed automatically, and for tar files, three compression schemes are available: bzip2, gzip, and compress. Ensure that the corresponding unpacking and decompression programmes are available on your system before selecting the retrieval scheme from the pull-down menu (default tar.gz).

The following tables may be useful for helping you decide on which packing and compression scheme to use. The National Host table refers to packed files containing *only* low resolution spectra (Low), *only* rebinned spectra (Rebin) and *equal numbers* of low resolution and rebinned spectra (L+R), with the packed file sizes normalised to unit spectrum content, and quoted in KBytes. The Principal Centre table refers similarly to concatenated high resolution and SILO files.

National Host			
Scheme	Low	Rebin	L+R
bzip2	6.6	6.3	6.1
gzip	6.5	6.4	6.5
ZIP	8.4	8.1	8.4
compress	10.1	9.5	9.5
tar	18.4	18.4	18.4

Principal Centre/Mirror			
Scheme	High	SILO	H+S
bzip2	236.5	61.3	150.3
gzip	238.9	78.9	158.9
ZIP	238.3	78.7	158.5
compress	307.2	93.6	203.3
tar	307.2	241.7	273.4

The most efficient compression is achieved by bzip2, but you should be aware that its compression/decompression cycle is more than ~5 times longer than for the other schemes. This is a small overhead compared to the savings in bandwidth for downloads of SILO images from the Principal Centre/Mirror, but is a consideration for downloads of high resolution, low resolution and rebinned spectra, where the bandwidth savings of bzip2 compared to gzip are marginal.

Especially, bzip2 is not recommended when retrieving HiRes wavelength cuts to avoid combining both sets of server overheads. Retrieval of the selected spectra from the National Host or Principal Centre/Mirror servers is effected by clicking the corresponding Retrieve Marked Data buttons.

You will be prompted to assign local filenames for the packed, compressed files from each server either before or after download, depending on the browser you use. Ensure that you choose different filenames for the downloads from each server; it is recommended that you name them according to the standard naming convention for the packing and compression scheme chosen (that is, file.tar.gz, file.tar.bz2, file.tar.Z, file.tar or file.zip).

Formatting a Text

You can access advanced formatting options by right-clicking the border of a text box. Select Format Text Box.

On the Colours and Lines tab, you can change the background colour and adjust the transparency. It also allows you to specify border style, colour, and weight.

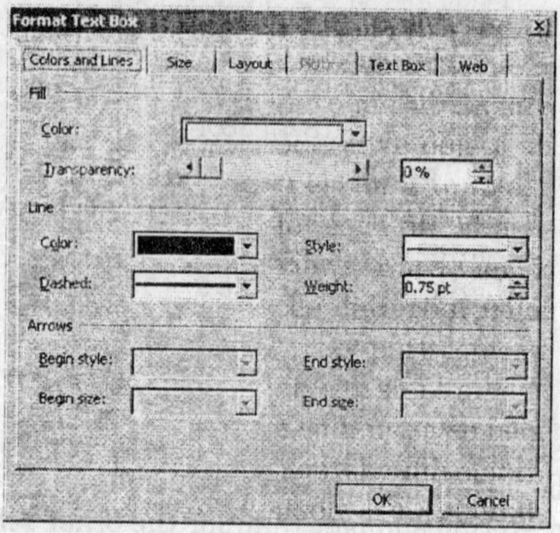

Handling Multiple Documents

Many end-user applications are document-centric (that is, they are tools for manipulating documents of one type or another). End users of these applications generally consider them merely a convenient way to modify a document. (Applications that are not document-centric focus on things like the programme itself; games are a good example of this). From the end user's perspective, it's easier to think of document-centric applications in terms of opening new documents, rather than in terms of running a programme. When you look at it this way, the programme just happens to start up when you open a document. Taking this perspective one step further, there should be nothing too strange about editing multiple documents at the same time.

However, as most programmers know, running multiple instances of one programme does not work all that smoothly. The two primary problems are that multiple instances do not cooperate nicely and they take up way too much memory. A Multiple Document Interface such as the GnomeMDI simplifies these problems by handling the user interface. So, let's take a closer look at how the GnomeMDI does this.

About GnomeMDI

GnomeMDI is actually not a widget but a simple object, because it derives directly from GtkObject, the main object of your application. Most likely, you will create only one of these and store it as a global variable. The document we will create here is the GnomeMDIChild, which is actually a second type of simple object altogether. (If your application were opening files, for example, there would be exactly one GnomeMDIChild for each file.) Each GnomeMDIChild can also have one or more views. Each view is a GtkWidget, which knows how to display the data that GnomeMDIChild stores. Now this is where the tricky part comes in. In order to use GnomeMDI, you must be able to store all data relevant to a file without having any view. You must also be able to update several views simultaneously. You should not therefore store any data in the view widget itself. You should always be able to generate another view, purely from the data stored in the GnomeMDIChild object. This is usually called the Model/View/Controller design.

So how does the design work? First off, you have to subclass GnomeMDIChild to add your data and methods to it. (Well, I lied; you don't really have to subclass it, although that's the better solution.) If you want to get started quickly you can use the GnomeMDIGenericChild class. But since you won't be able to override certain methods if you do, you will need to provide function pointers to GnomeMDIGenericChild. There is also no provision in the object for any data, so you have to use the gtk_object_set_data and gtk_object_get_data (or, as we will, use gtk_object_set_user_data and gtk_object_get_user_data). For these reasons, it is very hard to create pure Model/View/Controller architecture using GnomeMDIGenericChild. So, if you want to create a really well designed solution, you should subclass GnomeMDIChild. But for simplicity's sake, we will stick with GnomeMDIGenericChild here.

Creating a Simple Text Editor

Now we are ready to start. We will build a simple "text editor". It won't be a real text editor, because it won't load or save files. Our text editor will only work on memory buffers.

But it should show you how to deal with some of the issues that pop up when you work with multiple document interfaces.

Screenshot of Simple Text

Let's look where it all begins, our main function. After we initialize gnome, we'll create a new mdi object and set up its menubar template. Note that the "mdi" variable is a global of type *GnomeMDI* *. (Blue font is used in the code samples for comments, and red is used for highlights.)

Manipulation of Tables

What is a Table?

Tables are made up of cells. A horizontal line of cells is called a "row" and a vertical line of cells is called a "column".

You can use tables to set up side-by-side text paragraphs that wrap around independently or graphics such as charts that sit side-by-side.

Tables can be useful for creating newsletters, brochures, web pages and forms.

Tables play a crucial part in any Word document so it is important you can manipulate then quickly and avoid the time consuming mistakes.

A table offers an easy way to group paragraphs side by side and to arrange text beside charts or pictures

A table is just a collection of horizontal rows and vertical columns that are used to create a grid of individual cells.

Table cells can contain text, numbers, fields, graphics and many other elements.

Originally tables were used just to display numbers but now tables are suitable for a whole range of different tasks.

Table and Borders Toolbar

This can be quickly displayed by pressing the Tables and Borders button on the standard toolbar

Alternatively you can use (View > Toolbars > Tables and Borders).

Tables and Borders - Toggles the display of the Table and Borders toolbar.

© BetterSolutions.com

Using the Table Menu

Most of your commands can be accessed from the Tables drop-down.

Tables that span more than one page can easily have the same heading rows. Select the rows you would like to appear at the top of each page and press (Table > Headings).

You may find it easier to quickly draw your tables free hand using (Table > Draw Table). This may be quicker for drawing uniform tables to draw the outline.

You can insert a tab within a table by pressing (Ctrl + Tab). Just pressing tab will move you to the next cell or create a new row.

When you drag the edge of a column to adjust its width, the table width will not change, but other columns will reduce in width to compensate. To change the actual width of the table hold down Ctrl and Shift?

If you want to see the exact measurements of rows and columns as you drag their borders hold down the Alt key as you drag. To quickly move a row, position the insertion point in the row and press (Shift + Alt) with either "Up Arrow" or "Down Arrow" to move the row up or down.

Every cell contains an end-of-cell marker. To avoid copying the cell itself you must avoid copying this marker.

If you alter the cell height in a particular cell all the cells in that row are effected.

You can know control both the vertical and horizontal alignment at the same time from the shortcut menu when you right click a cell.

Select text and press (Ctrl + Alt + "K") to remove any extraneous paragraph marks.

You can make the borders in your tables white so no lines or gridlines appear regardless of the individuals options.

To add a double border to separate column headings from table entries, first apply single borders to all the sides, select the table choose (Format > Borders and Shading), and select the Grid under Setting. Select the first row of the table and change the line style of the border below the row

You can apply borders to paragraphs and graphics within a table cell in addition to the borders applied to the actual cells.

If you want to apply the same border to a group of paragraphs, all the paragraphs must have the same indents, otherwise they are placed in separate boxes.

You can easily convert text to a table by using selecting (Table > Convert > Text to table) and then selecting a seperator character.

You can link an Excel table into your document by copying the table to the clipboard and selecting (Edit > Paste Special) and choosing "Paste as Link".

Showing Gridlines

Gridlines are similar to table borders except that they are only visible on the screen and will not be printed.

(Table > Hide Gridlines)

(Table > Show Gridlines)

This is a toggle

Columns and Rows

To insert a row or column within a table, select the row or column after the position for the new row or column. Select Insert Row or Insert Column from the Table menu.

To insert a column to the right of the table, position the insertion point just outside the last column. Choose select column from the table menu, and then click the insert columns button on the standard toolbar.

1. Select the first row in the "States" table.
2. Select Insert Rows from the Table menu.
3. Select the last row in the "States" table.
4. Select Insert Rows from the Table menu.
5. Select the first column in the "States" table.
6. Select Insert Columns from the Table menu.
7. Select the last two columns in the "States" table.
8. Select Insert Columns from the Table menu.

Changing Column Width

You can adjust the width of a column, or you can adjust the width of all the cells in a column. To change the column width, click on the column width button. Drag the button to the left or right according to your needs. To change the width of all the columns select the entire table and drag the column width button you wish to change.

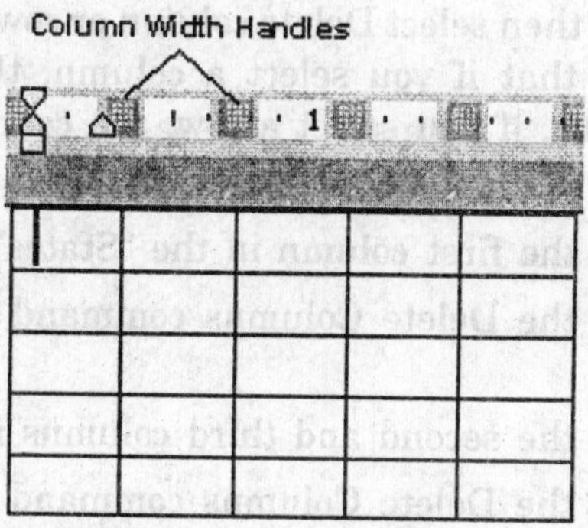

1. Click and drag the first column width button to the 1.5-inch mark.
2. Click on the Next Column width button to the 3-inch mark.

The mouse can also be used to change column widths. To select the column that you want to change, place the mouse pointer on the right border of the column. As you move the mouse pointer on top of the column border the pointer becomes a two-headed arrow (see example displayed in the left margin). When the mouse pointer is displayed as the two-headed arrow, press the mouse button and drag to reposition the column width.

As you drag the mouse, an outline of the new border shows the border position. When you have resized the column to a satisfactory width, release the mouse button. The entire column is resized accordingly.

1. Select the first column of the second table in your document.
2. Place the mouse in the right hand border of the column.
3. When you see the two-headed arrow appear, press and drag the mouse to increase the column width.
4. Select the second column and resize the column width using the mouse.

Deleting Columns and Rows

To delete a column or row, select the column or row you want to delete then select Delete column or row from the Table menu. Notice that if you select a column, the command is Delete Columns, if you select a row, the command is Delete Rows.

1. Select the first column in the "States" table.
2. Select the Delete Columns command from the Table menu.
3. Select the second and third columns in the table.
4. Select the Delete Columns command from the Tal·· menu.
5. Select the first row in the last table in your document.
6. Select the Delete Rows command from the Table menu.
7. Select the last row in your table.
8. Select the Delete Row command from the Table menu.
9. Click on the Undo button to restore the deleted rows.

Adding Borders

The table gridlines surrounding each cell are non-printing lines. To add printing lines or borders to a table, select the table followed by the Borders and Shading command from the Format menu. The Cell Borders and Shading dialog box appears. You can select a variety of border styles using the options listed in the Borders dialog box. Instructions for using the Cell Border dialog box are listed in the table below.

None	No borders.
Box - the outer boundary of the table is outlined with a border.	Select Box from the Presets selection box.
Shadow -the table is outlined with a shadow.	Select Grid from the Presets options.
3-D	
Custom - any boundary or set of boundaries can a border using any Line style.	In the Border selection box, select the boundary you want to add a border to, then click on the Line style that you want to use in the Line selection box.

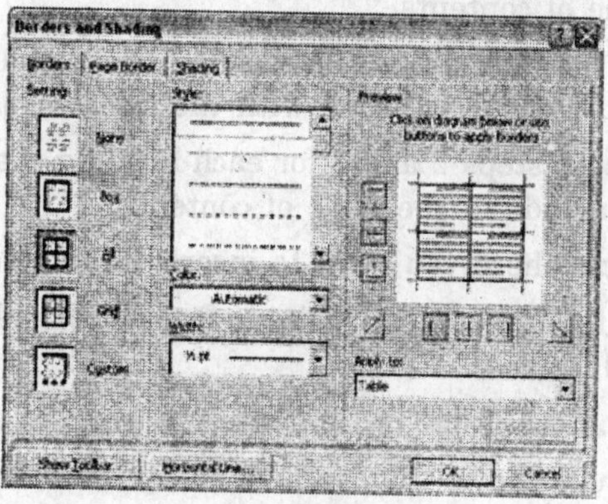

1. Select the entire "States" table.
2. Select Borders and Shading from the Format menu.
3. Select Grid from the Presets selection box and click on the OK button.
4. Select the next table in your document.
5. Select Borders and Shading from the Format menu.
6. Select Box from the Presets selection box and click on the OK button.

7. Select the next table in your document.
8. Create a custom border using the Presets and Line selection boxes in the Borders and Shading dialog box.
    1. Click where you want to insert the table of contents.
    2. On the Insert menu, point to Reference, and click Index and Tables.
    3. Click the Table of Contents tab.
    4. To use one of the available designs, click a design in the Formats box.
    5. Select any other table of contents options you want.

If you aren't currently using outline levels or built-in styles, do one of the following:

1. On the View menu, point to Toolbars, and click Outlining.
2. Select the first heading that you want to appear in the table of contents.
3. On the Outlining toolbar, select the outline level that you want to associate with the selected paragraph.
4. Repeat steps 2 and 3 for each heading that you want to include in the table of contents.
5. Click where you want to insert the table of contents.
6. On the Insert menu, point to Reference, and click Index and Tables.
7. Click the Table of Contents tab.
8. To use one of the available designs, click a design in the Formats box.
9. Select any other table of contents options you want.

If you've already applied custom styles to your headings, you can specify the style settings you want Microsoft Word to use when it builds the table of contents.

1. Click where you want to insert the table of contents.
2. On the Insert menu, point to References, and click Index and Tables.

3. Click the Table of Contents tab.
4. Click Options.
5. Under Available styles, find a style you've applied to headings in your document.
6. Under TOC level, to the right of the style name, enter a number from 1 to 9 to indicate the level you want that heading style to represent.

Note: If you want to use only custom styles, remove the TOC level numbers for the built-in styles, such as Heading 1.

7. Repeat steps 5 and 6 for each heading style you want to include in the table of contents.
8. Click OK.
9. To use one of the available designs, click a design in the Formats box.
10. Select any other table of contents options you want.

Tables and Footnotes

To create a four-column, five-row table:

1. Choose Table > Insert > Table from the menu. The Insert Table dialog box opens.

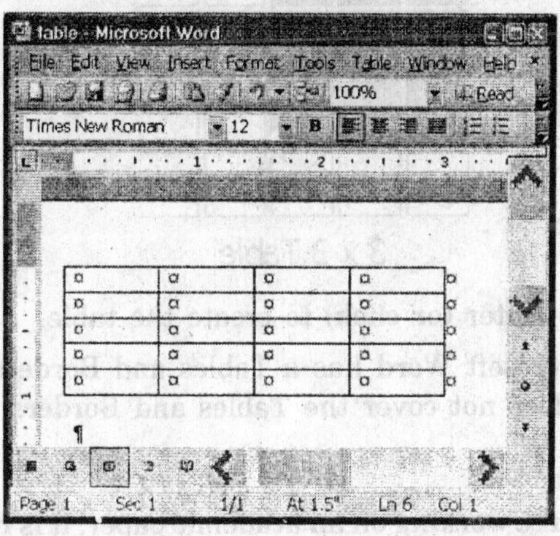

Alternate Method- Creating a Table by Using the Insert Table Icon

2. Type 4 in the Number of Columns field.
3. Type 5 in the Number of Rows field.
4. Select Auto in the Column Width field. Selecting Auto allows Microsoft Word to determine the size of your column widths. Alternatively, you can enter the column width you desire.
5. Click OK. Your table should look like the one shown here, with four columns and five rows.

You can also create a table by clicking on the Insert Table icon on the Standard toolbar.

1. Click the Insert Table icon.

2. Highlight the number of rows and columns you need. The maximum table size you can create by this method is a four-row by five-column table.

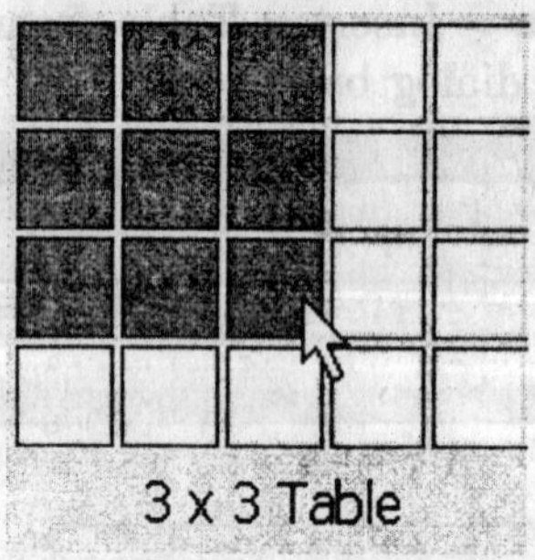

3. Press Enter (or click) to create the table.

Note: Microsoft Word has a Tables and Borders toolbar. This lesson does not cover the Tables and Borders toolbar.

Footnotes

When you're working on an academic paper, it is important to cite your references. Adding footnotes in Word is quite easy. Word automates the process so the numbering is always correct.

Plus, if you make changes to the document, you don't need to worry about the placement of the footnotes.

To insert footnotes, follow these steps:

1. Place the cursor where the footnote mark should be located
2. On the Insert menu, select Reference
3. On the Reference submenu, click Footnote...
4. Make sure Footnotes is selected in the Location section
5. Additionally, select Bottom of page, if it isn't already
6. Click Insert

   The footnote mark will appear at the selected location. Word will take you to the footnote section at the bottom of the page.
7. Enter the footnote text. Add formatting if desired

You can add footnotes in any order you want. Word automatically updates the numbering.

Table of Contents and Index

Creating a table of contents in a Microsoft Word document is a two-step process. First, identify the text that you want to appear in the Table of Contents. Second, tell Word to insert the Table of Contents. Having created your Table of Contents, you can then customize it in several ways, to suit your needs.

Step 1: Identify the text that you want to appear in the Table of Contents

In your document, click within the first major heading that you want to appear in the Table of Contents. Apply the Heading 1 style to that paragraph. The easiest way to apply the Heading 1 style is to click the Style box on the Formatting toolbar and choose Heading 1. If clicking the Style box doesn't appeal to you, there are several other ways to apply a style.

In the same way, apply the Heading 1 style to other major headings in your document. Apply the Heading 2 style to sub-headings, Heading 3 style to sub-sub-headings etc.

If you don't like the way the heading styles look (eg, you want a different font or font size or colour), don't format the text directly. Instead, modify the heading styles.

Step 2: Create the Table of Contents

Click where you want your Table of Contents to appear.

In Microsoft Word 2002 and 2003, choose Insert > Reference > Index and Tables. Click on the Table of Contents tab. (Elsewhere on this page, this is called the Table of Contents dialog.) Click OK.

In earlier versions of Word, choose Insert > Index and Tables. Click on the Table of Contents tab. (Elsewhere on this page, this is called the Table of Contents dialog.) Click OK.

Step 3: Customize the Table of Contents (if you need to)

* If you don't like the way your headings look (eg you want a different font, font size, colour, more or less spacing before or after the heading), don't choose Format > Paragraph or Format > Font. And don't use the font size or bold buttons on the toolbar. Instead, modify the Heading style.
* To change the font, font size, colour etc used to create the Table of Contents itself, you need to do two things in the Table of Contents dialog. First, make sure that, in the Formats box, you have chosen "From Template". Second, click Modify and modify the relevant TOC style. Word uses style TOC 1 for the top level of contents, TOC 2 for the next level etc.
* By default, Word shows three levels in your Table of Contents. That is, it puts the text from Heading 1, Heading 2 and Heading 3 in the Table of Contents. If you want to show more or fewer levels, in the Table of Contents dialog, change the number in the Show levels box.
* There are very good reasons for using the built-in Heading styles. But if you really need to use other styles (other built-in styles, or custom styles), you can

put them in your Table of Contents. In the Table of Contents dialog, click Options, and allocate your style(s) to the appropriate level(s).

* For sophisticated customization, you can edit the switches in the TOC field.

How to Create a Table of Contents for Several Documents?

* To create one table of contents for several documents, you need to do the following.
  - o Create a separate document to hold the table of contents (this is the ToC document).
  - o For ease, put all the documents, and your ToC document, in the one folder.
  - o In your ToC document, use an RD (Reference Document) field for each document that you want to include in your Table of Contents.
  - o To insert an RD field, do ctrl-F9 and, within the brackets that Word gives you, type RD "filename". For example { RD "Chapter 1.doc" }. You can't type the curly brackets by hand. You must do ctrl-F9.
  - o If you can't put all your files in one folder, you must use double backslashes and double quotes. For example, { RD "C:\\My folder\\Chapter 1.doc" }.
  - o In theory, you can use relative path names. But it never seems to work properly<g>.
  - o Use an RD field for each document that you want to reference, in order.
  - o Create the Table of Contents in this ToC document in the usual way.
  - o Remember the page number rule: "The Table of Contents will pick up whatever pagination appears in your document". It applies when using RD fields to create a ToC for many documents. You may have to set the starting page number manually in each document if you want pagination to run consecutively through your project.

Creating an Index in Word

Most long documents have an index. An index lists the ideas, topics, and terms discussed in the tome, so people can find the information they seek more easily. The good news is that adding an index to your document makes it vastly more useful to your readers. The bad news is that creating an index is a time-consuming and potentially challenging process. Although Microsoft Word includes the tools you need to create an index, the usefulness of the end product depends more on the person creating the index than on Word itself.

Know Thy Document

Before you start in on the mechanics of dealing with the index in Word, think about your document. If you are the author, it can be helpful to keep a list of terms and concepts off in a list somewhere as you are writing. If you aren't the author, it's helpful to just print out the document first and highlight potential index entries.

The goal is to gather up a lot of of the terms you'll enter into the index. Look for nouns for subject entries and verbs for procedural information. You'll notice that for procedures, most indexes use the -ing form of the verb, such as "copying files" rather than "copy files."

After you have a list of words, think of synonyms and ways people might look up the information. Those can be "see also" type entries like "how to copy files, see deleting files" or "making copy of files, see deleting files."

Add Entries

In Word, creating an index is a two-step process. First you add the entries throughout the text and then you generate the index itself. Word goes through the document and collects the entries into a list with the page numbers. If you've read the online help, you may have read about creating a "concordance file" that automatically marks index entries. It sounds like it would be a cool thing, but generally it's more trouble than it's worth because it's essentially a giant search activity. Only a human can determine when terms are contextually relevant.

For example, suppose you have a book about dog training. You might have an entry that points to a section on dealing with problem barking. If you did a concordance, Word would go through and find every time you used the word bark or barking. Now consider how many entries it would find that aren't relevant. Dogs bark for a lot of reasons. Deleting all the entries the concordance marked incorrectly is probably more work than just doing the index entries in the first place.

The XE Field

To create indexes, it helps to spend some time learning about fields. You use the Index Entry (XE) field to mark the text you want to incorporate into the index. This situation is one where you really should learn the keyboard shortcut. (The menu item is so deep it's absurd.) So to mark entries, follow these steps:

1. Highlight a word or words you want to add as an index entry. Or you can enter different text by placing the insertion point where you want the XE field code.
2. Press Alt+Shift+X. The Mark Index Entry dialog box appears.

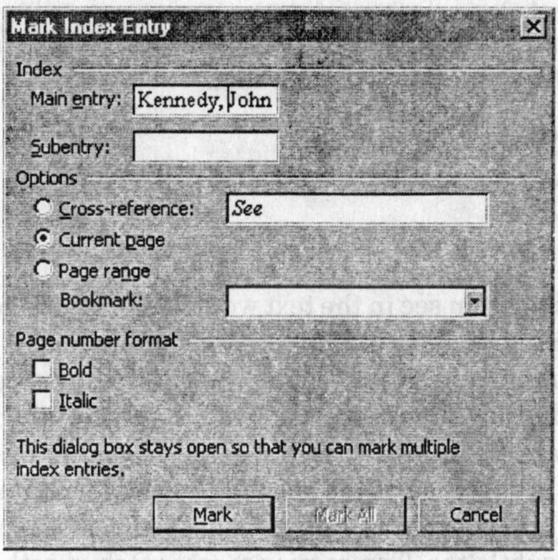

3. If you highlighted text, it appears in the Main Entry box. Otherwise, type your first-level index entry text.

You also can type a second-level entry in the Subentry box. If you need a three-level index, you can follow the subentry text with a colon and type the third-level entry text.

4. Click Mark. The Mark Index Entry dialog box stays open, so you can add more entries.

The way you add your index entries affects how they appear in the index. For example, if you put Kennedy, John in the Main Entry field, you'd end up with an index entry that looks like this:

Kennedy,

John, 7

You can create each entry individually and just ignore the subentry field if you want. When you show field codes, you see that the field looks like {XE "Kennedy,John"} in the text. Note that the comma in there is the one you typed in.

However, if you put Kennedy in the Main Entry Field and John in the Subentry field, you get:

Kennedy

John, 7

If you add entries for other Kennedys such as Robert and Rose too, together they'd look like:

Kennedy

John, 7

Robert, 9

Rose, 10

The fields you see in the text would be {XE "Kennedy:John"}, {XE "Kennedy:Robert"}, and {XE "Kennedy:Rose"}. Note that the last name and first name are separated by a colon. When you use the subentry field, you need to be careful that the text in the main field is exactly the same for similar entries. For example, in this case, if you spelled Kennedy wrong in an entry, you'd get an extra entry with the misspelling. Misspellings can be really subtle too. The entries must match exactly. You can't have extra spaces or change the case. Word treats "rose" and

"Rose" as two different entries. And "Rose Kennedy" (one space in between the words) is not the same thing as "Rose Kennedy" (two spaces in between the words).

As soon as you begin marking entries, Word shows field codes and hidden text, so you can see what's going on and make sure you have entered the entries correctly. ▯XE "fred" However, it's sort of confusing because showing the index entries actually expands out your document, so the page numbers may seem wrong. Be sure you hide field codes and hidden text before you generate your index. Choose Tools | Options and in the View tab, remove the checkmarks next to Field codes and Hidden Text.

Generate the Index

After you have defined all your index entries, you are ready to generate your index. In a short document, you can just add the INDEX field at the end of the document by choosing Insert | Index and Tables or Insert | Reference | Index and Tables, depending on your version of Word.

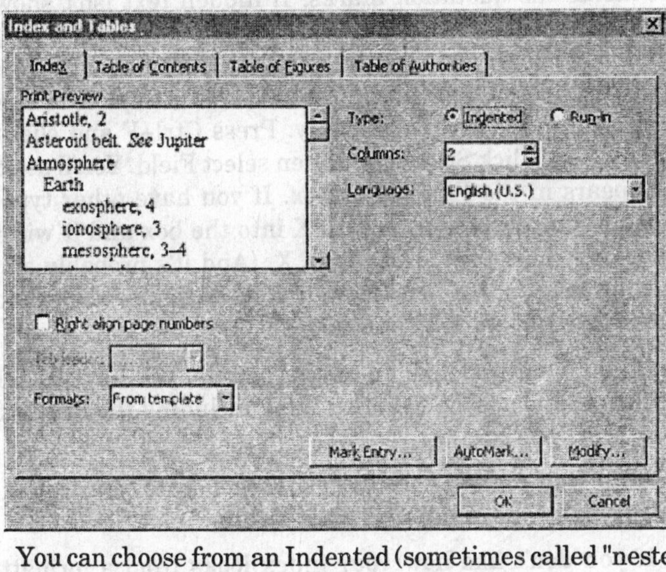

You can choose from an Indented (sometimes called "nested") or a Run-in Index. Basically, the Indented index looks somewhat like an outline.

Dogs

allergies (see also skin and coat)

contact dermatitis 228-229

flea-bite sensitivity 227-228

food allergies 227-228

In contrast, a run-in index appears in a paragraph format like so:

Dogs: allergies, 129; breeds, 188;

difference from cats, 210; housebreaking, 300

After you generate the index, it's virtually guaranteed that you'll find mistakes. So you need to go back and change the entries that have problems. Although it's tempting, don't edit your generated index. If you regenerate the index, your changes disappear. So you need to go back and edit the entries directly.

To edit the entries, you need to have hidden text showing. You can modify the index entry text directly by changing the text inside the quotation marks. If hidden text isn't showing press Ctrl+Shift+8 or press the Show/Hide button on the Standard toolbar, which is the one that looks like a paragraph icon. With hidden text showing, you also can use Word's Search feature to find a particular entry. Press Ctrl+F and click the More button. Click Special and then select Field. You'll see that ^d appears in the Find What box. If you have other types of fields in your document, put ^d X into the box and it will hop to the next field that starts with X. (And it's probably an XE index entry field!) If you know the entry name, add it too in quotes, such as ^d XE "storm".

If you want to delete an entry entirely, you have to delete the entire field code. Select the entry including the braces and press the Delete key.

After you make your changes, regenerate your index by clicking in it and pressing F9 to update fields.

If you don't like how your index looks from a formatting standpoint, you can change the built-in Index 1 through Index 9 styles so they match your document. This process is much like editing the Table of Contents styles. The styles correspond to the index level.

Sorting

Summary: Sort names and other text in your Microsoft Word 2003 documents.

Microsoft Word 2003 can sort text, such as a list of peoples' names, class names, names of inventory items, etc. However, the option is somewhat hidden under the "Sort" menu.

To sort text, such as a list of names:

1. Highlight the list of names with your mouse.
2. Choose "Table" then "Sort".
3. The "Sort Text" dialog box should appear. Most likely you will not have to make any changes. However, if you desire, click the "Descending" radio button to sort the text in descending order.
4. Click "OK" to close the dialog box.

Sorting Data in Microsoft Word

Most people seem to know that you can sort data in Microsoft Word, but don't know or remember how.

Simply select the data, and hit TableàSort. (Yes. Even if your data is not in a table.)

One of the most common reasons you'll get the error "Word found no valid records to sort"...

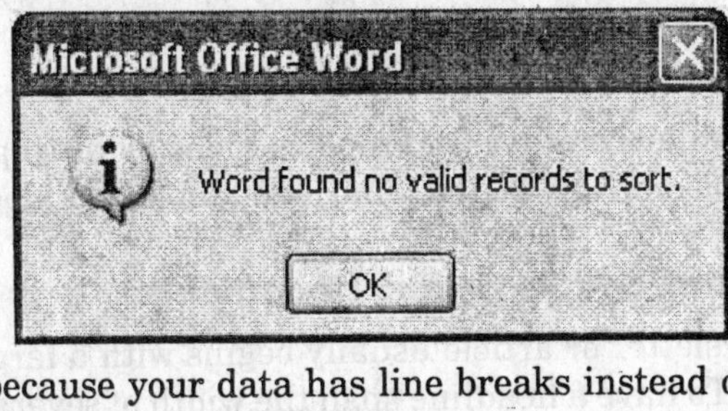

...is because your data has line breaks instead of carriage returns. Turn on your Show/Hide button to see what's breaking your lines.

The following shows line breaks instead of carriage returns.

hij↵
abc↵
efg↵
cde↵
¶

If this is true with your data—which is often the case when copying from the web—you can use Find and Replace to replace the line breaks with carriage returns, as shown:

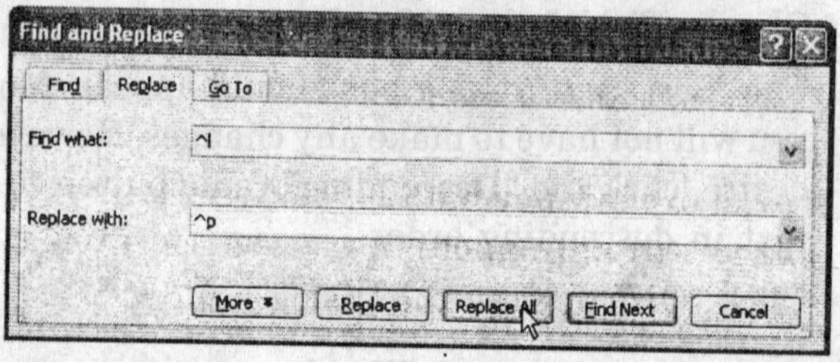

The Find what box contains a carat (^) and a lower-case letter L.

The Replace with box contains a carat (^) and a lower-case letter P.

Hit Replace All. Your data will now look like this.

hij¶
abc¶
efg¶
cde¶
¶

You can learn other find/replace codes by hitting the More and Special buttons of the Find and Replace dialog.

Formatting Sections and Documents

A newsletter or article usually begins with a larger title or headline. To have a headline span the width of several columns in MS Word, it must be formatted with a different number of columns.

Formatting Pages with Section Breaks

Whenever you have different page-level formatting applied to a single document, you need to break it into different sections with something called a "section break." In doing so, sections of a document can be formatted with different margins, page orientation, number of columns, headers and footers, page numbering, et cetera.

For example: in a newsletter with several pages, you may have a number of different sections: some with a two-column format, some with three columns. Other, longer reports may require you to have a beginning section containing the preface, table of contents, and so on, that use lowercase Roman numerals for page numbers, with the rest of the report beginning on page 1. Alternatively, you might have a very wide table with information spanning the months from January to December, and you want to have that page in landscape orientation, even though the rest of the report is portrait.

When you want to combine page-level formatting (such as orientation, margins, headers and footers) in one document, you must insert a section break to divide the document into different sections, each with its own formatting.

Applying a section break has one other important function. When a multi-column document is not long enough to fill a page, you wind up with one long column and a partial column. That's a rather awkward way to end. It's better to have two or three short columns, all the same length. To force Word to balance columns so that they end at the same length, insert a section break.

Using Different Column Formats

It's simple to apply a different number of columns to one section of text.

1. Select the text you want to change, such as the title or headline of an article.
2. Click the Columns button and drag to define the number of columns for the selection.

Behind the scenes, Word applies the new column format to the selected text and inserts a section break between it and the other text. Section breaks appear as double-dotted lines in Normal view or in Print Layout view when you click the Show/ Hide button.

After your document is divided into different section, you have another choice to make when you apply page-level formatting. For example, if you want to change the margins, the Page Setup dialog box offers an Apply To box where you specify whether you want to apply the settings to this section or the entire document.

UNIT-VII

Spreadsheet

Basics of Spreadsheet

- Finding your way around.
- Entering data.
- Graphing with spreadsheets.

Finding Your Way Around

Data is stored and displayed in cells. A cell is addressed by column letter and row number. Your current cell address is displayed in the address box. You move around in the spreadsheet by clicking a cell with the mouse or using the tab or arrow keys.

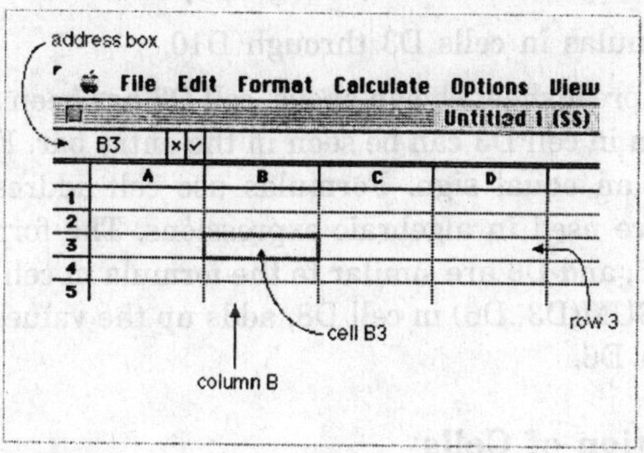

Entering Data

To enter data you will select a cell by clicking on it and then typing your data. What you are typing will show up in the entry bar. Press Return or Enter.

Hint: The X and check mark between the Address box and Entry bar can be used to cancel or accept an entry you've just typed.

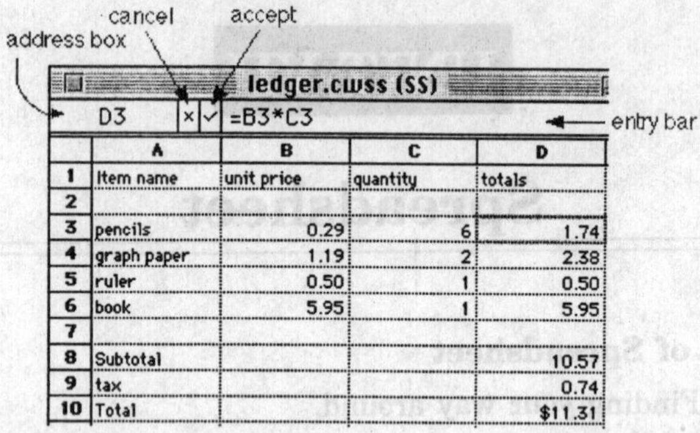

	A	B	C	D
1	Item name	unit price	quantity	totals
2				
3	pencils	0.29	6	1.74
4	graph paper	1.19	2	2.38
5	ruler	0.50	1	0.50
6	book	5.95	1	5.95
7				
8	Subtotal			10.57
9	tax			0.74
10	Total			$11.31

Open this spreadsheet. If you haven't done so already set your Web browser to use ClarisWorks as a helper application for these examples.

There are three types of data in the spreadsheet shown above:

- titles (or text) in column A and in row 1,
- numbers in cells B3 through C6, and
- formulas in cells D3 through D10.

In the spreadsheet shown above, cell D3 has been selected. The formula in cell D3 can be seen in the entry bar. Formulas begin with an equal sign. Formulas use cell addresses like variables are used in algebraic expressions. The formulas in cells D4, D5, and D6 are similar to the formula in cell D3. The formula, =SUM(D3..D6) in cell D8, adds up the values in cells D3 through D6.

Manipulation of Cells

Tool Could Manipulate Tiny Objects on a Chip

In a feat that seems like something out of a microscopic version of Star Trek, MIT researchers have found a way to use a "tractor beam" of light to pick up, hold and move around individual cells and other objects on the surface of a microchip.

The new technology could become an important tool for both biological research and materials research, say Matthew J. Lang and David C. Appleyard, whose work is being published in an upcoming issue of the journal Lab on a Chip. Lang is an assistant professor in the Department of Biological Engineering and the Department of Mechanical Engineering. Appleyard is a graduate student in Biological Engineering.

The idea of using light beams as tweezers to manipulate cells and tiny objects has been around for at least 30 years. But the MIT researchers have found a way to combine this powerful tool for moving, controlling and measuring objects with the highly versatile world of microchip design and manufacturing.

Optical tweezers, as the technology is known, represent "one of the world's smallest microtools," says Lang. "Now, we're applying it to building [things] on a chip."

Says Appleyard, "We've shown that you could merge everything people are doing with optical trapping with all the exciting things you can do on a silicon wafer ... There could be lots of uses at the biology-and-electronics interface."

For example, he said, many people are studying how neurons communicate by depositing them on microchips where electrical circuits etched into the chips monitor their electrical behavior. "They randomly put cells down on a surface, and hope one lands on [or near] a [sensor] so its activity can be measured. With [our technology], you can put the cell right down next to the sensors." Not only can motions be precisely controlled with the device, but it can also provide very precise measurements of a cell's position.

Optical tweezers use the tiny force of a beam of light from a laser to push around and control tiny objects, from cells to plastic beads. They usually work on a glass surface mounted inside a microscope so that the effects can be observed.

But silicon chips are opaque to light, so applying this technique to them is not an obvious move, the researchers say, since the optical tweezers use light beams that have to travel through the material to reach the working surface. The key to making it work in a chip is that silicon is transparent to infrared wavelengths of light—which can be easily produced by lasers, and used instead of the visible light beams.

To develop the system, Lang and Appleyard weren't sure what thickness and surface texture of wafers, the thin silicon slices used to manufacture microchips, would work best, and the devices are expensive and usually available only in quantity. "Being at MIT, where there is such a strength in microfabrication, I was able to get wafers that had been thrown out," Appleyard says. "I posted signs saying, 'I'm looking for your broken wafers'."

After testing different samples to determine which worked best, they were able to order a set that was just right for the work. They then tested the system with a variety of cells and tiny beads, including some that were large by the standards of optical tweezer work. They were able to manipulate a square with a hollow center that was 20 micrometers, or millionths of a meter, across—allowing them to demonstrate that even larger objects could be moved and rotated. Other test objects had dimensions of only a few nanometers, or billionths of a meter. Virtually all living cells come in sizes that fall within that nanometer-to-micrometers range and are thus subject to being manipulated by the system.

As a demonstration of the system's versatility, Appleyard says, they set it up to collect and hold 16 tiny living E. coli cells at once on a microchip, forming them into the letters MIT.

The work was supported by the Biotechnology Training Programme of the National Institutes of Health, the W.M. Keck Foundation and MIT's Lincoln Laboratory.

Say you have a column of text:

Dairy

Meat

Beverages

Produce

That you want to change into a row, like so:

Dairy
Meat
Beverages
Produce

Or maybe you have a row of data that you want to change into a column.

Moving the data manually, one item at a time, would be a tedious process. To save time, you can use the Paste Special command to quickly transpose a column of data to a row of data, or vice versa.

Columns and Rows

1. Copy the data in one or more columns or rows.
2. Before you paste the copied data, right-click your first destination cell (the first cell of the row or column into which you want to paste your data), and then click Paste Special.
3. In the Paste Special dialog box, select Transpose, and then click OK.

You'll find theTranspose check box in the lower-right corner of the dialog box:

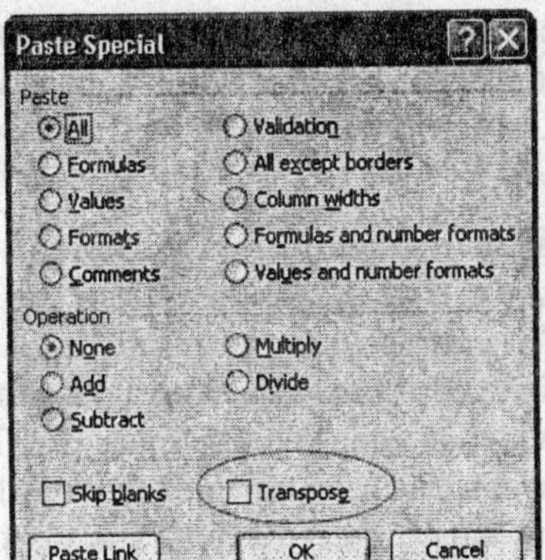

Starting with your first cell, Excel pastes the data into a row or column.

Notes :

- Columns and rows can not overlap. For example, if you select values in Column C, and try to paste them into a row that overlaps Column C, Excel displays an error message. When you go to paste a column or row, the destination area must be outside of the original values.
- If you copy and paste data from more than one column, Excel places the data from the leftmost column on top. For example, say you copy data from columns A and B of a worksheet, and you paste the data into another worksheet starting at row 1. Excel places the data from column A in row 1, column B in row 2, and so on.
- If you don't see the Paste Special command, make sure you right-click the first destination cell. You'll also find the command on the Edit menu. If you still don't see the command, make sure you're using Excel 2000 or later.

Tabulation of Bio data of Staff and Students of the School in which the Student Teacher is Attached for Practice Teaching

Tabulation of bio data of staff and students of the school in which the student teacher is attached for practice teaching.

The National Center for Education Statistics within the Institute of Education Sciences has released the report "New Indicators of Career/Technical Education Coursetaking: Class of 2005."

This Statistics in Brief uses data from the 2005 High School Transcript Study (HSTS) to examine the career/technical education (CTE) coursetaking of public high school graduates using new indicators of participation. These indicators examine the extent to which students participate in CTE and in specific occupational areas (such as agriculture and business) broadly (many students earning credits) versus deeply (many credits earned by participating students).

First, the brief looks at student participation across the three main CTE curriculum areas (family and consumer sciences education, general labour market preparation, and occupational education). Second, the brief looks at coursetaking within occupational areas, including occupational concentration. Finally, the brief examines coursetaking across occupational areas, including the areas that students tend to combine.

Findings indicate that high school graduates' use of the CTE curriculum is generally broad rather than narrow in the sense that most (70 percent) earn credits in both occupational education and either general labour market preparation or family and consumer sciences education, and most (58 percent) earn credits in more than one occupational area. Five occupational areas had the broadest participation (i.e., had the greatest number of graduates earning credits in the area): business; communications and design; manufacturing, repair, and transportation; consumer and culinary services; and computer and information sciences). The occupational areas with the deepest levels of participation were manufacturing, repair, and transportation; agriculture and natural resources; health sciences; and construction and architecture. Finally, some occupational areas were more likely than others to be taken together. For example, marketing coursetakers were more likely than other occupational!

Coursetakers to earn credits in business.

Student Progress Record

Strategies for Assessing and Keeping Records in the Classroom

There are many methods for documenting student progress. There isn't a single way that can be used for all subjects. Each subject, each assignment warrants its own method of grading or documentation depending on what the grade level expectation consists of.

Using traditional grading methods, rubrics, portfolios and anecdotal records make for a well-rounded assessment practice. Using these assessment practices in combination allows for a better look at a student's progress with standards.You will no doubt use traditional multiple choice, fill in the blank, true or false type assessments but for those assessments that aren't nearly as straightforward, other methods are necessary.

Anecdotal Records

Anecdotal records are a great way to document student behaviors and academic progress over time. They can be useful in diagnosing a student's difficulty in a particular subject area or simply to show mastering of a standard. Traditionally the teacher will take brief notes on a student's interactions within the classroom with subject matter and peers. By keeping such notes, the teacher has a point of reference for the planning of how instruction as well as an additional tool for communication to parents of their child's progress.

Maintaining a consistent system for taking anecdotal notes will ensure success when using this type of informal assessment. One method of keeping anecdotal records is to create a clipboard or file folder with note cards, one for each student, cascading down in an overlapping fashion. As you are observing, simply flip to the child's card that you are observing and jot down notes. As you fill up cards, file them away into the students class file and place a new card in its place.

If you are interested in taking notes on students in multiple subject areas, create separate folders/clipboards for each subject area. Consider using different colour note cards for each subject area to simplify finding specific notes when conferencing with a parent.

Portfolios

Portfolios are files or binders which hold samples of individual student work As students master specific standards, choose a sample that represents the student's progress and place it in the portfolio. At different points during the year, this portfolio can be used to conference with students regarding their progress as well as parents, administrators or other staff members providing services for students.

Portfolios are an excellent communication tool between all interested parties. Consider keeping a file just for student portfolios. This file should be seperate from a file kept with additional students information, communication with parents and graded work. The portfolio is a sample of standards progress, it is not an all inclusive file with all things pertaining to the student.

Rubrics

Rubrics are a great way to assess a students progress with standards in a detailed manner. For assignments that require more than a simple selection of the correct answer or filling in the blank, rubrics are the answer. Rubrics provide several focal points when grading subjective work. They also provide the teacher with a tool to ensure that grading is fair and consistent for all students. Rubrics provide a primary focus for otherwise ambiguous assignments.

Documenting student progress can be a daunting task due to the numerous options out there for doing so. By choosing a few set practices such as anecdotal records, portfolios and the use of rubrics in addition to standard, straightforward grading practices with multiple choice, fill in the blank, and true false answering, you simplify the process of keeping records. Additionally, you provide the parents and students with a consistent method of communicating progress when using a chosen few grading practices. The copyright of the article Methods for Documenting Student Progress in New Teacher Support is owned by Nicole Hempeck. Permission to republish Methods for Documenting Student Progress in print or online must be granted by the author in writing.

Tabulation of Results of an Academic Test

Students' performance is influenced by many factors, for example students' background and other factors related to students' learning process wherethey take the education programme. This means that the variety of students' background and study condition will result in variety of their academic achievement.

Introduction to Probability module is one of the compulsory modules, which given in the first semester. This module is counted as 3 SKS (SKS equal to module credit) at Department of Statistics FMIPA – ITS and students need at least "C" (score range between 56 and 60) for passing it. The lecture is held twice a week, each lecture is 100 minutes in duration, and the total number of lectures is 32 times.

Introduction to Probability module is a foundation for Introduction to Statistics method, Statistics Mathematics I, II, and III module. This research uses questionnaires distributed on week 2th, 12th, and 16th, combined with average mark of unexpected test, scheduled test, Mid-term examination mark, and Final-term examination mark. Students can be motivated to study diligently by several ways, such as keep remind them and organize unexpected tests. Change in high school study system does not always affect Mid-term examination or Final-term examination results.

From the correlation, it can be summarized the average mark of unexpected test does not have any correlation statistically with average mark of scheduled tests, Mid-term examination mark, and Final-term examination mark. On the other hand, average mark of scheduled tests statistically has correlation with Mid-term examination mark and Final-term examination mark. The correlations are 0.61 and 0.46 respectively. Students' performance is influenced by many factors, for example students' background and other factors related to students' learning process where they take the education programme. This means that the variety of students' background and study condition will result in variety of their academic achievement.

Introduction to Probability module is given in the first semester and it becomes one of the compulsory modules. This module is counted as 3 SKS (SKS equal to module credit) at Department of Statistics FMIPA – ITS and students need at least "C" (score range between 56 and 60) for passing it. The lecture is held twice a week, each lecture is 100 minutes in duration, and the total number of lectures is 32 times.

Introduction to Probability module is a foundation for Introduction to Statistics method, Statistics Mathematics I, II, and III module. Therefore, Introduction to Probability module is important to be well understood. Mid-term Examination and

Final-term Examination are held on week 8th and 18th respectively. Both of them are held after a reading week. Students' study system generally still follows their High School study system which is heavily relied on assignment/ tutorial from their teacher. They will study only if there is an examination/ test. Therefore, lecturer needs to motivate support students extrinsically by organizing 'unexpected' test, reminding them to continuously study, and require them to read more compulsory textbook so that they will get exercises other than those given by their lecturer. It is intended to force students to do excercises from books available at the library.

It is best that students read the material directly after the lecture and review it a day before the next lecture in order to understand a better the lecture. Further more, students need to be actively doing additional exercises at Department Library or Central Library. Because of the abovementioned reasons, it is needed to conduct a research on how is the study system of First Semester Student at university, especially on Introduction to Probability module. Result of this research is expected to provide contribution to Department of Statistics in particular and later it can be utilized by ITS as a step for motivating study system of ITS students in improving their results. Up to this moment, students' motivation to study and students' study system at university have not been evaluated yet. Thus, it is important to know it. The problem which will be researched in this paper is:

How to motivate students' study system at university, particularly on Introduction to Probability module?

The objective of this paper including:

1. Understanding how to motivate students' study system at university
2. Understanding whether the changes in High School study system will affect Mid-term and/ or Final-term result.
3. Whether there is correlation between average marks of the unexpected test, average mark of scheduled test, Mid-term examination mark, and Final-term examination mark.

The expected benefit is:

Make a contribution to identify effect of study system in High School to the marks of Mid-term examination and Final-term examination.

Discussion

Materials given in this module including : Principle of Multiplication; Permutation; Combination; Multinomial Coefficient; Sample Space; Axiom in Probability; Conditional Probability; Bayes; Independent Event; Discrete Random Variable and Continue Random Variable. Discrete Random Variable comprise of binomial distribution, Poisson geometric distribution, negative binomial distribution, hyper geometric, whereas Continuous Random Variable comprise of uniform distribution, normal distribution, normal approach for binomial distribution, gamma distribution, and Weibull distribution. Moreover, the module also includes these following materials:

Distribution with two random variables, independent two random variables, conditional distribution with discrete and continuous random variable

Expected score of random variable, variant and covariant, conditional expected score, moment generating function, probability generating function, and characteristics function

Central limit theorem, Chebyshev's inequality, weak law of large numbers, strong law of large numbers (Ross S, 1976)

By conducting unexpected test, each of which lasts 15-30 minutes, students are motivated to study and they will try to do exercises from books available at the library so that they will not face any significant difficulties during Mid-term and/or Final-term examination.

Lecture details on Introduction to Probability class are as follow:

1. At the beginning of the term all the materials that will be taught are explained together with the correlation of one material to another.

2. Scoring system is also explained at the beginning of the term which is 30% for Mid-term examination, 50% for Final-term examination, 10% for unexpected test, 10% for scheduled test, and 10% bonus for active student who can correctly answer questions. (Peraturan Akademik ITS, 2004)
3. Unexpected test, scheduled test, and Mid-term examination result are always returned to the students and discussed.
4. During an unexpected test, students are requested to write their target mark after they know the question
5. Lecture will be conducted by using OHP. However, students may also be requested to write on the board in front of class when solving the problems.
6. Students are always provided with examples for each of sub subject and they are asked to solve these in class. This will show whether students have understood the sub subject
7. In one semester three questionnaires will be distributed: first, to identify whether students always read materials before the next lecture; second, to recognize changes in study system after students knowing their mid-term examination result.
8. At the end of the term, student is requested to write comments regarding the lecture during the term.
9. At the end of the term, on week 18th (after reading week on week 17th) Final-term examination is held. All the lecture materials during one term will be tested.

Student's success during studies at university can be measured from each semester Grade Point Average (GPA) and Cumulative GPA at the end of the study together with the duration of study.

This research uses questionnaires distributed on week 2th, 12th, and 16th, combined with average mark of unexpected test, scheduled test, Mid-term examination, and Final-term examination. Unexpected test is held for 15-30 minutes to identify whether students have already studied, and understood materials given from previous lecture. In one semester, this test is held 6 times. Scheduled test is conducted 3 times before the end of the term. From the research done on students academic year 2007/2008 with odd matriculation number from Statistics Department FMIPA-ITS, the results are as follow:

Students with odd matriculation number in Statistics Department who is active in one semester are 41 students.

It can be seen that of those students 26.83% students have average unexpected test mark higher than average target mark, 51.22% students have Final-term examination mark higher than Mid-term examination mark or scheduled test, 36.59% students have Mid-term examination mark higher than Final-term examination mark. Information extracted from first questionnaire about study system:

1. In term of study system, 19.51% students still follow high school study system and 80.49% are already changed from their high school study system.
2. Result from cross tabulation of change in high school study system and students' effort to explore exercises other than assignment from lecture is 29.27% of those students have higher Final-term examination mark than Mid-term examination mark. On the other hand, 24.39% students have lower Final-term examination mark compare to Mid-term examination mark.
3. Result from cross tabulation of change in high school study system and students who do no have effort to explore exercises other than assignment from lecture is 12.2% of those students have higher Mid-term examination mark than Final-term examination mark. On the other hand, 9.76% students have lower Mid-term examination mark compare to Final-term examination mark.

Information extracted from second questionnaire about study system after Mid-term examination:

1. Cross tabulation result of change in high school study system, Final-term examination, and change after Mid-term examination:

– 9.76% students who start changing their study system, with Final-term examination mark 74, 7.32% of them have not been able to manage their time well.

– 9.76% students who start changing their study system, with Final-term examination mark 76, 7.32% of them have not been able to manage their time well.

– 4.88% students who have not started changing their study system yet, with Final-term examination mark 90, 2.44% of them have not been able to manage their time well.

– 2.44% students who keep their high school study system, with Final-term examination mark 70, have already studied well after Mid-term examination.

Regarding students who have not been able to manage their time well because of the large number of student activities attended, it also can be seen from the cross tabulation result that 34.15% students have their mark reduced and Final-term examination mark is lower than Mid-term examination mark.

2. Cross tabulation of change in high school study system and effort to search exercises other than lecture assignment after Mid-term examination results 21.95% students have Final-term examination mark higher than Mid-term examination mark.

It is made known from third questionnaire result about suggestion for Introduction to Probabilistic module that students want to have more exercises. However, when it is related to students initiative to search for exercises by themselves (on second questionnaire), 31.7% students have not tried to do other exercises than those given by the lecturer. It means that they rely solely on exercises from lecturer. In lecture, students are always reminded to study. It is aimed to motivate them.

In order to understand the relationship between unexpected test, scheduled test, Mid-term examination, and Final-term examination, one can see the correlation between average mark of unexpected tests, average mark of scheduled tests, Mid-term examination mark, and Final-term examination mark. It can be analyzed from the correlation that average mark of unexpected test does not have any correlation statistically with average mark of scheduled tests, Mid-term examination mark, and Final-term examination mark. On the other hand, average mark of scheduled tests statistically has correlation with Mid-term examination mark and Final-term examination mark. The correlations are 0.61 and 0.46 respectively.

Conclusion

The results are as follow:

1. Students can be motivated to study diligently by several ways, such as keep remind them and organize unexpected tests.
2. Change in high school study system does not always affect Mid-term examination or Final-term examination results.
3. From the correlation, it can be summarized the average mark of unexpected test does not have any correlation statistically with average mark of scheduled tests, Mid-term examination mark, and Final-term examination mark. On the other hand, average mark of scheduled tests statistically has correlation with Mid-term examination mark and Final-term examination mark. The correlations are 0.61 and 0.46 respectively.

Based on abovementioned results, the following suggestion can be presented:

In the future, studies in University can be improved by providing tutorial to add the chance for exercises

UNIT-VIII

Power Point

Basics of PowerPoint

This tutorial explains some of the basic features of Microsoft PowerPoint. Most of the screenshots were obtained from Microsoft 2000 for Windows, but will appear very similar in PowerPoint 97 for Windows and PowerPoint 98 for Macintosh, unless otherwise specified.

Start PowerPoint

Speaker Notes

Audio & Video

View Options

Background / Colour Scheme

Charts

Add a Slide

Headers / Footers

Transitions

Add / Modify Text

Graphics

Slide Show Animation

Start PowerPoint

- Launch PowerPoint. Usually on Windows computers you can click on the Windows Start menu / Programmes/ Microsoft PowerPoint. On Macintosh computers try looking for PowerPoint in the Applications folder of your hard drive, or there may be a special Microsoft Office menu near the right of your screen, or try looking under the Apple menu.. Check with your instructor if you are not sure how to launch PowerPoint on the computer you are using.

- The initial PowerPoint dialog window provides various starting points for working in PowerPoint:

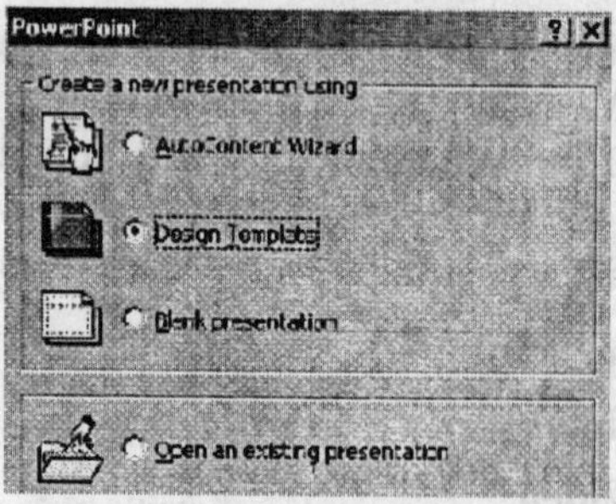

AutoContent Wizard: Formats a basic slide set by leading you through some basic questions.

(Design) Template: Choose a pre-designed slide layout (background and colour scheme).

Blank Presentation: Design a presentation from scratch.

Open an Existing Presentation: Locate an existing PowerPoint file to continue working on.

At any time in PowerPoint, you can start a new presentation by clicking on the PowerPoint File menu and selecting New, or open an existing file by selecting File / Open.

View Options

There are several ways to view your work in PowerPoint. To change the view use the View menu or the buttons in the lower-left corner of the screen.

2000:  97/98: 

	Normal	(PowerPoint 2000 only) Provides the text outline of the entire presentation on the left, the current slide on the upper-right, and speaker notes on the lower-right.
	Outline	Provides a large text outline area.
	Slide	Shows a graphic view of the current slide.
	Slide Sorter	Shows the entire set of slides (numbered) on the screen. Allows you to drag-and-drop slide icons to change their order.
	Notes Page	Provides a large area to view the speaker notes on a slide. This button is provided in PowerPoint 97/98, but not 2000. In 2000, to get this view, click on the **View** menu, and select **Notes Page**.
	Slide Show	Displays the presentation in full-screen mode starting with the slide which was last edited (so jump to slide 1 first if you want to see the entire presentation). Press the **Escape** key if you wish to exit the Slide Show before it ends.
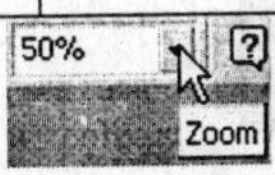 50% Zoom		The **Zoom** adjuster lets you alter how large your slides appear on the screen relative to full-screen presentation mode. Click on the **Zoom** drop-down list (in the toolbar near the top of the screen), or click on the **View** menu, and select **Zoom...** Select "fit", a default percentage, or type in your own number, according to your needs.

Add a Slide

In the Text Outline area, you can add a slide *before* or *after* an existing slide.

- To add *before* a slide position the cursor at the beginning of text of the slide in front of which you would like a new slide, and press the **Enter** key.
- To add *after* a slide, position the cursor at the end of the text of the slide after which you would like a new slide, and press the Enter key (if you had indented levels of text on the previous slide, use the Promote (left arrow) button in the toolbar at the top of the screen to move the text back to the left to force a new slide.

In Normal, Outline, Slide, or Slide Sorter view, select the slide *after* which you wish to insert a new slide. 

- Then click on the Insert menu, and select New Slide.
- When you add a new slide this way, the New Slide window appears, asking you to select a slide layout.

- Select whichever layout is appropriate for the content you will place on the new slide. The one selected in the example on the right is "Bulleted List". If the provided layouts don't meet your needs, select the bottom-right layout, "Blank", which will provide you with a new empty slide. However, no matter which layout you choose, you will be able to modify it later.

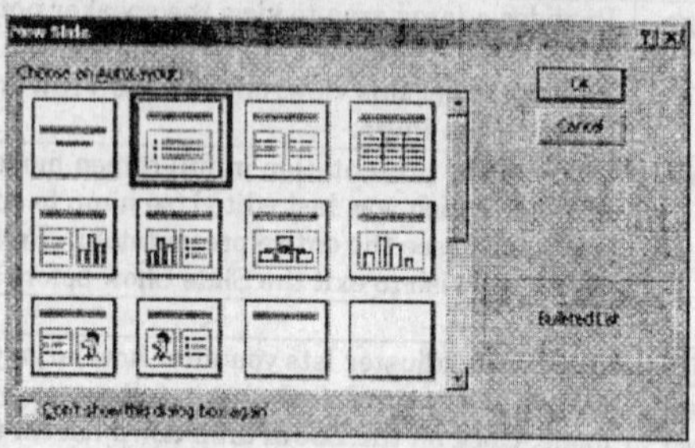

Creating a Presentation

After you open up Microsoft PowerPoint, a screen pops up asking if you would like to create a New Presentation or Open An Existing Presentation.

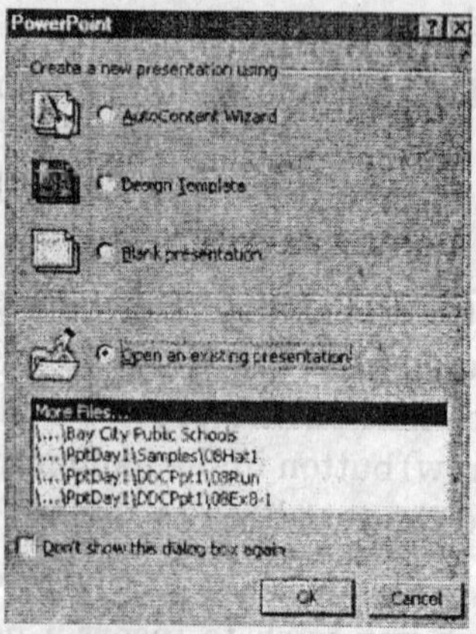

- ***AutoContent Wizard***
    - o Creates a new presentation by prompting you for information about content, purpose, style, handouts, and output. The new presentation contains sample text that you can replace with your own information.

Simply follow the directions and prompts that are given by Microsoft PowerPoint.

- ***Design Template***
  - o Creates a new presentation based on one of the PowerPoint design templates supplied by Microsoft. Use what is already supplied by Microsoft Power Point and change the information to your own.
- ***Blank Presentation***
  - o Creates a new, blank presentation using the default settings for text and colours. Go to next step: Creating A Blank Presentation

Opening An Existing Presentation

1. Select Open An Existing Presentation from the picture above
2. Click on your presentation in the white box below step 1
   - o If you do not see your presentation in the white box, select More Files and hit OK.
   - o Locate you existing Presentation and hit the Open button

Create a Blank Presentation

After you select Blank Presentation a window pops up asking you to select the layout of the first slide.

Pre-Designed Slide Layouts (Left to Right)

- Title Slide
- Bulleted List
- Two Column Text
- Table
- Text & Chart
- Chart & Text
- Organizational Chart
- Chart
- Text & Clip Art
- Clip Art & Text

- Title Only
- Blank Slide

Note: If you already know what you want in your next slide, it is a very good idea to choose one of the pre-designed layouts from above. However if you do not, then you can still insert what you want in throughout your Presentation anytime you desire. Just choose Blank Slide and insert items as you see fit.

Different Views That PowerPoint Demonstrates

There are different views within Microsoft PowerPoint that allow you to look at your presentation from different perspectives.

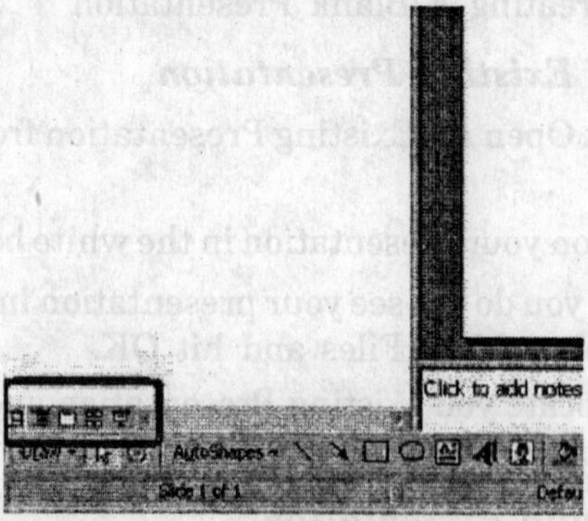

Normal View	Outline View	Slide View	Slide Sorter View	Slide Show View
Switches to normal view, where you can work on one slide at a time or organize the structure of all the slides in your presentation	Switches to outline view, where you can work with the structure of your file in outline form. Work in outline view when you need to organize the structure of your file.	Switches to slide view, where you can work on one slide at a time	Displays miniature versions of all slides in a presentation, complete with text and graphics. In slide sorter view, you can reorder slides, add transitions, and animation effects. You can also set the timings for electronic slide shows.	Runs your slide show in a full screen, beginning with the current slide if you are in slide view or the selected slide if you are in slide sorter view. If you simply want to view your show from the first slide: 1. Click **Slide Show** at the top of the screen 2. Select **View Show**

The Slide Manager Preparation of Different Types of Slides

- Inserting A New Slide
  1. Click Insert at top of screen
  2. Select New Slide
- Formatting A Slide Background
  - o You can format your slide to make it look however you would like, whether it be a background colour, picture, or a design template built into Microsoft PowerPoint. The next step will show you how to apply a Design Template, but the other items mentioned above can be accomplished the same way.
  1. Click Format at the top of the screen
  2. Select Apply Design Template
  3. Select Design you wish to apply
  4. Click Apply Button
- Inserting Clipart & Pictures
  0. Display the slide you want to add a picture to.
     1. Click Insert at the top of the screen
     2. Select Picture
     3. Select Clip Art
     4. Click the category you want
     5. Click the picture you want
     6. Click Insert Clip on the shortcut menu
     7. When you are finished using the Clip Gallery, click the Close button on the Clip Gallery title bar
     8. *Steps 1-4 are very similar when inserting other Pictures, Objects, Movies, Sounds, and Charts*

Adding Transitions to a Slide Show

You can add customized transitions to your slide show that will make it come alive and become appealing to your audience. Follow these steps when adding Slide Transitions.

1. In slide or slide sorter view, select the slide or slides you want to add a transition to.
2. On the Slide Show menu at the top of the screen, click Slide Transition

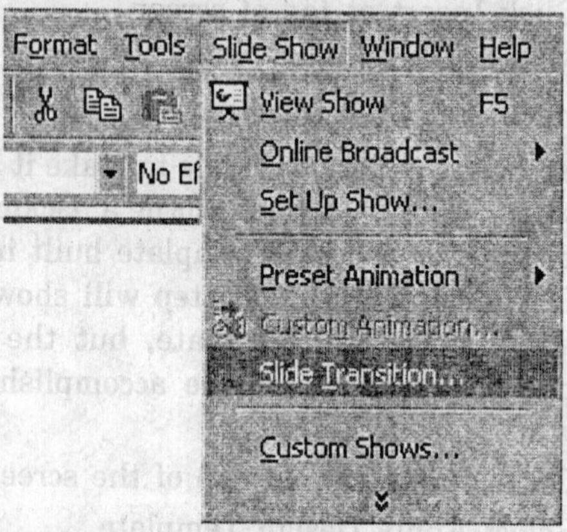

3. In the Effect box, click the transition you want, and then select any other options you want
4. To apply the transition to the selected slide, click Apply.
5. To apply the transition to all the slides, click Apply to All.
6. Repeat the process for each slide you want to add a transition to.
7. To view the transitions, on the Slide Show menu, click Animation Preview.

Slide Design

PowerPoint provides slide designs as a quick and easy way to create a background and design style for your fonts and bullets. There are various different slide designs that you can choose by going to the Slide Design pane in the Task Pane.

In the Task Pane:

1. Click on the down arrow in the top right corner. A list of all the different panes will appear.
2. Select Slide Design. The Task Pane will change and thumbnail images of each slide design will appear.

3. If you click on one of them, your slide will automatically apply that slide design.

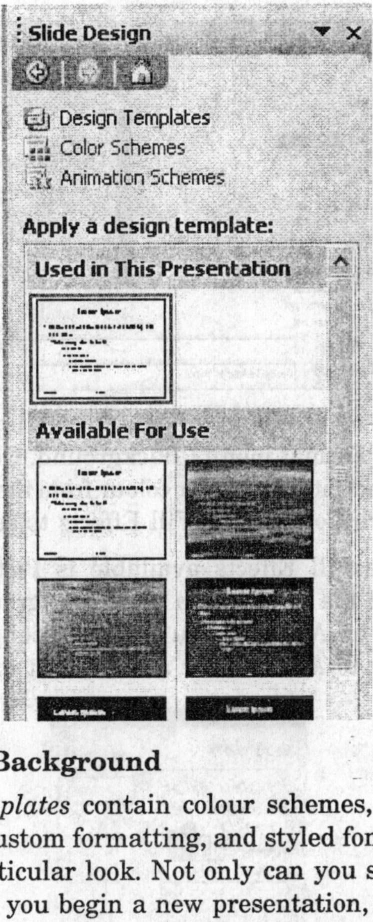

Colour and Background

Design templates contain colour schemes, slide and title masters with custom formatting, and styled fonts, all designed to create a particular look. Not only can you specify a design template when you begin a new presentation, you can choose a design template (for the whole presentation, not individual slides) any time while editing a presentation. To do this, click on the Format menu, and select Apply Design Template (Apply Design in 97/98). A window will open asking you to choose a design. Select one and click Apply.

The name of the template chosen will be displayed in the center of the status bar at the bottom of the PowerPoint screen. If the status bar is not visible, click on the Tools menu, select

Options (Preferences on Macintosh), click on the View tab, and ensure that Status bar is checked.

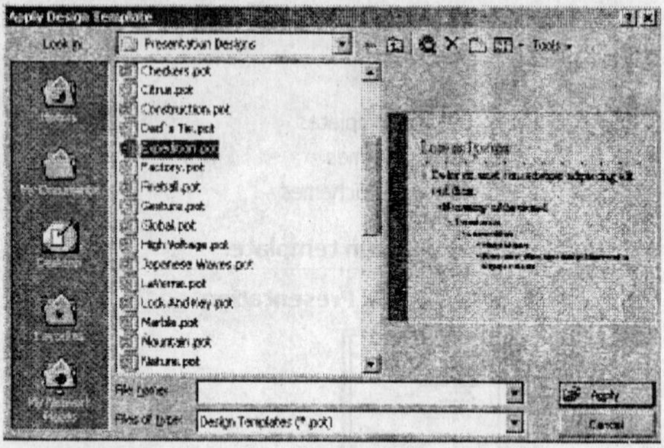

The *background colour of slides* can be customized by clicking on the Format menu / Background. Click on the drop-down list to select either another colour from the subset provided or click on More Colours and Fill Effects to see other choices.

One of the Fill Effects available is Picture (import an external image file to use as a slide background). When you are done, click on Apply (if you wish to alter just the current slide) or Apply to All (to alter all slides at once).

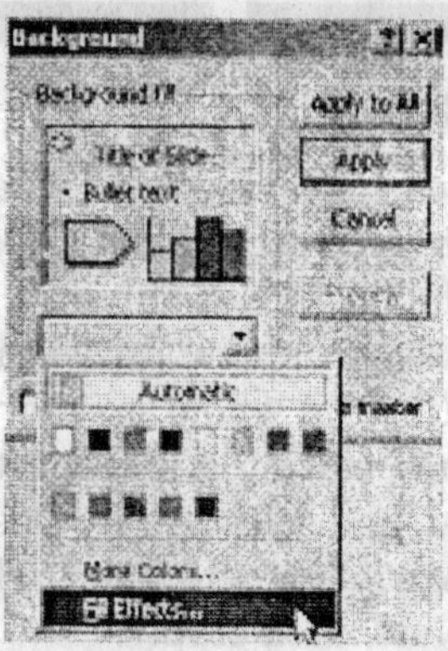

The *colour scheme for slides* can be customized by clicking on Format / Slide Colour Scheme. Either choose a preset scheme from the Standard tab or click the Custom tab, click on the desired component (e.g. Background), and click Change Colour (a colour selection window will appear). When you are done making colour choices, click on Apply (if you wish to alter just the current slide) or Apply to All (to alter all slides at once).

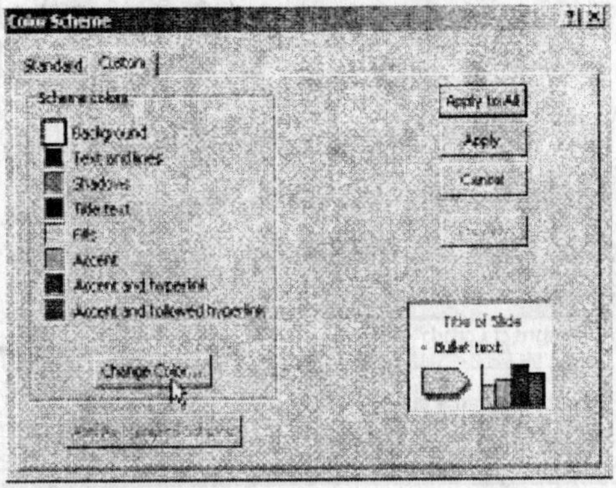

Headers/Footers

- On the View menu, click Header and Footer.
- On the Slide tab, you set options which affect what will appear at the bottom of slides:
  - o Date and time can be set to Update automatically (to reflect the last date the slides were modified) or Fixed (type a certain date such as when the presentation will be given).
  - o Selecting the Slide number option will automatically insert a sequence number.
  - o Selecting Footer (and typing text in the box below it) inserts fixed footer text.
  - o Selecting Don't show on title slide will omit the footer from the title slide (but it will appear on the other slides).
  - o Normally you click on the Apply to All button to make these changes throughout the presentation, but of course you can click Apply to affect just the current slide.
- Similar options are available on the Notes and Handouts tab, plus the option of adding a page header to your printouts.

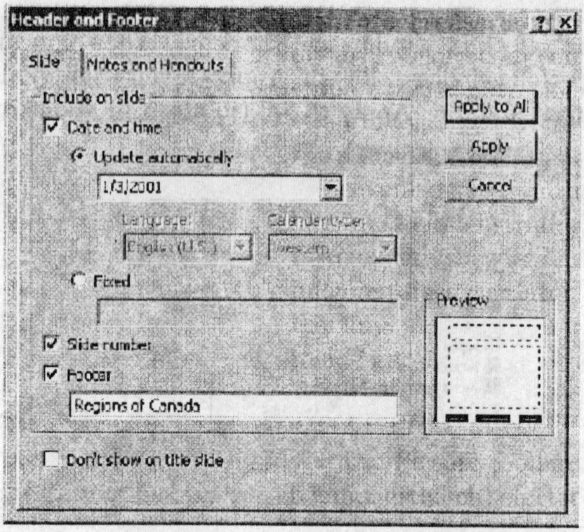

Manipulation and Presentation of Slides

Incorporating Images into a PowerPoint Presentation

Before discussing PowerPoint image manipulation, I would liketo summarize the basic steps used in producing an image slidewith PowerPoint. These steps have already been discussed indetail [8, 9], so they will only be reviewed briefly here.

The easiest method for adding an image is to use the InsertPicture button from the Drawing toolbar. If this toolbar isnot displayed, use View Toolbars to select it. After clickingInsert Picture, locate and select the image by browsing theInsert Picture dialog box.

Then click Insert (on the InsertPicture dialog box), or double-click the image icon itself toembed the image in the slide (Fig. 1). Another way to add animage is to use the Insert menu. On Insert, point to Pictureand then click From File (Fig. 2). The Insert Picture dialogbox will appear. Locate and select the image you want by browsingthis dialog box. Then click Insert or doubleclick the imageicon. An inserted image will be placed in the middle of theslide. Click on the image and position the mouse pointer overone of the corner handles to resize the image.

To decrease or increase the size, drag the mouse toward or awayfrom the center (Fig. 3). Three points must be emphasized aboutresizing. First, to maintain the central position of an image,hold down the Control key (CTRL) while dragging the mouse. Second, tomaintain width-to-height proportions and to prevent distortion,the use of side handles should generally be avoided in mostradiologic images. Finally, to resize an image to an exactlyspecified height and width, use the Format Picture button (discussedlater in this article). After inserting and resizing an image,move it to a desired position by clicking inside the image and draggingthe mouse.

The Picture Toolbar and Image-Manipulation Commands

The Picture toolbar appears by default after an image has beeninserted or selected. If the toolbaris not displayed, use the View menu to select it (View ToolbarsPicture). The Picture toolbar has 14 editing commandsavailable in the 2002 version of PowerPoint, but earlier versionslack some or most of them. The function of each command will beexplained. A general discussion of editing techniques and theirpractical applications is covered in the next article.

Insert Picture allows the user to insert a new image, usingthe steps just described for inserting a picture from the Drawingtoolbar. Colour changes the colour mode of an image. After selectingan image, click Colour, and choose an option from the pull-downmenu. The menu comprises Automatic (original settings), GrayScale, Black & White, and Washout. Gray Scale is the most helpfuloption in radiology presentations.

More Contrast, Less Contrast, More Brightness, and Less Brightnessadjust the contrast and brightness, respectively, of an image.To change contrast or brightness, select the image by clickingit. Then click the appropriate button (e.g., More Contrast)for the effect desired. Repeated clicking increases the effecton the image. A change can be reversed using Edit Undo or using theopposite function (e.g., Less Contrast).

Crop removes unwanted vertical or horizontal edges. To cropan image, select the image, and click Crop on the Picture toolbar.The shape of the side and corner handles will change

Position the cropping tool over the appropriate cropping handle,and drag it inward. To perform equal cropping on two sides simultaneously,hold down CTRL while dragging the handle inward. To turn off theCrop command, click the slide outside the image, or click Cropon the Picture toolbar.

Rotate Left rotates an image 90° counter-clockwise. To rotatean image, select it, and click Rotate Left. Other forms of rotation(Rotate Right and Free Rotate) and flipping (Flip Horizontaland Flip Vertical) are available on the Drawing toolbar. Line Style adds a frame around an image. After selecting theimage, click Line Style, and select one of the options fromthe pulldown menu. The frame can be customized by selectingMore Lines from the menu.

Compress Picture reduces image resolution to 96 or 200 dotsper inch or discards hidden portions of a cropped image. Compressionis helpful in reducing the file size. To compress an image orgroup of images, select the images, click Compress Picture,and choose from the options in the Compress Picture dialog box.

Recolor Picture can be used only for drawn pictures (vector-based graphics).Radiologic images are bitmapped graphics, so this command neednot be discussed.

Format Picture enables the user to apply fine adjustments inimage size, position, line style, brightness, contrast, andcropping. The previously described Colour, Free Rotation, andCompression commands are also available in Format Picture, whichalso allows certain effects such as resizing and cropping tobe reversed individually. To format, select the image, and click FormatPicture. A dialog box with multiple tabs will appear. The tabsinclude Colours & Lines, Size, Position, Picture, Text Box,and Web. Select the appropriate tab to adjust or modify features.For example, to restore the original dimensions of a resizedimage without reversing other changes, click Size Reset. TheLock Aspect Ratio box should be checked in radiologic images.

To make a fine adjustment in contrast, click the Picture tab,and then change the settings. The Picture tab can also be usedto restore a cropped image: Click the tab, and then click Reset;or reset the numbers to zero.

Set Transparent Colour is used to designate a transparent colorin an image. To set a transparent colour, select the image, andclick the Set Transparent Colour button. Click the colour thatis to be made transparent. Bear in mind, however, that mostapparently uniform colours in medical images (e.g., image background)have subtle differences in pixel values. Such differences may createinhomogeneity and noise in the areas in which colour was removed.Also, colour replacement affects all pixels with the same selectedcolor. As a result, colour may be inadvertently removed fromadditional areas. For these reasons, the Set Transparent Colorcommand has few practical applications in radiology presentations.

Reset Picture reverses all changes that have been made to animage and restores its original state. To reverse not all, butonly specific changes, click the Format Picture button on thePicture toolbar. (Note, however, that some options in the CompressPicture dialog box— e.g., Web/Screen and Print or Deletecropped areas of pictures—are irreversible.)

UNIT-IX

Internet

Meaning

The shared global computing network. A network based on standards including Internet Protocol (IP), Simple Mail Transfer Protocol (SMTP) and the Domain Name System (DNS), which enables global communications between all connected computing devices. It provides the platform for web services and the WorldWide Web.

The Internet is a global network of interconnected computers, enabling users to share information along multiple channels. Typically, a computer that connects to the Internet can access information from a vast array of available servers and other computers by moving information from them to the computer's local memory. The same connection allows that computer to send information to servers on the network; that information is in turn accessed and potentially modified by a variety of other interconnected computers. A majority of widely accessible information on the Internet consists of inter-linked hypertext documents and other resources of the World Wide Web (WWW). Computer users typically manage sent and received information with web browsers; other software for users' interface with computer networks includes specialized programmes for electronic mail, online chat, file transfer and file sharing.

The movement of information in the Internet is achieved via a system of interconnected computer networks that share data by packet switching using the standardized Internet

Protocol Suite (TCP/IP). It is a "network of networks" that consists of millions of private and public, academic, business, and government networks of local to global scope that are linked by copper wires, fiber-optic cables, wireless connections, and other technologies.

Importance

We talk a lot about the internet here at share marketing. Because the single greatest tool for sharing is the computer. So when this study came out, I was immediately intrigued:

In a study called Counting on the Internet, these are the subheads:

Most expect to find key information online

Most find the information they seek

Many now turn to the Internet first

From the PDF:

"With over 60% of Americans now having Internet access and 40% of Americans having been online for more than three years, the Internet has become a mainstream information tool."

It's not like this is news. But seeing the numbers confirms something that we've known for a long time. The Internet is a big part of our life. The writer's ended their strike because they will now be paid if I watch an episode of Life on my computer. I watched them all online.

Pew says people look online first for answers. Soon, they'll look to the computer for more things than we can think of. My 2-year-old already thinks of it as a phone. She uses Skype to see her family. Other things we have names for like TV, Radio, phone, datebook, watercooler, atlas, game console....all these things no longer have one meaning. You can do it all online.

The computer can be, and already is a TV (where you can find programming that isn't on TV), movie theater (check out Jaman), Radio (podcasts, ie radio shows from around the world, played anytime you want), phone (with camera), watercooler (Facebook). Next week, the computer might be something we only imaged—like a place to try on clothes that fit your avatar—with your friend from another time zone. Who knows?

Now this isn't meant to be a post talking about the greatness of the computer. It's meant to confirm something we already know: when thinking about reaching people, we can't ignore the computer.

More and more, our target isn't.

So why do we? When a job comes into an agency, why doesn't someone always ask how it will translate online?

Types of Networking

Main Network Types

- Ethernet
- FDDI
- Token Ring
- ARCnet
- AppleTalk

Other Network Types

- *Fiber Channel :* Operates at 256 Mbps or 1 Gbps. It was developed for peripheral devices like disk arrays, but is now used for point to point networking for full duples server to server communications. It is the lowest cost 1 Gbps network.
- *Gigabit Ethernet :* This type of ethernet places ethernet packets in fiber channel packets. The fiber channel network works like an ethernet bridge.

LAN

A local area network (LAN) is a computer network covering a small physical area, like a home, office, or small group of buildings, such as a school, or an airport. The defining characteristics of LANs, in contrast to wide-area networks (WANs), include their usually higher data-transfer rates, smaller geographic place, and lack of a need for leased telecommunication lines.

ARCNET, Token Ring and many other technologies have been used in the past, and G.hn may be used in the future, but Ethernet over unshielded twisted pair cabling, and Wi-Fi are the two most common technologies currently in use.

History

As larger universities and research labs obtained more computers during the late 1960s, there was increasing pressure to provide high-speed interconnections. A report in 1970 from the Lawrence Radiation Laboratory detailing the growth of their "Octopus" network, gives a good indication of the situation.

Cambridge Ring was developed at Cambridge University in 1974 but was never developed into a successful commercial product.

Ethernet was developed at Xerox PARC in 1973–1975, and filed as U.S. Patent 4,063,220. In 1976, after the system was deployed at PARC, Metcalfe and Boggs published their seminal paper-"Ethernet: Distributed Packet-Switching For Local Computer Networks".

ARCNET was developed by Datapoint Corporation in 1976 and announced in 1977- and had the first commercial installation in December 1977 at Chase Manhattan Bank in New York.

The Personal Computer

The development and proliferation of CP/M-based personal computers from the late 1970s and then DOS-based personal computers from 1981 meant that a single site began to have dozens or even hundreds of computers. The initial attraction of networking these was generally to share disk space and laser printers, which were both very expensive at the time. There was much enthusiasm for the concept and for several years, from about 1983 onward, computer industry pundits would regularly declare the coming year to be "the year of the LAN".

In reality, the concept was marred by proliferation of incompatible physical layer and network protocol implementations, and confusion over how best to share resources. Typically, each vendor would have its own type of network card, cabling, protocol, and network operating system. A solution appeared with the advent of Novell NetWare which provided even-handed support for the 40 or so competing card/ cable types, and a much more sophisticated operating system than most of its competitors. Netware dominated[8] the personal computer LAN business from early after its introduction in 1983 until the mid 1990s when Microsoft introduced Windows NT Advanced Server and Windows for Workgroups.

Of the competitors to NetWare, only Banyan Vines had comparable technical strengths, but Banyan never gained a secure base. Microsoft and 3Com worked together to create a simple network operating system which formed the base of 3Com's 3+Share, Microsoft's LAN Manager and IBM's LAN Server. None of these were particularly successful.

In this same timeframe, Unix computer workstations from vendors such as Sun Microsystems, Hewlett-Packard, Silicon Graphics, Intergraph, NeXT and Apollo were using TCP/IP based networking. Although this market segment is now much reduced, the technologies developed in this area continue to be influential on the Internet and in both Linux and Apple Mac OS X networking—and the TCP/IP protocol has now almost completely replaced IPX, AppleTalk, NBF and other protocols used by the early PC LANs.

Cabling

Early LAN cabling had always been based on various grades of co-axial cable, but IBM's Token Ring used shielded twisted pair cabling of their own design, and in 1984 StarLAN showed the potential of simple Cat3 unshielded twisted pair—the same simple cable used for telephone systems. This led to the development of 10Base-T (and its successors) and structured cabling which is still the basis of most LANs today.

Technical Aspects

Although switched Ethernet is now the most common data link layer protocol and IP as a network layer protocol, many different options have been used, and some continue to be popular in niche areas. Smaller LANs generally consist of one or more switches linked to each other—often with one connected to a router, cable modem, or ADSL modem for Internet access.

Larger LANs are characterized by their use of redundant links with switches using the spanning tree protocol to prevent loops, their ability to manage differing traffic types via quality of service (QoS), and to segregate traffic via VLANs. Larger LANS also contain a wide variety of network devices such as switches, firewalls, routers, load balancers, sensors and so on.

LANs may have connections with other LANs via leased lines, leased services, or by 'tunneling' across the Internet using VPN technologies. Depending on how the connections are made and secured, and the distance involved, they become a Metropolitan Area Network (MAN), a Wide Area Network (WAN), or a part of the Internet.

WAN

Wide Area Network (WAN) is a computer network that covers a broad area (i.e., any network whose communications links cross metropolitan, regional, or national boundaries). In contrast with personal area networks (PANs), local area networks (LANs), campus area networks (CANs), or metropolitan area networks (MANs) which are usually limited to a room, building, campus or specific metropolitan area (e.g., a city) respectively. The largest and most well-known example of a WAN is the Internet.

WANs [a] are used to connect LANs and other types of networks together, so that users and computers in one location can communicate with users and computers in other locations. Many WANs are built for one particular organization and are private. Others, built by Internet service providers, provide connections from an organization's LAN to the Internet. WANs are often built using leased lines. At each end of the leased line, a router connects to the LAN on one side and a hub within the WAN on the other. Leased lines can be very expensive. Instead of using leased lines, WANs can also be built using less costly circuit switching or packet switching methods. Network protocols including TCP/IP deliver transport and addressing functions. Protocols including Packet over SONET/SDH, MPLS, ATM and Frame relay are often used by service providers to deliver the links that are used in WANs. X.25 was an important early WAN protocol, and is often considered to be the "grandfather" of Frame Relay as many of the underlying protocols and functions of X.25 are still in use today (with upgrades) by Frame Relay. Academic research into wide area networks can be broken down into three areas: Mathematical models, network emulation and network simulation.

MAN

Metropolitan area networks, or MANs, are large computer networks usually spanning a city. They typically use wireless infrastructure or Optical fiber connections to link their sites.

IEEE Definition

The IEEE 802-2001 standard describes a MAN as being:

> *"A MAN is optimized for a larger geographical area than a LAN, ranging from several blocks of buildings to entire cities. MANs can also depend on communications channels of moderate-to-high data rates. A MAN might be owned and operated by a single organization, but it usually will be used by many individuals and organizations. MANs might also be owned and operated as public utilities. They will often provide means for internetworking of local networks. Metropolitan area networks can span up to 50km, devices used are modem and wire/cable"*

Authors Kenneth C. Laudon and Jane P. Laudon of Management Information Systems: Managing the Digital Firm 10th ed. define Metropolitan Area Networks (MAN) as:

> *"A Metropolitan Area Network (MAN) is a large computer network that spans a metropolitan area or campus. Its geographic scope falls between a WAN and LAN. MANs provide Internet connectivity for LANs in a metropolitan region, and connect them to wider area networks like the Internet."*

Implementation

Some technologies used for this purpose are ATM, FDDI, and SMDS. These older technologies are in the process of being displaced by Ethernet-based MANs (e.g. Metro Ethernet) in most areas. MAN links between LANs have been built without cables using either microwave, radio, or infra-red laser links. Most companies rent or lease circuits from common carriers due to the fact that laying long stretches of cable can be expensive.

DQDB, Distributed Queue Dual Bus, is the Metropolitan Area Network standard for data communication. It is specified in the IEEE 802.6 standard. Using DQDB, networks can be up to 20 miles (30 km) long and operate at speeds of 34 to 155 Mbit/s.

Several notable networks started as MANs, such as the Internet peering points MAE-West, MAE-East, and the Sohonet media network.[citation needed]

Internet—WWW

The World Wide Web (commonly abbreviated as "the Web") is a system of interlinked hypertext documents accessed via the Internet. With a Web browser, one can view Web pages that may contain text, images, videos, and other multimedia and navigate between them using hyperlinks. Using concepts from earlier hypertext systems, the World Wide Web was started in 1989 by the English physicist Sir Tim Berners-Lee, now the Director of the World Wide Web Consortium, and later by Robert Cailliau, a Belgian computer scientist, while both were working at CERN in Geneva, Switzerland. In 1990, they proposed building a "web of nodes" storing "hypertext pages" viewed by "browsers" on a network, and released that web in December. Connected by the existing Internet, other websites were created, around the world, adding international standards for domain names & the HTML language. Since then, Berners-Lee has played an active role in guiding the development of Web standards (such as the markup languages in which Web pages are composed), and in recent years has advocated his vision of a Semantic Web.

The World Wide Web enabled the spread of information over the Internet through an easy-to-use and flexible format. It thus played an important role in popularizing use of the Internet. Although the two terms are sometimes conflated in popular use, *World Wide Web* is not synonymous with *Internet*. The Web is an application built on top of the Internet.

Website

A website (or "web site") is a collection of related web pages, images, videos or other digital assets that are hosted on one web server, usually accessible via the Internet.

A web page is a document, typically written in (X)HTML, that is almost always accessible via HTTP, a protocol that transfers information from the web server to display in the user's web browser.

All publicly accessible websites are seen collectively as constituting the "World Wide Web".

The pages of a website can usually be accessed from a common root URL called the homepage, and usually reside on the same physical server. The URLs of the pages organize them into a hierarchy, although the hyperlinks between them control how the reader perceives the overall structure and how the traffic flows between the different parts of the site.

Some websites require a subscription to access some or all of their content. Examples of subscription sites include many business sites, parts of many news sites, academic journal sites, gaming sites, message boards, Web-based e-mail, services, social networking websites, and sites providing real-time stock market data. Because they require authentication to view the content they are technically an Intranet site.

Web Pages

A web page or webpage is a document or resource of information that is suitable for the World Wide Web and can be accessed through a web browser and displayed on a computer screen.

This information is usually in HTML or XHTML format, and may provide navigation to other web pages via hypertext links. Web pages may be retrieved from a local computer or from a remote web server. The web server may restrict access only to a private network, e.g. a corporate intranet, or it may publish pages on the World Wide Web. Web pages are requested and served from web servers using Hypertext Transfer Protocol (HTTP).

Web pages may consist of files of static text stored within the web server's file system (static web pages), or the web server may construct the (X)HTML for each web page when it is requested by a browser (dynamic web pages). Client-side scripting can make web pages more responsive to user input once in the client browser.

Internet Connectivity

The Internet Connectivity Evaluation Tool checks your Internet router to see if it supports certain technologies. You can use this tool on a PC running either the Windows Vista or Windows XP operating system. If you're planning to run Windows Vista, this tool can verify whether your existing Internet router supports advanced features, such as improved download speeds and face-to-face collaboration using Windows Meeting Space. The tool is intended to be run from a home network behind a home Internet (NAT) router. Running this tool from behind a corporate firewall or on operating systems other than those specified above won't produce accurate results. This tool requires administrator privileges to run.

The tests can require up to 10 minutes to complete and do not make any permanent changes to your router. For the most accurate results, your computer should be connected directly to your Internet router, using a wired connection.

Note: Although it is unlikely, testing might interrupt your Internet connectivity or cause your router to stop responding. If you require uninterrupted Internet access at this time (for example, if you are in the middle of downloading a large file, bidding on a time-sensitive Internet auction, or playing an online game), you should wait and do this testing at another time.

Browsing the Internet

What do I Need to Know?

A browser is a programme on your computer that enables you to search ("surf") and retrieve information on the WorldWideWeb (WWW), which is part of the Internet. The Web is simply a large number of computers linked together in a global network, that can be accessed using an address (URL, Uniform Resource Locator, e.g. http://www.veths.no for the Oslo Veterinary School), in the same way that you can phone anyone in the world given their telephone number.

URLs are often long and therefore easy to type incorrectly. They all begin with http://, and many (but not all) begin with http://www. In many cases the first part (http://, or even http://www.) can be omitted, and you will still be able to access the page. Try this with http://www.cnn.com.

URLs are constructed in a standard fashion. This may be of use to you. Take, for example, the address of this page:

http://oslovet.veths.no/teaching/internet/basics.html

The ".no" indicates that the server is in Norway. The page you have accessed is called basics.html, and it resides in a folder on the server called "internet", which is in the folder called "teaching". If the URL that you type does not work, and you have typed it correctly (no mistakes are allowed!), the reason may be that the host has renamed the web page, or moved it to another folder on the server, or you are not allowed access to that level.

Try removing the text of the URL stepwise from the right-hand end in this example, until you reach the main page:

http://www.bbc.co.uk/info/purpose/public_purposes/index.shtml.

It is possible, in many cases, to find your way back down through the hierarchy to the page you were interested in.

You don't need to know how the telephone network functions to be able to make a phone call. However, you ought to know how to use your telephone apparatus and the finesses (software) it contains. Your computer is the equivalent of the telephone, and a browser is the equivalent of the software that modern telephones contain. (A browser can also be used to handle electronic mail, create and edit information on the Internet, as l have done here, and to contact discussion groups. This presentation is limited to the use of browsers to surf the WorldWideWeb).

Searching the Web

If you don't know the telephone number of the person you wish to ring to, you need a telephone directory. The Web provides two methods of searching for pages providing information:

- sites presenting web pages sorted by category and subcategories, e.g. Yahoo (several sites, including http://www.yahoo.com and http://www.yahoo.no)
- sites offering search engines that return lists of web pages containing text that matches a search word or string, e.g. Google (http://www.google.com), AltaVista (http://www.altavista.com) and FAST Search (http://www.alltheweb.com).

Many web sites offer both, or a combination of, these alternatives.

Before you conduct a search, it is important to consider, among others, the following points:

1. Is your choice of search term is adequate, too restrictive or too general?
2. Is the search you have planned to undertake most suited for a search engine that categorizes web sites, so that you can browse through appropriate subcategories when the first results are returned?
3. Are you more interested in using a search engine that merely returns all the web pages it has found containing the search term?

4. Have you read the Search Help pages that most search pages offer? These will tell you how the search engine conducts the search, and therefore how you ought to plan your search.
5. Bear in mind the fact that engines differ in their coverage of the Internet, their speed and whether they are largely compiled manually by people or automatically by 'robots' that scan the Internet.

A search strategy must include knowledge of how the search engine you have planned to use handles Boolean Logic and other similar search terms, e.g.

- transgenic AND mice will find all pages covering transgenic mice, but not pages that only mention transgenic rats
- transgenic NOT mice will return pages on all species other than mice.
- "transgenic mice" will find pages that contain the phrase "transgenic mice", i.e. where the words are adjacent in the text, but will not return a page containing the text "transgenic rodents, including mice", for which transgenic NEAR mice would be necessary
- transgen* will return occurences of trangenesis, transgenic and transgenic (thereby increasing your chances of finding pages you are interested in), but will also return pages featuring the word 'transgender', which is probably not what you were looking for!

N.B. Not all search engines support all these options, some support many more, and all of them have a "default" function (e.g. AND or OR) which you must check before you start.

To illustrate the enormous implications that this may have for your search results, try out the following search strings in the AltaVista or Google search engines and note the number of web pages returned for each alternative:

- Karina Smith
- "Karina Smith"

- Karina and Smith
- KARINA and SMITH
- Karin* Smith
- Karin*Smith

Excellent reviews of these processes have been written by information specialist Krys Bottrill. These cover:

- Basic principles when searching the Web
- Choice of search terms and strategies
- Comparison of Search engines on the Web

Browsing Software

A web browser is a software application for retrieving, presenting, and traversing information resources on the World Wide Web. An information resource is identified by a Uniform Resource Identifier (URI) and may be a web page, image, video, or other piece of content. Hyperlinks present in resources enable users to easily navigate their browsers to related resources.

Although browsers primarily intended to access the World Wide Web, they can also be used to access information provided by web servers in private networks or content in file systems.

The major web browsers in order of usage according to Net Applications are Windows Internet Explorer, Mozilla Firefox, Apple Safari, Google Chrome, and Opera.

The history of the web browser dates back to late 1980s, when a variety of technologies laid the foundation for the first web browser, WorldWideWeb, by Tim Berners-Lee in 1991. That browser brought together a variety of existing and new software and hardware technologies.

The introduction of the NCSA Mosaic web browser in 1993 – one of the first graphical web browsers – led to an explosion in web use. Marc Andreessen, the leader of the Mosaic team at NCSA, soon started his own company, named Netscape, and released the Mosaic-influenced Netscape Navigator in 1994, which quickly became the world's most popular browser, accounting for 90% of all web use at its peak (see usage share of web browsers).

Microsoft responded with its browser Internet Explorer in 1995 (also heavily influenced by Mosaic), initiating the industry's first browser war. By bundling Internet Explorer with Windows, Microsoft was able to leverage its dominance in the operating system market to take over the web browser market; Internet Explorer usage share peaked at over 95% by 2002.

In 1998, Netscape launched what was to become the Mozilla Foundation in an attempt to produce a competitive browser using the open source software model. That browser would eventually evolve into Firefox, which developed a respectable following while still in the beta stage of development; shortly after the release of Firefox 1.0 in late 2004, Firefox (all versions) accounted for 7.4% of browser use. As of February 2009, Firefox has a 21.77% usage share.

Opera debuted in 1996; although it has never achieved widespread use, having less than 1% browser usage share as of February 2009 according to Net Applications, it has a substantial share of the fast-growing mobile phone web browser market, being preinstalled on over 40 million phones. It is also available on several other embedded systems, including Nintendo's Wii video game console.

Apple's Safari had its first beta release in January 2003; as of February 2009, it has a dominant share of Apple-based web browsing, accounting for just over 8% of the entire browser market.

The most recent major entrant to the browser market is Google's Chrome, first released in September 2008. As of February 2009, it has a 1.15% usage share.

Function

The purpose of a web browser is to display resources to the user. This process begins when the user inputs a Uniform Resource Identifier (URI), for example *http://en.wikipedia.org/* into the browser. The prefix of the URI determines how the URI will be interpreted. The most commonly used kind of URI starts with *http:* and identifies content to be retrieved over Hypertext Transfer Protocol (HTTP). Many browsers also support a variety of other prefixes, such as *https:* for HTTPS, *ftp:* for the File Transfer Protocol, and *file:* for local files. Prefixes that the web browser cannot directly handle are often handed off to another application entirely. For example, *mailto:* URIs are usually passed into the user's default e-mail application, and *news:* URIs are passed to the user's default newsgroup reader.

In the case of *http*, *https*, *file*, and others, once the content has been retrieved the web browser sets about displaying it. HTML is handed off to the browser's layout engine to be transformed from markup to an interactive document. Aside from HTML, web browsers can generally display any kind of content that can be part of a web page. Most browsers can display images, audio, video, and XML files, and often have plug-ins to support Flash files and Java applets. Upon encountering a file of an unsupported type or a file that is set up to be downloaded rather than displayed, the browser prompts the user to save the file to disk.

Features

Available web browsers range in features from minimial, text-based user interfaces with bare-bones support for HTML to rich user interfaces supporting a wide variety of file formats and protocols. Browsers which include additional components to support Usenet news, Internet Relay Chat (IRC), and e-mail are often referred to as "Internet suites" rather than merely "web browsers".

Most major web browsers allow the user to open multiple information resources at the same time, either in different browser windows or in different tabs of the same window. Major browser also include pop-up blockers to prevent unwanted windows from "popping up" without the user's consent.

Most web browsers can display a list of web pages that the user has *bookmarked* so that the user can quickly return to them. Bookmarks are also called "Favorites" in Internet Explorer. In addition, all major web browsers have some form of built-in web feed aggregator. In Mozilla Firefox, web feeds are formatted as "Live bookmarks" and behave like a folder of bookmarks corresponding to recent entries in the feed. In Opera, a more traditional feed reader is available which stores and displays the contents of the feed.

Furthermore, most browsers can be extended via plug-ins, downloadable components that provide additional features.

User Interface

Most major web browsers have these user interface elements in common:

- *Back* and *forward* buttons to go back to the previous resource and forward again.
- A *refresh* or *reload* button to reload the current resource.
- A *stop* button to cancel loading the resource. In some browsers, the stop button is often merged with the reload button.
- A *home* button to return to the user's home page
- An address bar to input the Uniform Resource Identifier (URI) of the desired resource and display it.
- A search bar to input terms into a search engine
- A status bar to display progress in loading the resource and also the URI of links when the cursor hovers over them, and page zooming capability.

Major browsers also possess incremental find features to search within a web page.

Privacy and Security

Most browsers support HTTP Secure and offer quick and easy ways to delete the web cache, cookies, and browsing history.

Standards Support

Early web browsers supported only a very simple version of HTML. The rapid development of proprietary web browsers led to the development of non-standard dialects of HTML, leading to problems with interoperability. Modern web browsers support a combination of standards-based and *de facto* HTML and XHTML, which should be rendered in the same way by all browsers.

URL Addresses

In computing, a Uniform Resource Locator (URL) is a type of Uniform Resource Identifier (URI) that specifies where an identified resource is available and the mechanism for retrieving it. In popular usage and in many technical documents and verbal discussions it is often, imprecisely and confusingly, used as a synonym for uniform resource identifier. The confusion in usage stems from historically different interpretations of the semantics of the terms involved. In popular language, a URL is also referred to as a *Web address*.

History

The URL was created in 1990 by Tim Berners-Lee as part of the URI. He regrets the format of the URL. Instead of being divided into the route to the server, separated by dots, and the file path, separated by slashes; he would have liked it to be one coherent hierarchical path. For example, http://www.serverroute.com/path/to/file.html would look like http://com/serverroute/www/path/to/file.html.

Syntax

Every URL is made up of some combination of the following: The scheme name or resource type, a registered domain name or internet protocol address, the port number, the pathname of the file to be fetched or the programme to be run, the query string, and with html files, an anchor for where the page should be displayed at. The combined syntax will look similar to this: resource_type://domain:port/filepathname?query_string#anchor

- The scheme name, or resource type, defines its namespace, purpose, and the syntax of the remaining part of the URL. Most Web-enabled programmes will try to dereference a URL according to the semantics of its scheme and a context-vbn. For example, a Web browser will usually dereference the URL http://

example.org:80 by performing an HTTP request to the host example.org, at the port number 80. Dereferencing the URL mailto:bob@example.com will usually start an e-mail composer with the address bob@example.com in the To field.

- o Other examples of scheme names include https: gopher:, wais:, ftp:. URLs that specify https as a scheme (such as https://example.com/) normally denote a secure website.

- The registered domain name or IP address gives the destination location for the URL. The domain google.com, or its IP address 72.14.207.99, directs you to where Google's website resides.
- The hostname and domain name portion of a URL are case insensitive since the DNS is specified to ignore case. http://en.wikipedia.org/ and HTTP://EN.WIKIPEDIA.ORG/ will both open same page.
- The port number is optional. If it is not provided, the default for the scheme will be used. For example, in your browser you could type http://google.com:80 which would bring you to google.com on port 80. If you left out port 80, your browser would navigate to the same location because port 80 is the default for HTTP.
- The file path name is the destination on the server for where to access the file or programme they are looking for. It may be treated as case insensitive by some servers, especially those that are based on Microsoft Windows. For example:
  - o http://en.wikipedia.org/wiki/URL is correct, but http://en.wikipedia.org/WIKI/URL/ will result in an HTTP 404 error page.
- The query string contains data to be passed to web applications such as CGI programmes. The query string contains name/value pairs separated by ampersands, with names and values in each pair being separated by equal signs, for example first_name = John&last_name = Doe.

- The anchor part when used with HTTP allows you to be directed to a specific location on the page after you have navigated there. For example, http://en.wikipedia.org/wiki/URL#Syntax would bring you to the beginning of the Syntax section of this page.
    - o On some sites, the anchor may have other functions; see: fragment identifier.

Absolute vs Relative URLs

An absolute URL is one that points to the exact location of a file. It is unique meaning that if two URLs are identical, they point to the same file. An example of this would be: http://en.wikipedia.org/wiki/File:Raster_to_Vector_Mechanical_Example.jpg

A relative URL points to the location of a file from a point of reference. This reference is usually the directory beneath the file. It is preceded by two dots (../directory_path/file.txt) for the directory above, one dot (./directory_path/file.txt) for the current directory or without the beginning slash(directory_path/file.txt), which is also the current directory.

URLs as Locators

In its current strict technical meaning, a URL is a URI that, "in addition to identifying a resource, [provides] a means of locating the resource by describing its primary access mechanism (e.g., its network 'location')."

Internet Hostnames

On the Internet, a hostname is a domain name assigned to a host computer. This is usually a combination of the host's local name with its parent domain's name. For example, "en.wikipedia.org" consists of a local hostname ("en") and the domain name "wikipedia.org". This kind of hostname is translated into an IP address via the local hosts file, or the Domain Name System (DNS) resolver. It is possible for a single host computer to have several hostnames; but generally the operating system of the host prefers to have one hostname that the host uses for itself.

Any domain name can also be a hostname, as long as the restrictions mentioned below are followed. So, for example, both "en.wikimedia.org" and "wikimedia.org" are hostnames because they both have IP addresses assigned to them. The domain name "pmtpa.wikimedia.org" is not a hostname since it does not have an IP address, but "rr.pmtpa.wikimedia.org" is a hostname. All hostnames are domain names, but not all domain names are hostnames.

Search Engines

A Web search engine is a tool designed to search for information on the World Wide Web. The search results are usually presented in a list and are commonly called *hits*. The information may consist of web pages, images, information and other types of files. Some search engines also mine data available in newsbooks, databases, or open directories. Unlike Web directories, which are maintained by human editors, search engines operate algorithmically or are a mixture of algorithmic and human input.

History

Timeline (full list)

Year	*Engine*	*Event*
1993	Aliweb	Launch
	JumpStation	Launch
1994	WebCrawler	Launch
	Infoseek	Launch
	Lycos	Launch
1995	AltaVista	Launch
	Open Text Web Index	Launch[1]
	Magellan	Launch
	Excite	Launch
	SAPO	Launch
1996	Dogpile	Launch
	Inktomi	Founded
	HotBot	Founded
	Ask Jeeves	Founded
1997	Northern Light	Launch

	Yandex	Launch
1998	Google	Launch
1999	AlltheWeb	Launch
	GenieKnows	Founded
	Naver	Launch
	Teoma	Founded
	Vivisimo	Founded
2000	Baidu	Founded
2003	Info.com	Launch
2004	Yahoo! Search	Final launch
	A9.com	Launch
	Sogou	Launch
2005	MSN Search	Final launch
	Ask.com	Launch
	GoodSearch	Launch
2006	wikiseek	Founded
	Quaero	Founded
	Ask.com	Launch
	Live Search	Launch
	ChaCha	Beta Launch
	Guruji.com	Beta Launch
2007	wikiseek	Launched
	Wikia Search	Launched
	Blackle.com	Launched
2008	Powerset	Launched
	Viewzi	Launched
	Cuil	Launched
	Boogami	Launched
	LeapFish	Beta Launch
	Musu	Beta Launch
	VADLO	Launch

Before there were web search engines there was a complete list of all webservers. The list was edited by Tim Berners-Lee and hosted on the CERN webserver. One historical snapshot from 1992 remains. As more and more webservers went online the central list could not keep up. On the NCSA Site new servers were announced under the title "What's New!" but no complete listing existed any more.

The very first tool used for searching on the (pre-web) Internet was Archie. The name stands for "archive" without the "v." It was created in 1990 by Alan Emtage, a student at McGill University in Montreal. The programme downloaded the directory listings of all the files located on public anonymous FTP (File Transfer Protocol) sites, creating a searchable database of file names; however, Archie did not index the contents of these sites.

The rise of Gopher (created in 1991 by Mark McCahill at the University of Minnesota) led to two new search programmes, Veronica and Jughead. Like Archie, they searched the file names and titles stored in Gopher index systems. Veronica (Very Easy Rodent-Oriented Net-wide Index to Computerized Archives) provided a keyword search of most Gopher menu titles in the entire Gopher listings. Jughead (Jonzy's Universal Gopher Hierarchy Excavation And Display) was a tool for obtaining menu information from specific Gopher servers. While the name of the search engine "Archie" was not a reference to the Archie comic book series, "Veronica" and "Jughead" are characters in the series, thus referencing their predecessor.

In June 1993, Matthew Gray, then at MIT, produced what was probably the first web robot, the Perl-based World Wide Web Wanderer, and used it to generate an index called 'Wandex'. The purpose of the Wanderer was to measure the size of the World Wide Web, which it did until late 1995. The search engine Aliweb appeared in November 1993. Aliweb did not use a web robot, but instead depended on being notified by website administrators of the existence at each site of an index file in a particular format.

JumpStation (released in December 1993) used a web robot to find web pages and to build its index, and used a web form as the interface to its query programme. It was thus the first WWW resource-discovery tool to combine the three essential features of a web search engine (crawling, indexing, and searching) as described below. Because of the limited resources available on the platform on which it ran, its indexing and hence searching were limited to the titles and headings found in the web pages the crawler encountered.

One of the first "full text" crawler-based search engines was WebCrawler, which came out in 1994. Unlike its predecessors, it let users search for any word in any webpage, which has become the standard for all major search engines since. It was also the first one to be widely known by the public. Also in 1994 Lycos (which started at Carnegie Mellon University) was launched, and became a major commercial endeavor.

Soon after, many search engines appeared and vied for popularity. These included Magellan, Excite, Infoseek, Inktomi, Northern Light, and AltaVista. Yahoo! was among the most popular ways for people to find web pages of interest, but its search function operated on its web directory, rather than full-text copies of web pages. Information seekers could also browse the directory instead of doing a keyword-based search.

In 1996, Netscape was looking to give a single search engine an exclusive deal to be their featured search engine. There was so much interest that instead a deal was struck with Netscape by 5 of the major search engines, where for $5Million per year each search engine would be in a rotation on the Netscape search engine page. These five engines were: Yahoo!, Magellan, Lycos, Infoseek and Excite.

Search engines were also known as some of the brightest stars in the Internet investing frenzy that occurred in the late 1990s. Several companies entered the market spectacularly, receiving record gains during their initial public offerings. Some have taken down their public search engine, and are marketing enterprise-only editions, such as Northern Light. Many search engine companies were caught up in the dot-com bubble, a speculation-driven market boom that peaked in 1999 and ended in 2001.

Around 2000, the Google search engine rose to prominence. The company achieved better results for many searches with an innovation called PageRank. This iterative algorithm ranks web pages based on the number and PageRank of other web sites and pages that link there, on the premise that good or desirable pages are linked to more than others. Google also maintained a minimalist interface to its search engine. In contrast, many of its competitors embedded a search engine in a web portal. By 2000, Yahoo was providing search services based on Inktomi's search engine. Yahoo! acquired Inktomi in 2002, and Overture (which owned AlltheWeb and AltaVista) in 2003. Yahoo! switched to Google's search engine until 2004, when it launched its own search engine based on the combined technologies of its acquisitions.

Microsoft first launched MSN Search (since re-branded Live Search) in the fall of 1998 using search results from Inktomi. In early 1999 the site began to display listings from Looksmart blended with results from Inktomi except for a short time in 1999 when results from AltaVista were used instead. In 2004, Microsoft began a transition to its own search technology, powered by its own web crawler (called msnbot).

As of late 2007, Google was by far the most popular Web search engine worldwide. A number of country-specific search engine companies have become prominent; for example Baidu is the most popular search engine in the People's Republic of China.

Exploring Websites

As the Internet continues to grow and develop, the traditional educational publishing field has been quick to adopt and supply elearning materials to education. The companion website materials for instructors which accompany the leading textbooks now make many of the new elearning tools readily available. These new teaching materials have been in existence for less than ten years and while their popularity is growing, most faculty have never given these materials a thorough review and many are not sure where they are or how to find them or use them with courses. This paper identifies companion websites for leading texts, catalogs features and evaluates these value-added materials related to coursework in Introduction to Computer Literacy.

Introduction

While publishers offer other textbook supplements like printed guides and test banks, CDs and DVDs with extra materials and premium services for a fee, this paper discusses companion websites that offer materials which students can access for free as part of the course. The basic procedures used for inventory and evaluation here however could be applied to any supplemental information and to other academic disciplines.

In a perfect world, faculty would like to be able to turn on their computers and with one click go to the website which accompanies the textbook for their course. It shouldn't take long to find the site, and faculty would hope to avoid wading through layers of menus and links to get to the actual course material. While publishing houses understand the importance of answering faculty inquiries quickly, some bumps are to be expected in in an area which is less than ten years old and which has undergone a period of enormous growth. Some faculty will fall by the wayside when paths to the companion websites are not clear and take too long to find.

It appears that the speed with which materials are being produced, reorganized and placed on the web is so fast that even web gurus are reluctant to discuss 'best practices' because today's practices may already be out of date. And the value of companion websites may already be out of date even when faculty reviewed them recently.

The list of companion website materials included major texts for courses that cover the Introduction to Computer Science Literacy. The texts were chosen based on their sales volume and are the top-selling books available in 2004. In the course of preparing this paper, it took numerous emails back and forth to illustrate the website access problem. When I sought to locate the companion website for a particular textbook, the publisher's rep assured me that the site could be found at a link which he attached and which turned out to be half Internet address and half email address. After three more emails the correct address was provided. One request ordinarily should be enough to obtain a link to a companion website. In a perfectly operating system, faculty wouldn't need guidance from a publisher's rep to find a companion site; their locations should be transparent.

In a second example, a publisher's rep provided a link to the companion website and later emailed back with an apology and an explanation that the old link no longer worked and asked us to try a new link. For another text, our search revealed two sites that were said to be the companion websites. A closer investigation of the two sites revealed that one site was apparently an early draft of what was to become the site to go with the textbook and was not meant to be available to faculty or students. Many faculty members stumbled across the draft site and were dismayed to find material that was not ready for prime time. Lastly, after finding a dead link on one site, it proved difficult to report the dead link to the publisher.

There were two links -one to 'Technical Feedback' and one to 'Editorial Feedback.' A message was sent to each with information about the dead link. The editorial feedback was never acknowledged and the reply from the technical support representative again did not acknowledge the website problem but instead focused on selling me a copy of the textbook.

Methodology

Texts included for review in the introduction to computer science-literacy were taken from searches of highest sales numbers in searches for computers and computer literacy. Dummies, Idiot and texts that were not available from academic publishers were discarded. The computer science programme at Saint Xavier University was then asked to review the list and use the 20 years of experience each faculty has in teaching literacy to see if the list was an appropriate list of best selling titles for literacy. The department searched the shelves of the departmental library and found no titles missing and chose not to add any titles since other books for introductory courses included non-literacy topics like programming .

Faculty members who do not adapt are often finding students vocally demanding some materials. In fact many publishers are now offering CD-ROM materials and companion websites for a fee to students even if the faculty chooses not to adopt such materials. Presently, many publishers give this material for free if the faculty requests it. This does save the students some time and money. There is some danger for the students when they make adoptions themselves, because often the materials need careful explanation and integration to be effective. A group of students were in the computer science lab downloading and printing online exams, unaware that if the exams were taken online they self-scored and gave remediation on readings from the text and page numbers for review. Even after it was pointed out to the group some could not understand how taking the tests online could be a time saving feature and good study aid.

As the push comes from students demanding materials and administrators promising all the latest and greatest additional teaching aids, many faculty members may feel overwhelmed! In the past, publisher's asked for reviews of text and even paid for long thorough well- thought-out reviews for their best selling text to make improvements and help faculty familiarize themselves with the book. Faculty members could depend on peer reviews of text for help in making adoptions for teaching. It does not appear that any publisher is making peer reviews available of the features on the websites to accompany the books. It would be so easy to add these reviews on the very page! Publishers do not have years of experience in marketing value added materials and even credible and reputable publishers have occasionally missed deadlines and pulled bad materials.

Websites for each book were easy to find by putting the ISBN number directly into the main webpage of the publisher. This keeps the search engine from giving endless multiple titles. Each book had its own page and that page linked to faculty resources. Publishers required a name and password to access the faculty resource page. The request forms for name and password were online and request for examination of the materials for faculty use were answered affirmatively in e-mail in about 24 hours. Even after names and passwords arrived one company had dead links at the invitation to take the product demo. Some books offered materials to be published shortly but had left the date in the link the year 2002. This type of poor marketing and website management may reflect the fact that so few faculty are reviewing the additional materials on the web before making adoptions of a book. It still appears as if many faculty members adopt the book and then assume that additional materials are all equal or are just an added extra needs no evaluation. A new faculty in the computer science department adopted a new book for a short session course, and then became alarmed and tried to cancel his adoption when he learned he would not get the teaching aids he had come to depend on with the previous text.

Many sites now require a User Agreement sign-off page before browsing on to the materials. These agreements restrict copy of materials or use of the materials without adoption of the text for a course. In order to keep these materials free of additional charges, faculty should respect these agreements. Even with a text that has literally every available teaching aid on the resource page, this is no indication that the materials are going to be easy to use for teaching. In some cases the materials may not be usable. Several publishers offer Blackboard or WebCT materials for the text. However, to put those texts on Blackboard or WebCT the faculty member must either get the institution to give a Systems Administrator clearance to the faculty member or must be willing to download and install the materials for the faculty member. Many institutions may find both solutions unworkable for different reasons.

Downloading Materials from Websites

To download material, log in using the username and password you were given when you purchased materials or entered the Shootout or the Jr Shootout.

If you don't have your username and password to gain access to your materials, contact dennis@texas-shootout.com.

Logging In

To log in, enter your username and password in the "Log In" box on the main page of our site.

Once you are logged in, you should see a blue box titled "Material List". This box should contain a list of materials available for you to download.

If you've logged in and don't see what you expect, email dennis@texas-shootout.com.

Downloading Material

After logging in, click on the "download" link next to the material you'd like to download. This should bring up a list of files that you can download. Click on a file's link to view it. If your browser is configured properly and you have Adobe Acrobat 5.0 or later installed, this should work. If that doesn't work and you have Acrobat 5.0 or later installed, try clicking on the file's link with the right mouse button to bring up a small menu box. From this menu box, choose "Save Target As" and save the file to your desktop or a directory. Then, try opening the file from there.

Material File Format

Materials are in PDF format and can be viewed and printed using Adobe Reader 5.0 later. Adobe Reader can be downloaded for free from adobe.com.

Problems or Questions

For some problems and questions, it might be best to talk with your local computer expert and/or try downloading and printing from a different computer system. If you have problems or questions about downloading, viewing, and printing material from our website that you can't resolve, email dennis@texas-shootout.com.

Exploring Websites Traffic With Google Trends For Website: Google Trend for Website can be used to track the popularity of a particular website or you can also compare the Statistics of your site with your competitor's site.

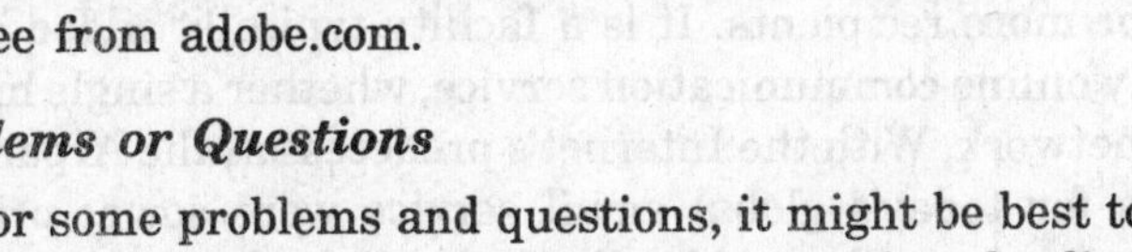

Here some of the Google Trend for Website features:

1. Compare traffic with up to 5 websites at one time.
2. Keywords which driving traffic to given website
3. View data for a specific country.
4. Related Websites

Previously Alexa ranking was the most popular for comparing websites traffic. However, some users have flagged Alexa data as erroneous.

Google Trend for Website is available for websites worldwide and it really going to help webmasters regarding SEO and comparing their sites with their rivals.

E-mail

Electronic mail—often abbreviated as e-mail or email—is a digital communication mechanism, designed primarily for human use, that consists of message content, an author and one or more recipients. It is a facility typically added quickly to any online communication service, whether a single machine or a network. With the Internet's predecessor, the Arpanet, the seeds for today's global email service were sown, primarily through a formally standardized encoding of messages, as RFC 733.

With the proliferation of the Internet since the early 1980s, the standardization produced the modern form of the service, with transport provided by the Simple Mail Transfer Protocol (SMTP), first published as Internet Standard 10 (RFC 821) in 1982, and a revision of RFC 733 to be Internet Standard 11 (RFC 822).

Network-based e-mail systems are based on a store-and-forward model in which e-mail computer server systems, accept, forward, or store messages on behalf of users, who only connect to the e-mail infrastructure with their personal computer or other network-enabled device for the duration of message transmission or retrieval to or from their designated server. Rarely is e-mail transmitted directly from one user's device to another's.

While, originally, e-mail consisted only of text messages composed in the ASCII character set, virtually any media format can be sent today, including attachments of audio and video clips.

Sending

Receiving Email Alerts: You can be notified when new articles or publications are available on IngentaConnect by setting up New Issue or Search Alerts. Five free New Issue Alerts can be set up. If you purchase a license you can set up unlimited new issue alerts and create alerts for your searches.

Receiving

Reading Messages	Working With Shortcuts	Replying to Messages	Forwarding Messages	Printing Messages	Flagging Messages

Reading Messages: Yahoo! Mail stores email messages in mail folders. Initially, all of your incoming email messages arrive in your Inbox folder (except suspected spam, which goes directly into your Spam folder). To read a message, you simply display a mail folder and click a message line.

Display in new window

- What's Next
- Learn More
- Help Topics

The folder list displays the number of unread messages in parentheses next to each folder name.

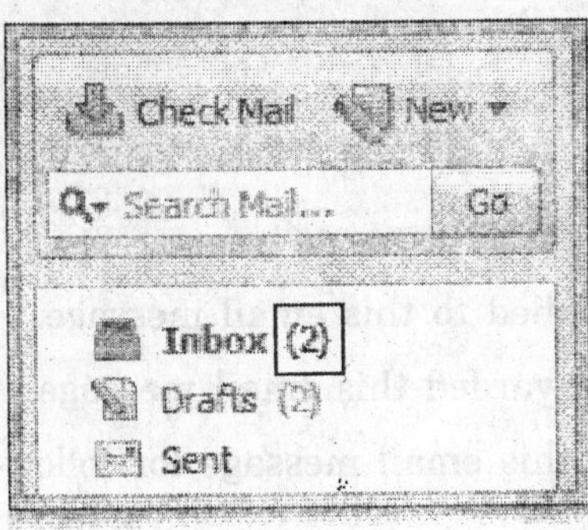

Click the Inbox link to display a list of your messages.

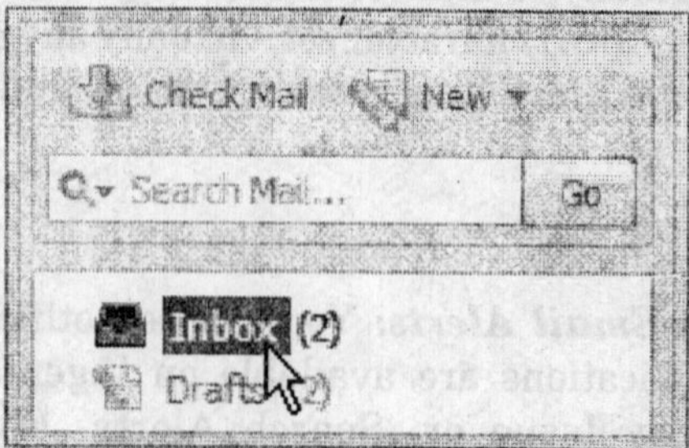

A list of the messages in your Inbox appears in the top portion of the Inbox tab.

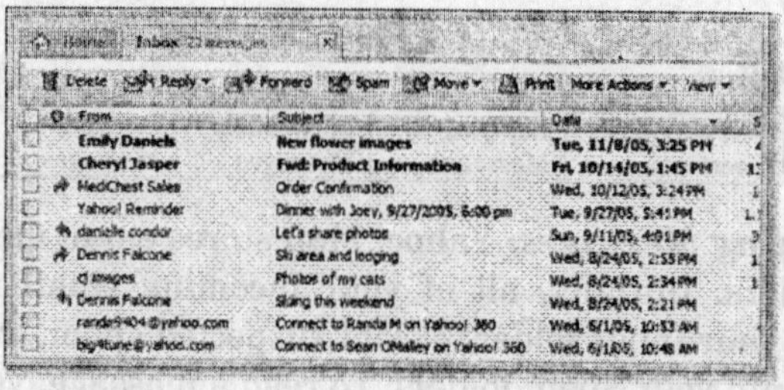

The subjects of the messages give you an idea of what each one is about. To get the whole story, read your messages.

You've probably noticed the little icons scattered around your Inbox and in open email messages.

These icons appear in mail folders to indicate special characteristics of messages:

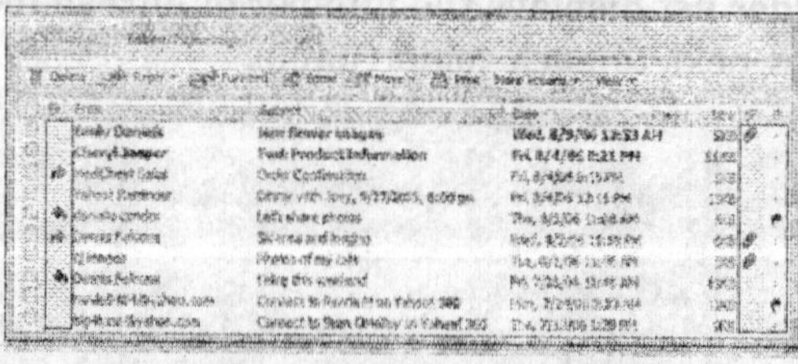

You have replied to this email message.

You have forwarded this email message.

You flagged this email message for follow-up.

This email message includes one or more attachments.

This email message is from a CertifiedEmail™ sender.

When reading an email message, you might see these icons in the header:

This person has a Yahoo! ID and is online. Click the icon to send the person an instant message using Yahoo! Messenger.

This person has a Yahoo! ID but is offline.

Verifies that the message is being sent from its claimed domain, such as "@yahoo.com".

Click the icon to add this person to your Yahoo! Contacts.

This person is in your Yahoo! Contacts. Click the icon to view the contact details for this person.

If you have a text-enabled mobile phone or other mobile device, click the icon to set up Yahoo! Mail to send you a text alert whenever you receive a message from this person.

This email message includes one or more attachments.

This email message is from a CertifiedEmail™ sender.

Most of these icons appear automatically. The flag is the only icon that you apply to a message by marking it for follow-up.

Storing Mail

It would be possible to have all email messages in one file, together with information in which folder each email should appear. This kind of mail storage could be, and sometimes is, implemented as a database, for example.

Another attempt would create one file for every email message and arrange them in a file system hierarchy representing the folders in the user interface. While this approach maybe has security benefits, it requires a lot of hard disk activity, which is slow.

Somewhere in between those two attempts lies another approach to storing email messages. We create a file for every mailbox and put all the messages in the corresponding folder in this file. This is the format used by most email clients, and it is called the mbox format.

The Mbox Format

If we use the mbox format to store emails, we put all of them in one file. This creates more or less long text file (Internet email always only exists as 7-bit ASCII text, everything else—attachments, for example—is encoded) containing one email message after the other. How do we know where one ends and another starts?

Fortunately, every email has at least one From-line at its very beginning. Every message begins with "From " (From followed by a white space character, also called a "From_" line). If this sequence ("From ") at the beginning of a line is preceded by an empty line or is at the top of the file, we have found the beginning of a message.

So what we look for when parsing an mbox file is, essentially, an empty line followed by "From".

As a regular expression, we can write this as "\n\nFrom .*\n". Only the very first message is different. It starts merely with "From " at the beginning of a line ("^From .*\n").

"From " in the Body

What if exactly the sequence above appears in the body of an email message? What if the following is part of an email?

...I send you the most recent report.

From this report, you need not...

Here, we have an empty line followed by "From " at the beginning of the line. If this appears in a mbox file, we unmistakably have the beginning of a new message. At least that's what the parser thinks — and why both the email client and we would be quite confused by an email message that contains neither sender nor recipient, but begins with "From this report".

To avoid such desastrous conditions, we need to make sure "From " never appears at the beginning of a line following an empty line in the body of an email.

Whenever we add a new message to a mbox file, we look for such sequences in the body and simply replace "From" with ">From". This makes misinterpretations impossible. The example above now looks like this and no more triggers the parser:

...I send you the most recent report.

>From this report, you need not...

This is why you may sometimes find ">From" in an email where you'd expect a mere "From".

Chating

Meet People Who Share YoPr passions

Chat rooms are a great place to meet and communicate with friends who share your interests. You'll find chat rooms for a world of topics from entertainment to sports, to politics and pop culture. Liven up your chats with emoticons, custom fonts and even voice.

UNIT-X

Web Designing

HTML

HTML, an acronym for HyperText Markup Language, is the predominant markup language for web pages. It provides a means to describe the structure of text-based information in a document—by denoting certain text as links, headings, paragraphs, lists, etc.—and to supplement that text with *interactive forms*, embedded *images*, and other objects.

HTML is written in the form of "tags" that are surrounded by angle brackets. HTML can also describe, to some degree, the appearance and semantics of a document, and can include embedded scripting language code (such as JavaScript) that can affect the behavior of Web browsers and other HTML processors.

History of HTML

Origins

In 1980, physicist Tim Berners-Lee, who was an independent contractor at CERN, proposed and prototyped ENQUIRE, a system for CERN researchers to use and share documents. In 1989, Berners-Lee and CERN data systems engineer Robert Cailliau each submitted separate proposals for an Internet-based hypertext system providing similar functionality.

The following year, they collaborated on a joint proposal, the WorldWideWeb (W3) project, which was accepted by CERN.

First Specifications

The first publicly available description of HTML was a document called *HTML Tags*, first mentioned on the Internet by Berners-Lee in late 1991. It describes 22 elements comprising the initial, relatively simple design of HTML. Thirteen of these elements still exist in HTML 4. HTML is a text and image formatting language used by internet browsers to dynamically format web pages. The semantics of many of its tags can be traced to early text formatting languages such as *runoff*. Runoff was developed in the early 1960s for the CTSS (Compatible Time-Sharing System) operating system, and its formatting commands were derived from the commands used by typesetters to manually format documents. Runoff was later incorporated into the UNIX operating system in more advanced formatting programmes such as roff, nroff, and troff.

Berners-Lee considered HTML to be, at the time, an application of SGML, but it was not formally defined as such until the mid-1993 publication, by the IETF, of the first proposal for an HTML specification: Berners-Lee and Dan Connolly's "Hypertext Markup Language (HTML)" Internet-Draft, which included an SGML Document Type Definition to define the grammar. The draft expired after six months, but was notable for its acknowledgment of the NCSA Mosaic browser's custom tag for embedding in-line images, reflecting the IETF's philosophy of basing standards on successful prototypes. Similarly, Dave Raggett's competing Internet-Draft, "HTML+ (Hypertext Markup Format)", from late 1993, suggested standardizing already-implemented features like tables and fill-out forms.

After the HTML and HTML+ drafts expired in early 1994, the IETF created an HTML Working Group, which in 1995 completed "HTML 2.0", the first HTML specification intended to be treated as a standard against which future implementations should be based. Published as Request for Comments 1866, HTML 2.0 included ideas from the HTML and HTML+ drafts. There was no "HTML 1.0"; the 2.0 designation was intended to distinguish the new edition from previous drafts.

Further development under the auspices of the IETF was stalled by competing interests. Since 1996, the HTML specifications have been maintained, with input from commercial software vendors, by the World Wide Web Consortium (W3C). However, in 2000, HTML also became an international standard (ISO/IEC 15445:2000). The last HTML specification published by the W3C is the HTML 4.01 Recommendation, published in late 1999. Its issues and errors were last acknowledged by errata published in 2001.

Editing Tools

Web Design Software

These web design software can be used to build a complete website without any prior technical skills. For beginners, try using a web design software that offers free web hosting. It will give you a chance to experiment with designing websites, as well as help you evaluate if the hosting service is right for you.

Comparison of Popular Web Design Software			
SOFTWARE	**ADVANTAGES**	**DISADVANTAGES**	**REMARKS**
Blue Voda	• Freeware • Microsoft Office interface	Designed for Microsoft Windows	Beginner Level
Nvu	• Freeware • Available for Win, Mac, Linux	On-going development	Beginner Level
Yahoo Geocities	• Includes Web Hosting • Free	Needs internet connection	Beginner Level
CoffeeCup HTML Editor 2006D	• Easy to use • Comes with photos, icons and templates	Cost US$50.00	Beginners - Intermediate Level
Microsoft FrontPage 2003	• Similar to other MS products • Produces "dirty" codes	Cost US$199.00	Intermediate Level
Dreamweaver 8	• Professional choice • Produces clean codes • Extensions and add-ons	• Expensive (US$399.00) • Difficult to learn at first	Advance Users

Digital Image Editing Software

If you can't afford to pay the US$600 price tag for the professional version of Adobe Photoshop software, than try these free digital image editing software. They're a lot easier to learn and use, and their functions are adequate for common digital image editing needs.

Comparison of Popular Free Digital Image Editing Software			
SOFTWARE	**ADVANTAGES**	**DISADVANTAGES**	**REMARKS**
Windows Paint	• Can edit simple pictures • retouch photos	Does not contain all the features of a commercial software.	Available on most windows platform
Google Picasa	• supports common editing techniques • User friendly	Picasa is free software from Google that allows you to edit and share your pictures. Does not contain all the features of a commerical software.	Freeware
PhotoFiltre	• Easy to use • Great photo effects	Does not contain all the features of a commercial software.	Freeware
FastStone Photo Resizer	• Converts photo file format • Allows watermarks and text to be added	Does not contain all the features of a commercial software.	Freeware

Web design tools and digital image editing software are two of the most important software for webmasters. A good HTML web design tool will allow you to layout pages by using drag and drop features, while a digital image editing software will allow you to easily manipulate images and photographs. Make sure that you are familiar with these two tools as they can greatly help you to design your own online tutoring website.

Other Software Tools for Website Design

There are many free software that can add more functionality and control to you website. During the initial website design process, you might like to add other features such as payment processing systems, voip voice tags, video, audio and slide show scripts generator software to improve the sites overall appeal. Adding more functionality means giving you more control over your website, and allows you to fully realize the full benefits of the internet. Here are some simple software that can be easily incorporated into your website design.

Hyperlink and Images

A "hyperlink" is, most commonly, an underlined word or phrase, or sometimes even a graphic image or icon, which has been tagged with a particular HTML command containing the specific address of another location. Usually, by placing the arrow on the hyperlink and clicking on it, the user will jump quickly or instantly from one location to another location (within the same document, in another document, or somewhere else on the World Wide Web). Occasionally, clicking on a hyperlink will elicit a sound, an image, an animation, or an executable piece of software.

In most internet documents, "unvisited" hyperlinks will be blue in colour. After the hyperlink has been activated or "visited," its colour should be changed to purple. On most browsers, these are the two *default* colours of "unvisited" and "visited" hyperlinks. (On some browsers, the "visited" hyperlink colour will be olive.) If you see a hyperlink to a location which your browser previously has visited, its colour should be the *visited* colour. (With some web browsers, hyperlinks which make a jump to another location within the *same document* are always the *visited* colour, whether those hyperlinks have been activated or not.) The colours of "unvisited" hyperlinks do not have to be blue, and the colours of "visited" hyperlinks do not have to be purple (or olive). If you will recall, the hyperlink you took to get to this page from the "Ted's HTML Tutorial" page was sort of a peach colour. The next time you see it, its colour should have been changed to sort of a dark tan colour, because it has been activated to bring you to this page. I chose and implemented those particular colours, thereby overriding the *default* colours.

All the "unvisited" hyperlinks in a document can be made any colour you wish, and all the "visited" hyperlinks can be made any (usually a different) colour. The commands to define the colour of every unvisited hyperlink and of every visited hyperlink are placed within the <BODY> tag, located near the beginning of the HTML source code document.

Most often, a hyperlink will jump to the beginning of another document. To do this, a pair of "anchor" (A) tags is required:

- *<A HREF="URL">text or graphic image</A>:* defines an "anchored hypertext reference" (commonly known as a hyperlink), including the unique URL (Uniform Resource Locator or web address) of the target location to which a browser will jump when that link is activated by clicking on it. The file that a hyperlink targets or "calls up" when activated (clicked on) can be an HTML document, a graphic image, a sound, a video, or an executable programme.

The <A HREF> tag may contain within it another parameter as part of the command:

- *TARGET="_blank": opens* up the linked page, specified by the URL, into a *new* browser window. (Without the TARGET="_blank" parameter, the new page will replace the existing page in the same browser window.)

Sometimes a hyperlink will jump to a certain location *within* another document, or even within the same document containing the hyperlink. In this case, two pairs of "anchor" (A) tags are required:

- *<A HREF="URL#name">text or graphic image</A>:* defines an "anchored hypertext reference" (commonly known as a hyperlink), including the unique URL (Uniform Resource Locator or web address) of the target location to which a browser will jump when that link is activated by clicking on it. In addition to the standard URL, a "name" attribute must be included which takes the browser to a specific location within the linked document.

The "name" attribute is used only if the target is located within another document or the same document. (In the specific case that the target of the hyperlink is within the *same* document as the hyperlink, only the "#name" aspect of the address needs to be listed: <A HREF="#name">. In this case, the initial URL information is unnecessary.)

- *<A NAME="name">(optional header, text, or graphic image)</A>:* defines an "anchored name" or "called name anchor" (target) to which a browser will jump when a hyperlink (<A HREF="URL#name">) with that target's address and name is activated. The <A NAME>

& </A> tags may be placed next to each other; any text or image between them is optional (although if the tags are located within a list or a table, there should be text between them).

Some browsers will not recognize adjacent pairs of anchored name tags (<A NAME=""> </A> <A NAME=""> </A> <A NAME=""> </A>). Therefore, it is recommended that something (such as a space, letter, word, or graphic) be inserted between one set of <A NAME=""> </A> tags and another set adjacent to it. (Placing the empty, meaningless <!> tag between adjacent sets of anchored name tags will work; the <!> tag is *invisible* on a browser, and it takes up *no space*.)

Note: The "name" attribute of both the anchored hypertext reference tag (<A HREF="URL#name">) and the anchored name tag (<A NAME="name">) *must match exactly*; otherwise, the link will not occur. Moreover, the "name" attribute of the <A HREF="URL#name"> tag *must* contain the "#" symbol for the link to work properly.

Note: Some browsers will *not* link to a <A NAME></A> tag which is located inside of a list or a table, although a link is more likely to be successful if text is placed between the <A NAME> and </A> tags.

Creating a Web Pages

Getting Started

There are basically two ways to make a web page. The first way is to create the page(s) offline and then upload them to your Internet Service Provider (ISP) via FTP. The second way is to create your web page(s) online using a Telnet programme by accessing your UNIX account, if you have one.

If you are creating your web page(s) offline, do so in any text editing or word processing document. Make sure that when you save your document, you save it as a "text", "plain text" or "text only" document. Otherwise it will not be read properly by a web browser. Once you have created your page(s), you will need to contact your ISP about how to go about uploading them to your server.

If you have a UNIX account, you can create your web page(s) online. You first need to get a programme that can access your UNIX account. I recommend Telnet for the Mac or Ewan for Windows 95/98.

Once you can access your account, you need to make a new directory called "public_html". You can do this by typing:

mkdir public_html

After this, change your directory to this new directory called "public_html".

cd public_html

If you want to, you can make other directories, one for all the web pages that you make, and one for all of the graphics that you have. Follow the same steps as above to do this.

Next, you need to think of a filename for your page (this is not a title, but what will be in the URL). A common filename for a main web page, is "index". Once you've decided on this, add ".html" to the end of it. Then type (i.e.)

pico index.html

Of course, use your page's filename, instead of this one. Next, you need to gain some knowledge of the many HTML commands. Lucky for you, I've already gotten some of the basic commands for you. Follow the index below, to decide what to put on your page, and how to do it. Once you've gotten started, exit your page. You can do this by pressing **control-x**. Then you need to type:

chmod 744 index.html

Only do this with the filename of your page. You only need to do this the very first time that you leave your web page. This command will make sure that nobody else can delete your page. You will need to do this to any other pages that you make in the future. Then, look at your page on the WWW. Lets say that your server is "www.domain.com", your username is "username", and the name of your page is "index.html". The URL would normally be:

http://www.domain.com/~username/index.html

However, you will need to contact your ISP for your URL.

If you have made separate directories for pages and graphics, then you need to include that in the URL also. Lets say that you made a directory for all of your web pages, called "Pages". The new URL would be: **http://www.domain.com/~username/Pages/index.html**

Title

The first thing to put on your web page, is a title. The title is what will show up in the very top of the window. Let's say that your title is going to be "John Doe's Web Page", you would type:

<title>John Doe's Web Page</title>

In HTML, every command is surrounded by <'s, and >'s. And in most commands, you need to tell the web browser when to end this command. You do this by putting a back slash (/) in front of the ending command, as in above. Since HTML isn't case sensitive, <title> is the same as <TITLE>, which is the same as <TiTLe>. Next, you need to decide what you want to put on your page. Text, links, graphics, and text fields, are just a few ideas. Follow the table of contents above to decide how, and what to put on your page.

Text

Headings: HTML has six levels of headings, numbered 1 through 6, with 1 being the largest. Headings are displayed in larger, or smaller fonts, and usually bolder. If you wanted to type "Hello", this is what you would type for each heading, and what the outcome is:

<h1>Hello</h1>

Hello

<h2>Hello</h2>

Hello

<h3>Hello</h3>

Hello

<h4>Hello</h4>

Hello

<h5>Hello</h5>

Hello

<h6>Hello</h6>

Hello

Paragraphs

Whenever you have more than a sentence of writing, you should have paragraphs. Personally, I don't see what the difference is, but I do it anyway, because then I can find a certain spot better when programing. To Make a paragraph of "This is a web page. How do you like what I've done? Please e-mail me with any suggestions at a@a.com", type:

<P>This is a web page. How do you like what I've done? Please e-mail me with any suggestions at a@a.com</P>

HTML Tags

If you're doing business on the Internet, taking the time to learn how to design your own web site and write your own HTML code (hypertext markup language) will play a major role in your success. Not only will learning HTML coding provide you with the freedom to update your own HTML documents, but it will also save you a great deal of money, as you will be able to avoid hiring a professional web designer.

If you're looking for some HTML tags to spice up your web site, you've come to the right place. You will find a variety of HTML codes and tips to assist you below. However, before reviewing the HTML tags, if you're new to HTML and web site design, the following section will assist you in creating an HTML web page. For additional web site design information, make sure you don't miss the web design articles and tutorials at the bottom of this page.

Creating an HTML Page

A web page is created using a language called, Hypertext Markup Language, better known as HTML Code. You can write your own coding within a plain text editor, such as Note Pad, or use an HTML editor, which will write the code for you.

HTML codes, also referred to as HTML tags, are enclosed by the lesser than (<) and greater than (>) brackets and may be written in capital or lower case letters.

The opening bracket is followed by an element, which is a browser command, and ends with the closing bracket.

<**font** size=2>

An element may also be followed by attributes, which are words describing the properties of the element, and further instruct the browser.

<font **size=**2>

Attributes are only contained in the opening HTML tags to the right of the element and are separated by a space and followed by an equal (=) sign.

The value follows the equal sign and is enclosed in quotes.

<font size=**2**>

Basic HTML Document Code Structure

Begin writing your HTML tags by creating your document's basic layout. Copy and paste this code into your text or HTML editor.

<html>

<head>

<title>Your Page Title</title>

</head>

<body>

This area will contain everything that will be visible through a web browser, such as text and graphics. All of the information will be HTML coded.

For a complete list of HTML codes, tags and examples, see the HTML chart below.

</body>

</html>

<html> - Begins your HTML document.

<head> - Contains information about the page such as the TITLE, META tags for proper Search Engine indexing, STYLE tags, which determine the page layout, and JavaScript coding for special effects.

<title> - The TITLE of your page. This will be visible in the title bar of the viewers' browser.

</title> - Closes the HTML <title> tag.

</head> - Closes the HTML <head> tag.

<body> - This is where you will begin writing your document and placing your HTML codes.

</body> - Closes the HTML <body> tag.

</html> - Closes the <html> tag.

How to Copy and Paste HTML Tags / Codes

To copy and paste the HTML tags / codes from the HTML chart below into the HTML of your web page, place your mouse pointer over the beginning of the HTML code you would like to copy. Next, click and hold your left mouse button and drag your mouse over all the HTML code you would like to copy (Example of highlighted text). Your HTML code should now be highlighted. Go to "Edit" - "Copy" on your web browser's toolbar and then place your cursor within your HTML code where you would like to place the code. Right click on your mouse and go to "Paste." Your HTML code should now be displaying within your HTML document.

Tables

Example

A simple HTML table, containing two columns and two rows:

```
<table border="1">
<tr>
<th>Month</th>
<th>Savings</th>
```

```
</tr>
<tr>
<td>January</td>
<td>$100</td>
</tr>
</table>
```

(more examples at the bottom of this page)

Definition and Usage

The <table> tag defines an HTML table.

A simple HTML table consists of the table element and one or more tr, th, and td elements.

The tr element defines a table row, the th element defines a table header, and the td element defines a table cell.

A more complex HTML table may also include caption, col, colgroup, thead, tfoot, and tbody elements.

Browser Support

The <table> tag is supported in all major browsers.

Frames

Introduction to Frames

HTML frames allow authors to present documents in multiple views, which may be independent windows or subwindows. Multiple views offer designers a way to keep certain information visible, while other views are scrolled or replaced.

For example, within the same window, one frame might display a static banner, a second a navigation menu, and a third the main document that can be scrolled through or replaced by navigating in the second frame.

Here is a simple frame document:

```
<!DOCTYPE HTML PUBLIC "-//W3C//DTD HTML 4.01
Frameset//EN"
```

```
"http://www.w3.org/TR/html4/frameset.dtd">
<HTML>
<HEAD>
<TITLE>A simple frameset document</TITLE>
</HEAD>
<FRAMESET cols="20%, 80%">
<FRAMESET rows="100, 200">
<FRAME src="contents_of_frame1.html">
<FRAME src="contents_of_frame2.gif">
</FRAMESET>
<FRAME src="contents_of_frame3.html">
<NOFRAMES>
<P>This frameset document contains:
<UL>
<LI><A href="contents_of_frame1.html">Some neat contents</A>
<LI><IMG src="contents_of_frame2.gif" alt="A neat image">
<LI><A href="contents_of_frame3.html">Some other neat contents</A>
</UL>
</NOFRAMES>
</FRAMESET>
</HTML>
```

that might create a frame layout something like this:

```
________________________________________

| | |
| | |
| Frame 1 | |
```

```
| | |
| | |
|————| |
| | Frame 3 |
| | |
| | |
| | |
| Frame 2 | |
| | |
| | |
| | |
| | |
________________________________
```

If the user agent can't display frames or is configured not to, it will render the contents of the NOFRAMES element.

Layout of Frames: An HTML document that describes frame layout (called a *frameset document*) has a different makeup than an HTML document without frames. A standard document has one HEAD section and one BODY. A frameset document has a HEAD, and a FRAMESET in place of the BODY. The FRAMESET section of a document specifies the layout of views in the main user agent window. In addition, the FRAMESET section can contain a NOFRAMES element to provide alternate content for user agents that do not support frames or are configured not to display frames.

Elements that might normally be placed in the BODY element must not appear before the first FRAMESET element or the FRAMESET will be ignored.

Forms

Introduction to Forms: An HTML form is a section of a document containing normal content, markup, special elements called *controls* (checkboxes, radio buttons, menus, etc.), and labels on those controls. Users generally "complete" a form by modifying its controls (entering text, selecting menu items, etc.), before submitting the form to an agent for processing (e.g., to a Web server, to a mail server, etc.)

Here's a simple form that includes labels, radio buttons, and push buttons (reset the form or submit it):

```
<FORM action="http://somesite.com/prog/adduser" method="post">
<P>
<LABEL for="firstname">First name: </LABEL>
<INPUT type="text" id="firstname"><BR>
<LABEL for="lastname">Last name: </LABEL>
<INPUT type="text" id="lastname"><BR>
<LABEL for="email">email: </LABEL>
<INPUT type="text" id="email"><BR>
<INPUT type="radio" name="sex" value="Male"> Male<BR>
<INPUT type="radio" name="sex" value="Female"> Female<BR>
<INPUT type="submit" value="Send"> <INPUT type="reset">
</P>
</FORM>
```

Note. *This specification includes more detailed information about forms in the subsections on form display issues.*

Controls

Users interact with forms through named *controls*.

A control's *"control name"* is given by its name attribute. The scope of the name attribute for a control within a FORM element is the FORM element.

Each control has both an initial value and a current value, both of which are character strings. Please consult the definition of each control for information about initial values and possible constraints on values imposed by the control. In general, a control's *"initial value"* may be specified with the control element's value attribute. However, the initial value of a TEXTAREA element is given by its contents, and the initial value of an OBJECT element in a form is determined by the object implementation (i.e., it lies outside the scope of this specification).

The control's *"current value"* is first set to the initial value. Thereafter, the control's current value may be modified through user interaction and scripts.

A control's initial value does not change. Thus, when a form is reset, each control's current value is reset to its initial value. If a control does not have an initial value, the effect of a form reset on that control is undefined.

When a form is submitted for processing, some controls have their name paired with their current value and these pairs are submitted with the form. Those controls for which name/value pairs are submitted are called successful controls.

Control Types

HTML defines the following control types:

buttons

Authors may create three types of buttons:

- submit buttons: When activated, a submit button submits a form. A form may contain more than one submit button.
- reset buttons: When activated, a reset button resets all controls to their initial values.
- push buttons: Push buttons have no default behavior. Each push button may have client-side scripts associated with the element's event attributes. When an event occurs (e.g., the user presses the button, releases it, etc.), the associated script is triggered.

Authors should specify the scripting language of a push button script through a default script declaration (with the META element).

Authors create buttons with the BUTTON element or the INPUT element. Please consult the definitions of these elements for details about specifying different button types.

Note. Authors should note that the BUTTON element offers richer rendering capabilities than the INPUT element.

Checkboxes

Checkboxes (and radio buttons) are on/off switches that may be toggled by the user. A switch is "on" when the control element's checked attribute is set. When a form is submitted, only "on" checkbox controls can become successful.

Several checkboxes in a form may share the same control name. Thus, for example, checkboxes allow users to select several values for the same property. The INPUT element is used to create a checkbox control.

Learning from Cyber Resources

The Internet has created a whole new world of social communications for young people who are using e-mail, social networking Web sites, instant messaging, chat rooms and text messaging to stay in touch with friends and make new ones.

While most interactions are positive, increasingly kids are using these communication tools to antagonize and intimidate others. Cyberbullying can be much more severe in its effects than offline bullying because the targets feel they have no escape. Also, given the wide scope of the Web, there can be many more witnesses to the bullying.

School administrators and teachers are struggling to address this issue with students. When real-world bullying occurs in a schoolyard or classroom, teachers are often able to intervene, but online bullying takes place off the radar screen of adults, making it difficult to detect in schools and impossible to monitor off school property.

Despite this, schools are increasingly being expected to address issues relating to cyberbullying. Dr. Shaheen Shariff of McGill University emphasizes that schools have a responsibility "to adapt to a rapidly evolving technological society, address emerging challenges, and guide children to become civic-minded individuals". According to Shariff, schools must support a preventive approach to cyberbullying that includes developing informed policies and providing pedagogy that is grounded in scholarship in order to grant *equal learning opportunities* to all students.

The Lessons

To help educators address this issue in their classrooms, Media Awareness Network has developed a series of lessons, in English and in French, to give students a better understanding of the ethical and legal implications of cyberbullying and to promote positive Internet use. Intended to support and enhance school-based anti-bullying and empathy-building programmes, *Cyberbullying: Encouraging ethical online behaviour* comprises the following:

Introduction to Cyberbullying: Avatars and Identity

Grades 5-6: With the layering of identity through the use of nicknames and avatars, as well as a sense of anonymity, it is easy for young people to sometimes forget that real people—with real feelings—are at the heart of online conversations. In this lesson, students are provided with opportunities to explore this concept and discuss the importance of using empathy and common sense when talking to others online.

Understanding Cyberbullying - Virtual vs. Physical Worlds

Grades 7-8: In this lesson, students explore the concept of cyberbullying and learn how the attributes associated with online communication may fuel inappropriate or bullying behaviour. Connections between other contributing factors to bullying—online and offline—are also reinforced as students develop an understanding of the role played by bystanders and the ways in which our own responses may fuel or stop this kind of behaviour. As a class, students establish a class "code of (N)ethics" for online conduct.

Cyberbullying and the Law

Grades 7-8 and Grades 9-12 (two lessons): In these lessons, secondary and middle school students learn about and discuss the legal aspects of cyberbullying. They review a variety of hypothetical scenarios and a case study, and consider the seriousness of the situations, who is legally responsible, what action (if any) should be taken and by whom. To determine this, students will seek answers to the following questions: How does cyberbullying differ from offline bullying? What aspects of a cyberbullying case make it a cause for legal action? What determines whether it is a civil or a criminal matter? How should rights to freedom of expression, guaranteed under the Canadian Charter of Rights and Freedoms, be balanced against rights to security of person? When and how are schools responsible for cyberbullying cases?

Cyberbullying and Civic Participation

Grades 7-8: This lesson allows students to explore the concept of civic participation in the creation of Canadian laws through a study of the consultation process found in the *Canada Gazette*. Students will create their own *School Gazette* by proposing and discussing rules against cyberbullying at school.

Promoting Ethical Online Behaviour: Our Values and Ethics

Grades 7-9: In this 3-part lesson, students learn about online privacy and ethical behaviour by exploring their digital footprints to better understand how our online interactions may not be as anonymous as we think they are. In Part One, students create a digital map of their Web-based activities and the various characters and personas they assume online. In Part Two, students further assess the privacy and ethics of their online activities by applying their cyber-portraits to a questionnaire and, in Part Three, students look at areas in their virtual lives where they can make improvements.

Bibliography

Abdulaziz, M.H. : *Language in Education: A Comparative Study of the Situation in Tanzania, Ethiopia and Somalia*, Netherlands; Philadelphia, 1991.

Adas, Michael : *Machines as the Measure of Men: Science, Technology, and Ideologies of Western Dominance*, Ithaca, Cornell University Press, 1989.

Aggarwal, Santosh : *Three Language Formula: An Educational Problem*, New Delhi, Sian, 1991.

Altbach, Philip G. and Gail Kelly : *New Approaches to Comparative Education*, Chicago, The University of Chicago Press, 1986.

Aspray, William: *John von Neumann and the Origins of Modern Computing*, Cambridge, MA: The MIT Press, 1990.

Augarten, Stan: *Bit By Bit: An Illustrated History of Computers*, New York: Ticknor & Fields, 1984.

Bass, Thomas A: *The Eudaemonic Pie*, New York, Random House, 1985.

Baumann, P. R.: *Computer assisted instruction programs in geography: five climate programs*, Publications in Geography, Oneonta, New York, 1970.

Beniger, James R.: *The Control Revolution: Technological and Economic Origins of the Information Society*, Cambridge, MA: Harvard University Press, 1986.

Bentley, T. : *Learning beyond the Classroom: Education for a Changing World*, London, Routledge. 1998.

Borst, Arno: *The Ordering of Time: From the Ancient Computus to the Modern Computer*, Chicago, IL: University of Chicago Press, 1993.

Bottery, M. : *The Ethics of Educational Management: Personal, Social and Political Perspectives on School Organization*, London, Cassell, 1992.

Brand, Stewart: *The Media Lab: Inventing the Future at MIT*, New York: Penguin, 1987.

Brockman, John: *Digerati: Encounters With the Cyber Elite*, San Francisco, HardWired, 1996.

Burke, Colin: *Information and Secrecy: Vannevar Bush, Ultra, and the Other Memex*, Metuchen, NJ: Scarecrow Press, 1994.

Caffarella, R.S. : *Planning Programs for Adult Learners, A Practical Guide for Educators, Trainers and Staff Developers*, San Francisco, Jossey-Bass, 1994.

Campbell-Kelly, Martin and William Aspray: *Computer: A History of the Information Machine*, New York: Basic Books, 1996.

Casey, Steven: *Set Phasers on Stun and Other True Tales of Design, Technology, and Human Error*, Santa Barbara, CA: Aegean Publishing, 1993.

Cavazos, Edward and Gavino Morin: *Cyberspace and the Law: Your Rights and Duties in the On-Line World*, Cambridge, MA: The MIT Press, 1994.

Cenkner, William : *A Tradition of Teachers: Sankara and the Jagadgurus Today*, Delhi, Motilal Banarsidass, 1983.

Chandler, Alfred D.: *The Visible Hand: The Managerial Revolution in American Business*, Cambridge, MA: The Belknap Press of Harvard University Press, 1977.

Chumbow, B.S. : *The Place of Mother Tongue in the National Policy of Education,* Port Harcourt, Nigeria, 1990.

Clapp, Doug: *The Macintosh Reader*, New York: Random House, 1992.

Cole, J. P.: *Situations in Human Geography: a Practical Approach*. Oxford: Basil Blackwell.

Collins, A., Warnock, E. H. and Passafiume, J. J.: *The Psychology of Learning and Motivation: Advances in Research and Theory*, New York: Academic Press, 1975.

Corn, Joseph J. and Brian Horrigan: *Yesterday's Tomorrows: Past Visions of the American Future*, Baltimore, The Johns Hopkins University Press, 1996.

Cortada, James W.: *The Computer in the United States: From Laboratory to Market, 1930-1960*, Armonk, NY: M. E. Sharpe, 1993.

Cowan, Ruth Schwartz: *A Social History of American Technology*, New York, Oxford University Press, 1997.

Crichton, Michael: *Electronic Life: How to Think About Computers*, New York: Alfred A. Knopf, 1983.

Dasgupta, Subrata: *Creativity in Invention and Design: Computational and Cognitive Explorations of Technological Originality*, New York, Cambridge University Press, 1994.

Donaldson, Gordon A. : *Cultivating Leadership in Schools*, New York, College Press, 2001.

Dvorak, John C.: *Dvorak Predicts: An Insider's Look at the Computer Industry*, New York: McGraw Hill, 1994.

Edwards, Paul N.: *The Closed World: Computers and the Politics of Discourse in Cold War America*, Cambridge, The MIT Press, 1996.

Elliott, J. : *Action Research for Educational Change*, Milton Keynes, Open University, 1991.

Evers, C. & Lakomski, G. : *Knowing Educational Administration*, Oxford, Pergamon, 1991.

Feigenbaum, Edward A.: *Computers and Thought*, New York: McGraw-Hill, 1963.

Fishman, Katherine Davis: *The Computer Establishment*, New York: McGraw-Hill, 1981.

Flink, James J.: *The Autmobile Age*, Cambridge, MA: The MIT Press, 1993.

Fordham, P., Holland, D. and Millican, J. : *Adult Literacy, A Handbook for Development Workers*, Oxford, Oxfam, 1995.

Galbraith, M.W. : *Education Through Community Organizations*, San Francisco, Jossey-Bass, 1990.

Gibson, R. : *Critical Theory and Education*, London, Hodder & Stoughton, 1986.

Giroux, H. : *Critical Theory and Educational Practice*, Geelong, Australia, Deakin University, 1983.

Glass, Robert L.: *Software Creativity*, Prentice Hall PTR, 1995.

Goldstine, Herman H.: *The Computer: From Pascal to von Neumann*, Princeton, Princeton University Press, 1972.

Goodlad, John I. : *Educational Renewal: Better Teachers, Better Schools*, San Francisco, Jossey-Bass, 1994.

Hafner, Kate and Matthew Lyon: *Where Wizards Stay Up Late*, New York: Simon and Schuster, 1996.

Hahne, Harry: *Bible and Computers: Desk and Discipline, The Impact of Computers on Biblical Studies: Proceedings of Association Internationale Bible et Informatique in Amsterdam August 1994*, Paris-Genéve: Champion-Slatkine, 1995.

Hanson, Dirk: *The New Alchemists*, Boston: Little, Brown, 1982.

Hardy, Henry Edward: *The History of the Net. Master's Thesis*, Grand Valley State University School of Communications, 1993.

Hawkes, Nigel: *The Computer Revolution*, New York: E.P. Dutton, 1972.

Heims, Steve J.: *The Cybernetics Group*, Cambridge, MA: The MIT Press, 1991.

Heller, Robert: *The Fate of IBM*, London: Little Brown, 1994.

Hollingdale, S. H., and G. C. Tootill: *Electronic Computers*, Baltimore: Penguin Books, 1967.

Houk, Neil B.: *Church Bytes*, Deerhaven Press, 1984-.

Hsu, Jeffrey: *A Comprehensive Guide to Computer Bible Study. Up-to-Date Information on the Best Software and Techniques*, Dallas: Word, 1993.

Hughes, John J.: *Bits, Bytes and Biblical Studies*, Grand Rapids, Mi.: Zondervan, 1987.

Jayasuriya, J.E. *Education in Korea: A Third World Success Story*, Colombo, Associated Educational Publishers, 1980.

Kahin, Brian and James Keller: *Public Access to the Internet*, Cambridge, MA: The MIT Press, 1995.

Kawasaki, Guy: *The Computer Curmudgeon*, Indianapolis: Hayden Books, 1992.

Kelly, Kevin: *Out of Control: The New Biology of Machines, Social Systems, and the Economic World*, Reading, MA: Addison Wesley, 1994.

Kennedy, K.J. : *Citizenship Education and the Modern State*, Washington, D.C: Falmer Press, 1997.

Kidder, Tracy: *Soul of a New Machine*, New York: Avon, 1981.

Kraft, Robert A.: *Computer Assisted Tools for Septuagint Analysis*, 1986.

Latour, Bruno: *Aramis, or the Love of Technology*, Cambridge, MA: Harvard University Press, 1996.

Lee, J.A.N.: *Computer Pioneers*, Los Alamitos, CA: IEEE Computer Society Press, 1994.

Lee, Yoonmi : *Modern Education, Textbooks and Image of the Nation: Politics of Modernization and Nationalism in Korean Education, 1800-1910,* New York, Garland, 2000.

Leebaert, Derek: *Technology 2001: The Future of Computing and Communications*, Cambrdige, MA: The MIT Press, 1991.

Levy, Steven: *Hackers: Heroes of the Computer Revolution*, New York: Dell, 1984.

Lewis, Charles: *Premises and Prospects: TCP/IP and the Internet*, B.A. Thesis, New College of the University of South Florida, 1996.

Linzmayer, Owen W.: *The Mac Bathroom Reader*, San Francisco: SYBEX, 1994.

Lubar, Steven: *InfoCulture*, Boston, Houghton Mifflin, 1993.

Malone, Michael S.: *The Microprocessor: A Biography*, Santa Clara, CA: TELOS, 1995.

McCarty, Willard: *Humanities Computing Yearbook*, Oxford: Clarendon Press, 1988.

McConnell, C. : *Community Education: The Making of an Empowering Profession*, Edinburgh, Scottish Community Education Council, 1996.

McGivney, V. and Murray, F. : *Adult Education in Development, Methods and Approaches from Changing Societies*, Leicester, NIACE, 1991.

Miall, David S.: *Humanities and the Computer: New Directions*, Clarendon Press, Oxford, 1990.

Nias, J. : *Seeing anew: Teachers' Theories of Action*, Australia, Deakin University, 1987.

Pagels, Heinz R.: *The Dreams of Reason: The Computer and the Rise of the Sciences of Complexity*, New York: Bantam, 1988.

Petroski, Henry: *The Pencil: A History of Design and Circumstance*, New York: Alfred A. Knopf, 1992.

Poster, C. and Kruger, A. : *Community Education in the Western World*, London, Routledge, 1990.

Poswick, Ferdinand R.: *Bible and Computer: Interpretation, Hermeneutics, Expertise*, Paris-Genéve, Champion-Slatkine, 1992.

Pournelle, Jerry: *The User's Guide to Small Computers*, New York: Baen, 1984.

Pursell, Carroll: *White Heat: People and Technology*, Berkeley, CA: University of California Press, 1994.

Ranson, S. & Stewart, J. : *Management for the Public Domain*, New York, St, Martin's Press, 1994.

Rheingold, Howard: *The Virtual Community: Homesteading on the Electronic Frontier*, Reading, MA: Addison-Wesley, 1993.

Rogers, A. : *Adults Learning for Development*, London, Cassell, 1992.

Rose, Frank: *West of Eden: The End of Innocence at Apple Computer*, New York: Penguin, 1989.

Sangwan, Satpal : *Science, Technology, and Colonisation: An Indian Experience, 1757-1857*. New Delhi, Anmika Prakashan, 1991.

Schneider, Ben Ross Jr.: *My Personal Computer and Other Family Crises*, New York: Macmillan, 1984.

Schultze, Quentin J.: *Internet for Christains. Everything You Need to Start Cruising the Net Today!*, Muskegon, Mi.: Gospel Films, 1995.

Seth, Michael J. : *Education Fever: Society, Politics, and the Pursuit of Schooling in South Korea*, Honolulu, University of Hawai Press, 2002.

Simkins, T. : *Non-formal Education and Development*, Manchester, Manchester University, 1977.

Southworth, G. : *Looking into Primary Headship: A Research based Interpretation*, London, Falmer, 1995.

Starratt, R.J. : *Centering Educational Administration: Cultivating Meaning, Community and Responsibility*, Mahwah, Lawrence Earlbaum, 2003.

Stenhouse, L. : *Authority, Education and Emancipation*, London, Heinemann, 1983.

Stross, Randall: *The Microsoft Way: The Real Story of How the Company Outsmarts Its Competition*, New York: Addison-Wesley, 1996.

Stuart C. Shapiro: *The Encyclopedia of Artificial Intelligence*, John Wiley & Sons, 1992.

Sudnow, David: *Pilgrim in the Micro-World: Eye, Mind, and the Essence of Video Skill*, New York: Warner, 1983.

Talstra, Eep: *Computer Assisted Analysis of Biblical Texts*, Amsterdam: Free University Press, 1989.

Thomas, A. : *Educating Children at Home*, London, Cassell, 1998.

Tyagi, P.N. : *Education for All: A Graphic Presentation*, New Delhi, National Institute of Educational Planning and Administration, 1991.

Warner D. and Palfreyman D. : *Higher Education Management: The Key Elements*, London, The Society for Research into Higher Education and Open University Press, 1996.

Wiggins, Grant : *Educative Assessment: Designing Assessments to inform and Improve Student Performance*, San Francisco, Jossey-Bass, 1998.

Index

□□□